TEENAGERS

The AGONY

The ECSTASY

The ANSWERS

AIDAN MACFARLANE
ANN McPHERSON

TEENAGERS

The AGONY

The ECSTASY

The ANSWERS

LITTLE, BROWN AND COMPANY

A *Little, Brown* Book

First published in Great Britain in 1999
by Little, Brown and Company

Copyright © Aidan Macfarlane and Ann McPherson 1999

The moral right of the authors has been asserted.

A CIP catalogue record for this book
is available from the British Library.

C FORMAT ISBN 0 316 64713 6

Typeset in Berkeley by M Rules
Printed and bound in Great Britain by
Clays Ltd, St Ives plc

Little, Brown and Company (UK)
Brettenham House
Lancaster Place
London WC2E 7EN

About This Book

Families may feel that, when it comes to bringing up a teenager, they could do with a whole team to help – a psychiatrist, a full-time cook, half a dozen bouncers, a substance abuse counsellor, and someone to operate a fleet of washing machines. They could instead choose to read this book.

It is a book that you can buy at a railway station and read on the way home in the train. It is a 'pick up and be instantly gripped and entertained' sort of book. What *Men Are From Mars and Women Are From Venus* did for helping to explain adult relationships, *The Agony, The Ecstasy, The Answers* does for relationships between parents and their adolescents. It is based on a series of interviews with parents and teenagers on how to get things right; on areas of conflict and how these may be resolved. Each chapter also contains relevant facts from research, and a summary list of suggestions which parents and teenagers may find helpful.

This book is for:

- parents who want to get maximum enjoyment out of their teenagers

- parents who want to maximise their teenagers' potential

- parents of teenagers who are giving them grief and want to understand why

- parents who want to be reassured by the fact that the conflicts they are having with their teenagers are archetypal and universal

- parents who want to be as well informed as their teenagers on drug taking, sex, relationships, feelings about their parents (and all the other things which may not be normally talked about within families)

- parents who will use this book to say 'look, read this, it will tell you how I feel about things' in order to open up communication

- teenagers who will give it to their parents and say 'look, read this, it will tell you how I feel about things' in order to open up communication

In fact, it is for any parent of the approximately seven million young people aged ten to nineteen living in the UK at any one time, most, but not all, of whom will be living at home with two parents (natural or step). These young people represent about one in five of the whole population. But they are a fluid 'through put' generation, as some 800,000 new ten-year-olds each year grow up from being nine years old, and the equivalent number of nineteen-year-olds disappear into 'young adulthood'. The major changes that occur in this mass of young people are rapid, and tend to cover a finite time period, which one young person has defined as the time 'between puberty and poverty'.

Who wrote this book and what it's about

The two authors, Aidan Macfarlane and Ann McPherson, have been writing books for young people for over ten years. The most famous ones are *The New Diary of a Teenage Health Freak* and *The Diary of the Other Health Freak*, which have sold over half a million copies in the UK, have been turned into two television series for Channel 4, and have been translated into twenty-two languages around the world.

With a further five books for teenagers between them, they now turn to revealing the secrets of teenage life to parents. By interviewing more than forty parents and their offspring, they show how parents view their teenagers and how teenagers view their parents, in order to enable each to understand the other's viewpoint. As the interviews indicate, the two may not always be compatible, but the book shows how these relationships can be improved.

What do young people consider important in their lives? What do they like best about their parents, and what do they hate most? Why do they experiment with drugs? What do they think about sex? How does what they need from their parents change as they grow older? Alongside the answers to these questions is what parents think of their teenagers' behaviour, what they like best and hate most about their offspring, and how they think they might have done better if they were to try again.

The names of the characters in the book have been changed to protect confidentiality.

Acknowledgements

First and foremost we should like to express our enormous gratitude to all the many parents and young people that we interviewed for the book and are unable, for reasons of confidentiality, to name. It is their willingness, openness and thoughtfulness in sharing their experiences with us that have made this book. Then, in no particular order, but with large portions of gratitude for all their help, we should like to thank:

Bliss teenage magazine for putting in an advertisement asking teenagers what they think of their parents

The many, many teenagers who responded to the advertisement

Keith Hawton, a leading authority on suicide in young people, for all the information that he provided us with

Klim McPherson – for his patience and support during the book's writing

Rosie Roberts – for her support and self-esteem building

PAPRYUS – for their help over the issues of bereavement

The Brook Advisory Centre and the Family Planning Association for information about contraception and sexually transmitted infections

Marny Leech – for yet again tolerating our whims and doing such an excellent job on copy-editing – the sixth book she has done for us. The work she performs on our behalf is truly miraculous.

Imogen Taylor – for her encouragement as our editor at Little, Brown

Our children – Sam, Magnus, Tess, Tamara, Beth, Gus – from whom we have learned over the years

Felicity Bryan – for all her support over the years as our agent

Fiona Palmer for all her help and much else besides over the years

Magnus Macfarlane and Phil Robson for information about drug taking among young people and information about the drugs themselves

Debbie Waller, who is a leading authority on eating disorders in young people and provided us with invaluable material on the subject

Julia Allen and Adèle Wright for all the information they collected about adolescents while working for the National Adolescent and Student Health Unit

Chris Donovan for all the work he has done over the years for adolescents and for his help and support while we were writing the book

John Coleman – Director of the Trust for the Study of Adolescence for the information we gathered from the many excellent publications from the Trust

John Balding – for information gathered from the many terrific publications and surveys put out by the Schools Health Education Unit, Exeter

The Office of National Statistics for all the statistics that their publications have provided us with

David Jones for his extremely helpful advice on child sexual abuse

Lyz Greenall and Toni Belfield for advice on contraception

Frances Campbell for all her wise words and reflections on marriage, divorce and separation

Susan Macrae for information on divorce, separation and step-parents

Jackie Maxmin, Rachel Miller and Liz Minton for supporting us at times when others were less helpful

The Child Growth Foundation for allowing us to use their growth chart information

Many thanks to Tat Armstrong Gray for her brilliant contribution

The following books and pamphlets helped to provide us with invaluable background information:

Butler, Gillian and Hope, Tony, *The Mental Fitness Guide: Manage Your Mind*, Oxford University Press, 1995.

Coleman, Dr John, *Teenagers: Survival Guide for Parents*, produced by Carlton Central.

Health Education Authority, *Young People and Health: the Health Behaviour of School Aged Children*, BMRB International, 1996.

Social and Community Planning Research and Dept of Epidemiology and Public Health, University of London, *Health Survey for England: The Health of Young People '95–97*, The Stationery Office Publications Centre.

Macfarlane, Aidan (ed.), *Adolescent Medicine*, Royal College of Physicians of London, 1996.

Balding, John, *Young People in 1996*, Schools Health Education Unit, University of Exeter, 1997.

Robson, Philip, *Forbidden Drugs: Understanding Drugs and Why People Take Them*, Oxford Medical Publications, 1994.

Macfarlane, Aidan, Macfarlane, Magnus and Robson, Philip, *The User*, Oxford University Press, 1996.

Rodgers, Bryan and Pryor, Jan, *Divorce and Separation: the Outcome for Children*, Joseph Rowntree Foundation, 1998.

Ferri, Elsa and Smith, Kate, *Parenting in the 1990s*, Family Policy Studies Centre, 1996.

Roberts, Helen and Sachdev, Darshan (eds), *Young People's Social Attitudes: Having Their Say – the Views of 12 to 19 year olds*, Barnardo's, 1996.

Confidentiality and People Under 16 Guidance, issued jointly by the BMA, GMSC, HEA, Brook Advisory Centres, FPA and RCGP. No date given.

Durex Global Sex Survey, 1997.

Teenagers and Divorce. A Relate Teen Conference, 1997.

Burghes, Louie, *Lone Parenthood and Family Disruption: the Outcomes for Children*, 1994.

Family Planning Association and its Contraceptive Education Service leaflets and publications.

Advice for Parents, Children and Staff in Schools. Anti Bullying Campaign.

Contents

What Young People Can Do at Different Ages

At seven, children can:
– open and draw money from a National and Trustee Savings
  Bank Account

At ten, children can:
– be convicted of a crime (if it can be proved they knew
  what they were doing was wrong)
– be searched, fingerprinted, photographed (and have sam-
  ples taken) by the police
– be detained 'during Her Majesty's pleasure' for a specified
  period if guilty of homicide

At twelve, children can:
– buy a pet
– be trained to take part in dangerous performances

At thirteen, children can:
– work part-time (but only in certain jobs and subject to
  various conditions)

– be convicted of rape or other offence involving sexual intercourse

At fourteen, children can:
– have an air weapon (air rifle, gun or pistol)
– drive and ride in an agricultural tractor or machine
– go into a pub but not buy or drink alcohol
– be convicted of a criminal offence as if an adult (although sentence and trial are different)
– ride a horse without protective headgear on a road

At fifteen, children can:
– open a Giro account (with a guarantor)
– see a category '15' film
– if boys, be sent to young offender institution and, under certain circumstances, to prison

At sixteen, young people can:
– leave school and work full-time (but not, for example, in a bar, licensed premises or a betting shop)
– leave home (with parental consent)
– probably leave home without parental consent (but if considered at risk action may be taken, for example, care proceedings)
– marry with parental consent (or the court's permission)
– join a trade union
– if a girl, legally consent to heterosexual sexual intercourse (a boy can consent at any age)
– apply for a passport (with one parent's consent) and be deleted from a parent's passport
– buy cigarettes, tobacco, cigarette papers, explosives (including fireworks) and liqueur chocolates
– drink beer, port, cider or sherry with a meal in the dining area of a pub or hotel
– buy lottery tickets, scratch cards and Premium Bonds
– enter and live in a brothel (this is also allowed up to the age

of four, but not between four and sixteen)
- sell scrap metal
- become a street-trader
- drive an invalid carriage, moped and certain tractors
- if a boy, join the armed forces (with parental consent)
- get a national insurance number
- be used for begging
- fly solo in a glider
- apply for legal aid, advice and assistance

At seventeen, young people can:
- drive a motorcycle, car or small goods vehicle and a tractor on the road
- buy or hire a crossbow, any firearm and ammunition
- fly a plane
- apply for a helicopter pilot's licence
- be tried for a criminal offence as an adult
- be interviewed by the police without an appropriate adult present
- if a girl, join the armed forces (with parental consent)

At eighteen, children reach the age of majority and can do most things, such as:
- vote
- marry (without parental consent)
- serve on a jury
- make a will
- join the armed forces (without parental consent)
- apply for a passport (without parental consent)
- buy and drink alcohol in a bar
- work in a bar
- be tattooed
- own land
- donate blood and body to science with parental consent
- bet and go into a sex shop
- enter into binding contracts

– change their names
– not be made a ward of court
– see a category '18' film
– pawn goods at a pawn shop
– if a man, consent to homosexual acts in private (provided both parties are over 18) The law may change in the year 2000

At twenty-one, young people can:
– stand in a local or general election
– apply for a liquor licence
– drive a lorry or a bus

There is no legal minimum age below which:
– a child or young person may not lawfully baby-sit but those who have parental responsibility for the child being baby-sat must ensure that the young person baby-sitting is capable and will provide adequate care for the younger child

Quotations from Parents and Teenagers

PARENTS ON TEENAGERS

'If we knew that the end result was going to be OK, then there would be no problem sticking with it.'

'The trouble is, you want them to turn out as you want, and they want to turn out as they want; the relief is that the mismatch gets less as time passes. You just need to accept that.'

'They are fantastically interesting and fun to be with and generally very stimulating.'

'Sometimes I am seized by an utter sense of helplessness and a sense that whatever we have tried to do and are doing will make no difference.'

'You can't just suddenly say, "Right it is over to you, you have to take all the responsibility for your life now." '

'. . . can make our lives either heaven or hell.'

'He sussed us out for a couple of arseholes when he was about ten and we are a complete embarrassment to him the whole time.'

'. . . rituals – I think rituals are useful.'

'Ambition in an adolescent is the best contraceptive.'

'So it's a difficult knife-edge of getting the right balance between helping and not being over-protective – allowing them to have responsibility and being able to stand back. You can't do it for them . . .'

'. . . what bench-mark should we use against which to judge the outcome?'

'I love bits of all of them, but the whole of none of them.'

'It's knowing that there is a fine line between wanting something done so much that you help them to do it and pushing them into doing exactly the opposite.'

'I've felt that I have wanted to have privacy from the children about certain things, but there is a fine line between being private and being secretive.'

'It's not just knowing the facts about drugs; you also have to get your feelings about them under control.'

'They have the ability to turn anywhere they live into instant and complete squalor.'

'As for sex, most of us parents probably don't want to know what they are up to; but if we do, and we find out, then we have to be prepared for it to be considerably more than we had thought, whatever it is.'

'. . . you need to have quantity time in order to have quality time. Quality time with your children occurs when you least expect it. It may happen when you are on the way to the lavatory . . .'

'When the current interest is fifty different types of teenage magazines and forty-five different types of pearlised nail varnish, and hours spent in the bathroom making-up, and then taking it all off again – it is so different from what I was like as a teenager, I can be partly envious of it and partly furious.'

'To have teenage magazines with articles instructing them how to suck their boyfriend off, and whether to swallow or not, I find that quite upsetting. It takes away the excitement, and the privacy of discovering all that for yourself . . .'

TEENAGERS ON PARENTS AND ON LIFE

'I absolutely don't think that parents know what we get up to at our age.'

'My mother knows when I'm lying – she seems to have an instinct for it.'

'What parents would be horrified by is all the snogging and drinking, vomiting and smoking.'

'It would be great if parents listened a bit more to their kids, and then offered some kind of compromise deal rather than just being totally dictatorial.'

7

'Parents have this really bad habit of being right.'

'The best thing about Mum is that she is always there for me and if I am in any trouble she will just back me up all the way.'

'When Dad's teasing he doesn't know when to stop. He'll carry on till I cry sometimes, but maybe it's his way of showing affection.'

'We're good friends really and my parents are very persuadable when I really want something and try hard.'

'The best thing about being a teenager is being independent if I want to be but always being able to come back home when I want to.'

'. . . they've got good respect for me, and are loving and caring, and that's what matters.'

'If you pull someone you don't really like, well it's OK, but if you pull someone you really like, it's a million times better.'

'The best thing my parents do is that they make it obvious that they really, really care about me and my brother.'

'I think that parents should definitely chill out a bit – after all they're not going to whip their kids every night to keep them in shape.'

'I definitely think that the kind of society I am growing up in is different from that of my parents.'

'I do play my parents off against one another.'

'I think that my parents know more than they let on, but don't do anything about it because they know they have to trust me a bit, and that is right because we are, on the whole, pretty sensible.'

'If I was to give parents advice I would say "Don't be so hard on your kids especially if you know that they won't be totally stupid and always do things which you are worried about." '

'Unless parents really scare their children into obeying them, then they are likely to try most things. There is certainly a tendency to try things which parents are saying "don't do" about, because if they say that, the thing must be good to try.'

'My older sister tried to kill me a couple of times when I was about seven. One time she locked me in the airing cupboard and pumped its temperature up to over 40 degrees to try and see if she could cook me – no laughing matter . . .'

1

Present and Future Dilemmas in Parenting Teenagers

Many of the most basic dilemmas for parents of teenagers are as old as the human race itself. Yet they are continually and subtly changing and being reinvented in the light of contemporary pressures within our society. These changes have both positive and negative aspects – as this book, and the experiences of parents recounted in it, will bear witness to.

Of age-old significance is the fact that as teenagers change and become independent, parents have to change too. Having been at least partly in control when their children were small, they now find themselves to some extent having to adapt to their teenagers' wishes, rather than making decisions on their behalf.

'I do think that teenagers are interesting, and what they do is interesting, and that's what I enjoy. The downside is that as teenagers grow older, they want to be with you less and less. It was quite hurtful at first when my son didn't any longer want to do things with me or my husband. For

*instance, this is the first year that my son has said he is
not coming with us on holiday, which makes me feel very
sad, even if I do understand why he wants to go on
holiday with his friends. I suppose it represents a change
which I know is irreversible.'*

This is from Abbie Scully, who is the mother of Fiona, fourteen, and Rory, sixteen. Abbie runs a 'head-hunting' agency
(partly from home) and is married to a computer expert, Ian,
who works for a multinational computer firm in Belgium and
is an 'absent father' for much of the time. Abbie and Ian live
in separate houses in the same village.

From the traditional parental roles of close physical contact
and emotional support – hugs, kissed grazed knees, reading
books together at bedtime, walking together to and from
school, cooking regular meals and sitting down and eating
them as a family – gradually you have to move to a looser,
more independent, but still interdependent form of living
together. You have to be there for your children 'just in case',
but your teenagers are somewhere else much of the time,
'finding themselves' out there. For some, like Abbie, these
changes can be a sudden shock.

*'My son Rory now refers to our family as being entirely
dysfunctional and I think that he may be right; but perhaps
all families are dysfunctional in some way or other. Rory
was wonderful up to the age of fifteen, but something
happened on his fifteenth birthday. I don't know whether it
was hormones or what, but he suddenly became distant,
self-centred and moody. I thought we had a wonderful
relationship until then, but he began being very rude, using
hideous obscenities which he said he got from me!'*

'Having time' for your children as they grow older can be
another cause of anxiety. The trouble is that 'time' becomes
more and more when your teenager wants it to be, rather than

time that is convenient for you; and this need for time gets increasingly intermittent and unpredictable, as Abbie explains.

'Although there are still odd moments of quality time, as a working mother I long ago stopped deluding myself that I could come home and say, "I am going to have quality time now." You really need to have quantity time in order to have quality time. Quality time with your children occurs when you least expect it. It may happen when you are on the way to the lavatory and you happen to bump into your son and have the most amazing conversation. You suddenly think, "Gosh, we are still connected after all." But I do in many ways regret that I worked so hard when the kids were young. People say that childhood is short, but sometimes you don't believe it when you are caught up in working, because it doesn't suit you to think about it. But you can't just say to your kids, "Oh no, not now, I am busy, can you tell me about that later?" because that moment is lost for ever.'

Then there is their freedom and their friends; and certainly with the latter, not necessarily the friends that you would choose for them, but the ones they choose for themselves. Picked up off the street, met at discos, brought home from school – though they do occasionally turn out to be allies, according to Abbie:

'I get on well with Rory and Fiona's friends, and I like them very much, especially when they say that they don't think I'm too bad. They don't understand why Rory is so rude to me, but the rudeness is, I have to admit, mutual. With my daughter Fiona, since she turned twelve, there have been many more arguments about her freedom and her friends. She wants to go everywhere, do everything, and have friends who I'm not too thrilled with – ones that steal and are into drugs. It's not because she is a girl that I

feel she shouldn't have as much freedom as she wants, but more because she's not that streetwise and is an attractive little creature in a miniskirt.'

Another recurrent and difficult dilemma is that of control. It is a dilemma which has changed enormously over the last few years with the advent of Children's Rights and the concept that physically punishing children and teenagers is no longer acceptable. However, the difficult but, rightly, much sanctified idea of controlling by trying to be positive and praising the good in your offspring doesn't always work, as almost every parent has experienced.

'All in all, Rory is a highly intelligent guy but he has an "authority" problem. He is very anti anything which even slightly smells of authority. Personally, I don't think I ever have been authoritarian, but I do think that if your mother asks you a favour you might say "yes" occasionally. I blame puberty and all those hormones. I do try and compliment him on the rare occasions when I come home and find that he has done something off his own bat, and that does seem to please him. But it is the saddest thing in my life that we have these rows. It is a complete shock.'

So what is the fall-back position when being positive does not work? How do you use a judicious mixture of bribery, per-suasion, cajoling, threatened sanctions and actual punishment when all else fails? There are no easy answers because adolescents, being human, are infinitely variable as to what they will respond to – both individually and over time.

'I've threatened to take away his allowance and then would have to recant because he needed things. There is a problem about imposing sanctions because you can't really say, "Go to your room without any dinner", which we used to in the good old days. They just wouldn't listen.

*After all, it can be scary having a violent argument with a
teenager who is bigger and stronger than you are and is
screaming at the top of his voice. At the end I feel totally
drained; my heart is thumping, I'm impotent with rage
and totally upset. That's definitely one of the main
problems that remain with Fiona and Rory: sanctions.
How should I punish my kids and what hold do I have
over them? But maybe I haven't asked them enough about
how to handle these situations.'*

So the first solution might be asking the teenagers themselves
what they will best respond to. However benign most parents
try to be most of the time, no parent has an inexhaustible
supply of patience, and there will always be a breaking point:

*'I've always had a breaking point where I totally lose it. It
must make the children nervous though, not knowing
when I am going to blow! We have these slanging
matches, and he has started to refer to me as "the bitch"
to other people; but then I shout at him, "You fucking
bastard, how can you fucking well dare to talk to me like
that", so we are as bad as each other.'*

One area where 'control' is particularly relevant for contemporary parents is the age at which young people are exposed
to what appears to be an 'adult' menu of hedonism: sex, illegal drugs and alcohol. Research shows that initiation in all
these areas is happening at a younger and younger age, but
there is little evidence that teenagers are becoming emotionally mature earlier in order to cope with these attractions,
even though they are going through puberty earlier.

The average age of puberty in boys is now twelve years,
and 95 per cent of boys have reached puberty by fourteen. In
boys, the first changes are the testes getting bigger, followed
by the growth of pubic hair, then underarm and body hair,
followed by facial hair. The penis gets longer and thicker and

about a year after this ejaculation begins. Boys begin to sweat more and smell more because of the development of special apocrine sweat glands. It is somewhat obvious to those in close contact with adolescent boys, but alas not always to themselves, that they can no longer get away with such infrequent attention to their daily toilet! Voice breaking tends to occur after all the other changes.

The average age at which puberty starts in girls is younger – eleven and a half years, and it has occurred in 95 per cent of girls by just over thirteen. Breast development starts first and can start as early as eight or nine. Pubic and underarm hair growth starts at the same time, or shortly after. Periods begin later and have normally begun between the ages of ten and sixteen.

Because of earlier puberty, reflected by an ever-increasing sexual explicitness in both male and female dress, and in magazines such as *Bliss*, *More*, and *Just Seventeen*, the courtship scene is not one familiar to most parents from their own teenage experience.

> 'With Fiona's current interest in fifty different types of teenage magazines and forty-five different types of pearlised nail varnish, and the hours spent in the bathroom making up and then taking it all off again – so different from what I was like as a teenager – I can be partly envious and partly furious. The music scene, the boys scene, is just so strange to me. To have teenage magazines with articles instructing girls how to suck their boyfriend off, and whether to swallow or not, I find that quite upsetting. It takes away some of the excitement, and the privacy of discovering all that for yourself.'

The age of first sexual experience (kissing and cuddling) has dropped by two years over the last twenty years, and now occurs, on average, at around twelve to thirteen years of age. This can be a dilemma for many parents, as Abbie points out:

'I can't blame boys though. It is very difficult for them, because guys do just sometimes get carried away with sex, and my daughter and her friends go around looking absolutely gorgeous with low-cut tops and bras showing out of them – all very tempting. It must be very hard to be near them and keep your hands off! I reckon that my greatest fear with my daughter is sex, and my biggest problem with my son is lack of communication and hostility. The sex thing is difficult though. I feel that I've been open with them about it from really early on, but they don't ask me about it now; and if I start on about sex, they turn me off again, because they don't want to hear about it from their mother! What's even worse is if I start talking about my own sex life, or lusting after someone. It's, "Go away, we don't want to hear about that." '

Likewise, exposure to illegal drugs is occurring earlier, with almost weekly reports in the press of children as young as eight or nine being offered drugs, or even bringing them to school themselves.

'Then there is the boredom for them of living in a village. One tends to think that it is kids brought up in the city who will have all these temptations, but actually it's almost worse in village life because there are no alternative activities. I've read somewhere that drug taking in villages in England is greater than in the urban areas of the cities.'

Cannabis, in its various forms, remains by far the most common drug experimented with by young people, followed by amphetamines and then ecstasy. Natural hallucinogens (magic mushrooms), solvents, cocaine and heroin come much further down the line. The present trend will continue into the new millennium, with new and stronger forms of hybrid cannabis plants being continually developed, along with experimentation with a wider range of synthetically developed drugs. It is a strange fact that drug taking in rural communities is on average higher than in urban communities – perhaps because of the boredom mentioned by Abbie, or because of the increased ease of 'growing your own'.

On a more mundane and daily front, meals can be another source of friction and one sign, frequently remarked upon by parents, of their teenagers' growing independence. Disagreements centring around meals are crucial for Abbie, as they seem to represent, for her at least, a loss of 'control' over the traditional family life-style.

'Since Rory was fifteen he prefers to skip meals or eat them in front of the television or take them up to his room, rather than eat with us. I've given up the fight against television and video now, and that's sad as I feel there is no family life anymore. But perhaps the microwave was the final death knell for family meals.'

This anxiety about meals has many aspects. The facts do show that most teenagers skip meals – especially breakfast – and that snacks provide up to 30 per cent of the energy they need. But research involving teenagers keeping food diaries found that, despite the grazing and the convenience foods, their diets were varied and nutritious. On the whole, they did eat all the different foods that they needed: protein, fats and carbohydrates. Yet the dilemma is that research also shows that teenagers who spend more time with their family are less likely to smoke or to try illicit drugs; are more likely to leave school later with qualifications; and (for girls) are less likely to get pregnant before the age of eighteen.

Another aspect of this dilemma over family meals is the increasing anxiety for parents, particularly when it comes to daughters, over eating problems.

> *'Another niggling worry with my daughter is that she*
> *might get eating problems, so I lean over backwards not to*
> *mention anything about her size or shape, especially*
> *when she is in my room trying on clothes.'*

If there is one thing that young people say they would like to change it is the size and shape of their bodies. More girls than boys want to lose weight generally, and boys would like to be taller and heavier, and have more muscles and a bigger chest! One in four eleven-year-old girls think they are too fat, and by the age of sixteen this rises to one in two girls. At all ages girls feel less confident about their appearance than boys. Overall, boys feel more confident than girls at all ages, with six out of ten boys feeling confident compared with four out of ten girls.

Feeling guilty appears to be something you cannot avoid as a parent. There is a tendency to think 'Oh, if only I had done something differently then this or that would never have happened.' In fact, one doesn't know that there wouldn't have been other, worse problems, because you see people who seem to have been brilliant parents and yet their teenagers seem to be screwed up, and you see other people who seem to be very bad parents and yet their teenagers seem to be brilliant. What is more, although guilt can be based on logic, it also has this knack of appearing to be totally irrational:

> *'The guilt creeps in mainly about not being there enough*
> *for them; or being present but not really there. I work*
> *from home a great deal, and when you have the accounts*
> *in front of you and are working with a calculator, you*
> *might as well be on another planet. I also feel guilty about*
> *not being patient enough, and I've never been a parent*
> *who devoted myself to driving the kids everywhere,*
> *because I do have other bits of my life which are*
> *important to me. Even when I do drive them, I have to*

pretend I am not there, as they seem to be embarrassed about me in front of their friends.'

What of modern and future teenagers? What do they see as their major dilemmas? Fiona, who is fourteen, is Abbie and Ian's daughter. She is coping with her parents living separately and is both aware of, and coping with, their needs as well as her own. She is well informed, investigative and always trying to tap into more freedom.

Many children have to deal with their parents living apart. Two in every five marriages end in divorce and the UK has the highest divorce rate in Europe. Although most children will survive into adulthood without major problems, whether their parents are living together, separated or divorced, children living with their two birth parents do report an overall higher satisfaction with life in general. However, many children, like Fiona, become philosophical about their parents separating, particularly as so many of their friends are experiencing the same thing:

'At first, when Mum and Dad separated, Dad was a bit upset and I was not sure about going round to his house, because I didn't know what to say to him that would help. I don't mind them living apart now. I don't know how they got married in the first place, they are like cheese and chalk together. Dad mainly talked to my brother about it and then Rory got upset because he didn't want to take sides or anything. Mum and Dad's relationship was a bit of a scabby area but they're much more friendly now. Anyhow, most of my friends seem to have parents who are divorced, and most of them don't get on so well with one another as my parents do!'

On the positive side, one of the features of young people is their enormous adaptability to new situations, and how quickly they learn to use the social surroundings they find themselves in to their own advantage. On the negative side, life is stressful enough for young people without having their parents add to it.

> '*I can't say that I actually like my parents living apart, even if I do understand it. But nowadays Dad, when I am with him, is more relaxed than Mum about letting me do things. Even so, I'm the youngest in my family and they do seem to want to keep me a baby. They don't seem to realise I am no longer that young. Like sometimes I'm trying to put my point of view across and they say, "We don't want to hear your point of view, Fiona – we just want you to do what we say," and I'm like, "But I'm not five any more." They're restrictive about everything, they over-react and shout at me, though most of the time we do try and compromise. It's funny, because me and my brother know one another much better than my parents do, so we have to stick up for one another. If we didn't have each another, I think we would both go crazy with our worries.*'

The worries of teenage boys and girls are slightly different, in both the type and quantity of the worry! When fifteen-year-old boys were asked what they worried about most, the way they looked, their families, their careers, being unemployed, and money, topped the list – in that order. For girls it was the way they looked, their families, their friends, and school. Girls worry significantly more than boys and, for instance, in spite of the fact that 'the way I look' was the top worry for boys and girls, it was a worry for six out of ten girls and only three out of ten boys.

A major concern of teenagers is their families and, within their families, how unpredictable the behaviour of their parents can be. Teenagers like stability at home as they go out to explore and experiment with the world. They need to have a fall-back position, both geographically and emotionally. The dilemma for parents is endlessly trying to be patient and to understand their teenagers' behaviour, but sometimes something has to give. Trying to discuss with teenagers what drives you mad about their behaviour, before you go completely spare, is better than appearing as if everything is sweet and happy and then suddenly losing your temper. But life cannot always be that well controlled, as Fiona observes:

> *'Mum can be very unpredictable. She gets really angry about things I wouldn't think she should get angry about – say, if she comes home and Rory or I have had friends round and things are in a bit of a mess. She goes berserk, which just doesn't seem reasonable to me.'*

There is also the embarrassment for many teenagers of having to cope with their parents in public. If teenagers are self-conscious about themselves, they are frequently doubly so about their parents, who may project a completely different image from the one their offspring would wish. But even Fiona finds redeeming features:

> *'Mum's clothes are the most embarrassing thing about her for me, and I won't go into town with her if she doesn't wear some decent clothes. By decent clothes I mean . . . well, just not her clothes really! The most embarrassing thing about Dad is his massive bald patch, but he wears nice clothes, even though he's a bit old. What hair he has is grey. I suppose that just happens when you get on, and even though I tell him to dye it, he won't. His laugh is the best thing, and nowadays he occasionally tells the funniest jokes and can have my friends in hysterics. It's fine going into town with him because he wears casual clothes and that's OK.'*

It is natural that, as teenagers try to develop their own identity, they can become extremely uncertain of themselves. This self-consciousness and uncertainty can express itself in aggression and moodiness.

> 'What worries me most about me is the way I look. I've become very self-conscious and think I look so ugly. I hate it that I may be fat as well. My brother gets at me, because I put on make-up, and he says, "Why are you putting on make-up? It's just to impress the boys," but it's not – it's to make me feel better – it really is. If I look in the mirror without make-up on, I just think, "Oh no, I look so ugly." There are so many pretty girls in our year and I hate that. I can't stand anything about the way I look, even though my boyfriend thinks I look great. But you don't just go out with someone for their looks, do you?'

Young people give 'money' as a major concern. The chief dilemmas are: how much they should get from their parents; whether it should be paid weekly or monthly; what it should cover in the way of day-to-day expenses (clothes, lunches, travel and so on); should this money be used as a method of control; and should it be used to teach them good money management for the future.

> 'Money is a constant source of argument between me and my dad and my mum; and what is worse is that they don't always agree between themselves. Sometimes that's great, because I can persuade Dad that Mum's not giving me enough. I also like to have a bit of independent money by working – though sometimes that gives stress to my mother who thinks it is interfering with my school work.'

For teenagers, like adults, there are many dilemmas revolving around cultural issues. Sometimes these are to do with race, at other times to do with class differences; and they can create conflict for children, as Fiona observes from her own experience.

'Most of my friends are allowed to play on the street, but not Rana – she doesn't even have a boyfriend. Her parents would climb the wall if she so much as looked at a boy. It's awful for her, like she lives one second away from the centre of our village and when me and two friends went to call for her, she opened the door and said, "Come inside." We did because we know she's not allowed out, so we don't force her. But then she said, "Let's go to the village and get some sweets," so we did. Then we said, "Since it's such a nice day, let's sit on the bench and eat them." Rana said OK but every second she was saying, "Let's go now. Let's go," because she was terrified her parents would get mad at her for being out so long. After school she goes straight home, while the rest of us just hang around and chat. I would hate to be her. I've only seen her once this holidays, in spite of the fact that every time I do see her I say, "Hi Rana, do you want to come round today?" She always says, "No, I can't." Her sister, who is seventeen, had a boyfriend once and her parents found a Valentine's card from him, and they kicked her out of the house. They are still into arranged marriages, but Rana says she's not going to have that, and she's going to choose who she'll marry. She cut her hair recently and her parents were even horrified at that. I reckon she must feel really cut off, the way her parents behave with her.'

Friendships and sexual relationships are also high profile for young people:

'Boys of my age or older are nice. I think they're really friendly to you when you reach fourteen. Before, when we were with younger boys, they used to call us names and trip us up and be as rude as they could be. I could never understand that, and I still don't. Now that they are starting to get to a more mature stage, they are not being so stupid. Loads of my friends are boys now, and they are

24

just like my girlfriends, but not quite as close.

'*It can be awkward with boys because you don't always know whether they want to go out with you, or just be your friend. If you do end up being really good friends, you usually then find out that they fancy you, and then it's, "No way, why does this have to happen?" because you just wanted a friendship. But it's not really serious. You go out with one, have a laugh, and then go on to another one.*

'*Boys do try and push the sex as far as they can, and some of my friends aren't virgins any more which I think is really stupid as we are only young – but that's their decision. Most boys are really sweet and don't push it but wait till we're ready. The boys who went with the girls who aren't virgins boast about what they did and it's all around the school next day because the boys want to impress their friends and tell them what it was like. The girls either want to just tell their best friends, or show off about it, depending on the girl. I am sure sex will be on the agenda for me next year though.*'

The dilemmas highlighted in this chapter, and how to find solutions, are dealt with in greater detail in later chapters, mostly through quotations from parents and teenagers themselves. At the end of each chapter, there is a list of suggested 'tips' to help parents and teenagers to cope with this period of time – which can be so rewarding if it is handled right. The last word of advice before the tips in this chapter goes to Fiona:

'*My advice is for parents to be more understanding. Don't be over-protective, let kids try things, and when necessary reach a compromise. Like, "If you want to do this, then you have to do that . . ." Work it out. Try to be positive with them and try not always to be angry, because then they won't tell you stuff. My mum would much rather I told her about things, but I have loads of friends whose parents just lose it if something goes wrong, so they just don't get told. Sometimes kids will do things to rebel, just to show their parents that they don't have to do what they say. Try to have a good relationship with them and don't always be getting into arguments. If you get to know them well, then you'll know that you can trust them not to do anything stupid.'*

What parents can do to adapt to their teenagers' changing needs:

- don't assume that looking after teenagers is necessarily going to be hell – for many people it turns out to be a very rewarding time

- don't lose your nerve – for almost all of us things will be OK in the long run; but there is no denying that sometimes it does take a lot of nerve!

- young people want to test the limits of what they are allowed to do, and in order to test those limits, they need limits to be set (by parents, teachers, others). Rules and rituals are important and need to be negotiated between parent and teenager

- expect a 'fair' degree of, but not 'absolute', honesty from teenagers about what they are up to

- bottling things up and then exploding is not a sensible way of dealing with things! Try discussing what upsets you, in a normal conversational tone, before you hit the roof

- don't be afraid to express your own feelings and your own views about sex, drugs and other matters, but remember also to listen to their views on the subject

- try to avoid issuing orders to your teenagers. If they refuse point blank, everyone loses face. Negotiate, negotiate, negotiate

- you need to have your own clear set of values (hopefully agreed between both parents) and you should explain what they are to your teenager, and why. Their set of values may well be different, so get them to explain what their values are, and why

- you need to tell your children you are getting separated (when you definitely are) but they don't need to be told all the details (the bedroom door can be kept closed!)

On a practical note, if your son's testes have not started getting bigger by fourteen, then puberty is delayed and it is worthwhile seeking a medical opinion. If your daughter has no breast development by fourteen or periods by sixteen, you may also want to seek a medical opinion.

Some facts for teenagers:

- the best protection against parents stressing you out is for you to have someone outside the immediate family with whom you can share your feelings of frustration, anger, happiness – a friend, neighbour, grandparent, or teacher

- parents are very useful. They provide the roof over your head, the hot water, the heating, the telephone rental bill, clean towels in the bathroom, the washing machine for your clothes, the television, the video, the food on the table (or in the refrigerator if you can't wait!)

- the best thing about being a teenager is being independent *if you want to be*, but always being able to come back home.

If you want that home to be one that you *want* to come back to, you need to keep your parents at least a little bit happy – and that takes care

- ask your parents how they behaved at your age with their parents, and try to look interested when they reply

- learn to say 'sorry' when you have done something wrong, and as soon as possible. This has a remarkable effect on soothing troubled waters (one can't say sorry too often!)

- if you are going to do things which you know will upset your parents, don't go out of your way to rub your parents' noses in the fact

- remember that one day *you* will be the parents of teenagers

2

When Living With Teenagers Is Wonderful

The period between ten and eighteen years can be fun, an involving, compelling and challenging time, when teenagers move from dependence to independence. Watching them experimenting with the huge menu that life provides, discovering that they are able to cope with these challenges, taking new initiatives and feeding back their discoveries to their parents, can and should give parents immense pleasure; even if other parents feel that it is enough if they have managed to bring children up through adolescence and are still friends with them.

As teenagers gradually find their own feet, their own values, their own personality, one recurring, entirely natural thought that all parents seem to have is expressed here by John Roberts:

'So far they are wonderful, sociable, on the whole trustworthy and well behaved, and have passed all their exams extremely successfully. What more could we ask? But when looking to see if we managed to make a success

*or not of bringing the children up through adolescence, the
question is what bench-mark should we use?'*

John is a maths teacher at a grammar school in
Buckinghamshire. He is married to Gail, who is a pharmacist,
and they have two children. Emma is eighteen and David is
nearly fifteen.

How should parents judge the outcome of bringing up
their teenagers? Exam results? Employment, happiness, sat-
isfactory family life? Probably a combination of all these
things; but just as important are the simple satisfactions of
daily life with them: their sociability, their curiosity, their
ability to cope, their consideration of other people's needs,
their delight in what you took pleasure in at their age. When
it comes down to it, John's view of his children may give the
ultimate criteria.

> *'The children are fantastically interesting, stimulating and
> fun to be with. I am enjoying their increasing
> independence immensely because it means I don't have to
> worry about them so much.'*

This 'letting go' is not always easy. It can be difficult for parents to know how much they should be doing for their
teenagers and how much they should be giving them their
independence and allowing them to discover for themselves.
John again:

> *'There is a territory between being responsible for them
> and they being responsible for themselves. It's knowing
> that there is a fine line between wanting something done
> so much that you help them to do it and pushing them into
> doing exactly the opposite because you're showing them
> how much you want it done.'*

Many things help to make life with teenagers more fun, one

of which is doing things with them that you yourself enjoyed at the same age:

'I have this image of them both lying in bed, reading before they go to sleep. We've always considered reading as a kind of luxury, which we get a lot of pleasure from. We read to them every night when they were little – both Gail and I were read to as children. Reading aloud to your kids intuitively feels important and the research shows that it is important too. We read them everything: Wind in the Willows, Peter Rabbit, Alice in Wonderland; *and as they got older,* Swallows and Amazons, Ballet Shoes *and then books like* Sherlock Holmes *– very traditional, the stuff we had read to us by our parents when we were young . We went on reading to them till they were eleven or twelve years old, but it's a changing world and I doubt whether the next generation will do the same, though there will be an awful lot of old people around to do the reading!'*

This raises an interesting point about the role of grandparents. Overall the number of children and old people who are dependent (not working) compared with the number of people working is projected to go up from 64 dependents for every 100 people working in 1994 to 68 people dependent for every 100 working by the year 2031; but there will be a fall in the number of dependent children and a rise in the number of dependent elderly people. Grandparents will need a role, and will continue to play a large part in family life, not least in continuing the emphasis on family rituals, as suggested by John's wife Gail, who works as a pharmacist:

'The other thing is rituals. I think rituals are useful. Some are religious, and some family; some we've invented ourselves, and some they get from their grandparents. We do many things the same every day, and the children say

*those things are important – daily rituals like getting
them to tidy their rooms, getting off to school every
morning, trying to eat together every night, sitting
around reading before going to bed – it's all quite
structured.'*

It is worth remembering, when living with teenagers, not
only that you went through adolescence yourself, but also
that all other parents are, or will be, involved in the same
activities, pleasures and concerns. However, this sharing of
experience between parents of teenagers is more difficult as
your children get older. When they are young their life is an
integral part of yours. You meet other parents at the school
gates, over cups of tea in the afternoon, and at parents'
evenings. As children become teenagers and more independent, only the last of these meeting places survives on a
routine basis. Gail again:

*'If I was advising other parents, I'd say it is crucial not to
get isolated from the realisation that the worries about
what your teenagers are doing are universal. If I had read
a book saying, "Look, this is what happens to all parents,
don't worry about it, it will come right in the end", I don't
think I would have been so stressed about some of the
things that I did get stressed out about, and I could have
enjoyed the terrific things about them more.'*

A source of great amusement for parents can be how different
their teenagers are from one another, as Gail points out, drawing on her own experiences:

*'Emma's eighteen, and behaves herself well, is very keen to
please us, and still thinks we are perfect. David, on the
other hand, sussed us out for a couple of arseholes when
he was about ten and we are a complete embarrassment to
him the whole time. For example, when we drop him off*

with his friends he doesn't allow us to have the radio on in the car, because of the kind of music we like. What we wear, what we say, what we do, is all a complete embarrassment, which I can only laugh at because that is the way I felt about my own parents.'

Gail fully realises that though her teenagers do, on occasion, stretch her to the limit, none the less, like most things in life, the best things are worth working at and waiting for:

'David has always stretched us since the age of about two, but is now an extremely competent, capable and good fun teenager and still interestingly challenging. There is no question about it, looking at both of them, and what fun they are, it has been worth it ten times over, even if it has been bloody hard work!'

Although Gail is not calculating in terms of money when she says 'worth it', it is estimated that by the age of seventeen, the cost of bringing a child up is £50,000, excluding anything extra like private education or private medical costs. Depending on your beliefs as to the importance of the role of parenting, this may appear cheap or expensive; but it is certainly worth it when everything is going well, and when you consider that most long-term outcomes for teenagers are extremely positive.

There are other rewards to be had from the differences between teenagers in the same family. John again, who sees the differences between his two children from another perspective:

'I always thought that David had the potential for being a great deal more sociable than Emma, and now I think that's being realised. He's got a terrific sense of humour which is a total saving grace, so when he's feeling confident he's great.'

Gail responds by highlighting the differences between the two as she sees them:

'David can make our lives either heaven or hell – but mainly heaven. I do so love everything going right and I don't want rows or anguish. There aren't many but there are occasions when I want to shout at them both. David's reaction to being shouted at is that he goes absolutely ape, and Emma's is to sulk for days. On the whole, the sulk is easier to deal with. David yelled at us the other day, "I can't believe that I'm even related to you!" He's really looking forward to the independence of leaving home, but when he does I bet he'll come round and use all the home comforts like our washing machine, and I will love him all the more for that.'

Perhaps most central to a successful outcome is parents acknowledging how important family life remains as their teenagers get older. Asked who the adult is they get on best with, four out of ten teenage boys and three out of ten teenage girls say their mother and father equally; two out of ten boys and three out of ten girls say their mother; and just over one in ten boys and just under one in ten girls say their father. Hardly anyone else rates, except for older (adult) brothers and sisters.

This success of family life involves that all too valuable commodity 'time', which both John and Gail emphasise, even though John, when working during term time, exceeds fifty hours work a week. Research shows that fathers who work more than fifty hours a week are often less involved in family activities. One in four fathers work these hours in the UK at the present time.

'One thing I feel really proud of is that, in spite of my school work, I gave my kids a lot of time when they were young. There is no easy way round this and it did mean

giving up a lot of other things. At weekends I used to take them with me whenever remotely possible – shopping and even into work. It slowed me down, and they often got bored, but they were there and there were educational and bonding opportunities all the time.'

Gail expresses similar feelings:

'Having time for them is absolutely crucial, and that is difficult when you are both working and does demand a great deal of organisation. If I had more children, I would worry less, value them more, and be with them every step of the way. I think we ought to value and respect our children more highly than anything else. Both our ambitions are to bring up two really nice kids. If we achieve that, we've done well.'

Less central, but still of great importance, is parents remembering what adolescence was like for themselves, and recognising similarities in their own children, as John does when discussing what life was like for him at the same age:

'Emma is into "the meaning of life". It is almost as if a new mental set is suddenly sparked off in teenagers, which begins with them questioning the meaning of life. I remember going through exactly the same sort of phase when I was seventeen. I became deeply religious, ardently so. I fell in love with an avid Christian girl in my class which lasted for eighteen months, until I discovered sex as well as love and got over it! Emma is reading a huge amount of philosophical stuff – Sartre, and that Persian philosopher bloke whose name I can never remember. I'm very sympathetic over all this, and told her that my philosophical period was precipitated by an unrequited love affair. She admitted that was probably her reason as well.'

There is no single way of relating to adolescents in such a way that you remain friends, they achieve their independence, and everyone feels positive about it. Parents, even within the same family, will manage this in different ways, make different contributions and, at the same time, help and support each other when the occasional surprising revelation occurs!

> *'I'm good at getting Emma out of her moods and we do work through things together. I think that I am generally closer to the children than John is, especially over their emotional and sex lives. They are both very open about their sexual feelings now; and David talks to me about his feelings of insecurity. In fact he talks with me about just about everything, though obviously I don't know what he isn't talking to me about! It was a shock for both John and myself the other day when they suddenly told us they'd both smoked cannabis! Perhaps we're total innocents after all, but we discussed it, and found a way through in which we were able to tell the children how we both felt about it.'*

Such revelations can be positive if parents use them to seek more information to help educate themselves in areas where they may not be well informed. Gail and John should not be too surprised on the cannabis smoking front, as more than one in five of fourteen and fifteen-year-olds have tried cannabis, rising to nearly half of fifteen and sixteen-year-olds. Looking at it the other way round, five out of ten fifteen to sixteen-year-olds have not tried illegal drugs. (Many more facts about drug taking in young people are given in Chapter 5.) Open discussion about illegal drugs (as well as other subjects like sex, relationships, alcohol and tobacco) well before the age when teenagers are first likely to be exposed is a good general policy to follow. Trying to be well informed about the subject, independently of what your teenagers may come up with in the way of information, is helpful on occasions. Their views may be biased!

School life plays a central role in the successful passage of teenagers towards adult life. Although most research shows that parents are the most powerful influence on young people, nevertheless how children get on at school, how satisfied parents are with the education being provided, what the child's peer group at school is like, all play a part; but according to Gail, parents may worry too much about school.

'Parents are a lot more interested in school than children are, and parents are more interested in how their kids are doing, but on the whole most kids survive school OK. At least, John thinks so. It's all to do with the expectations that parents have for their children, and how they are doing in comparison with other children. We worried endlessly at first, with the result that our children both started out in the private sector and then switched to the state sector. Emma did brilliantly in the private system and was in danger of becoming a snotty little shit; and I was concerned about the private school ideal that the sunshine shone out of their arses. The kids' schooling was the closest that John and I ever came to a full-blown bust up. At one stage, John even wanted them to go to boarding school so we could live the grand social life with them safely tucked away – travel, go to endless parties, do the social round.'

Sorting out the question of schools for teenagers is obviously a major problem for parents, and continues to be of concern throughout school life, not least because of the ever-increasing emphasis put on final exam results. John, as a teacher, recognises that a lot more goes on at school than straightforward classroom education:

'I am ashamed that I ever thought that private education was what they should have, and me a teacher too! I just can't imagine how I came up with crap like that. It would

have been a disaster, and they would have been imbued with a whole range of beliefs which wouldn't have been our beliefs. It took them a year back in the state sector to adapt. In fact, Emma made a small fortune that year selling her homework to other kids, which was probably better than selling dope. It took a lot of effort to change the way she thought, the way she spoke, the way she related to other people, but she did it, and she did it really well. David is a total non-conformist and we are told by the school that he is "disruptive", which turns out to mean that he often refuses to agree with what the teacher says and wants to argue about everything. He also does things like wearing his raincoat inside out, just to be different. There is a rider on my belief that most kids survive school, because we are in the position that if the going gets too rough for them, we can afford to send them privately, and that's an option that is only open to a very, very small proportion of society as a whole.'

In judging the success of what parents want to achieve a big question remains: what is the final hoped-for outcome of putting all that time and effort into bringing teenagers up? In broad terms it would probably include, for most parents, having them in their twenties settled with a decent job, living with someone who makes them feel good about themselves and whom they make feel good, and a couple of children of their own. But for others, just generally being happy and enjoying what they are doing would be fine. This should not mean forgetting the more immediate pleasures that Gail enjoys:

'With Emma, the joy has been seeing her satisfaction in working at school, being interested in her work, enjoying acquiring knowledge, doing something she considers she is doing well – that is what gives me pleasure. She used to come in from school smiling, saying, "I've done some

really interesting work today." That's more than enough satisfaction.'

This delicate balance between enjoying your teenager at the time and looking at the long-term outcome has also to involve how your teenager feels about it all. If he feels good – valued and respected – then so will you. John and Gail's son David is now nearly fifteen. He is amused when describing his life and his parents' attitudes towards his behaviour. Even when admitting that his parents do not always know what he is up to, he shows humour and insight into the practicalities of his life.

> 'The best thing about being a teenager is being independent if I want to be, but always being able to come back home when I want to. I get much more freedom than when I was younger – if I want it. I have an elder sister, so I think my parents are more relaxed second time around with me. It's little things like being able to go to town by myself and do other things younger than when my sister could. She was eleven or twelve when she was allowed to, and I was eight or nine, so that's a good thing. But maybe it's just because they are less protective of me being a boy.'

One thing from teenagers' point of view that rates high in smoothing their passage towards independence is, not surprisingly, money. It represents, as it does in adulthood, a certain degree of status, and the freedom to experiment with the things money can buy. How teenagers come by the money they have to spend, and how they choose to spend it, is different for boys and girls. Fourteen to fifteen-year-old boys, on average, get a combined total from pocket money and paid work of £11.40 per week; girls get an average of £10.60. Three times as many girls as boys spend money on presents for their friends, and they are much more likely to buy magazines, cosmetics, cigarettes and pets. More boys than girls spend money on sports items, computer games and arcade gambling. David manages a mixed economy and finds other benefits to earning his cash:

> '*It's good being given an allowance. I get £50 a month for everything, without any other hand-outs from Mum and Dad. The thing about my allowance though is that it's tied in to keeping my room tidy, so the bad thing is being made to tidy my room. My parents negotiated that: no tidy room, no allowance, and that's annoying – but it's their house, I guess. To be more independent of their money and to swell my income, I've started baby-sitting our neighbours' kids, who are incredibly well behaved. I did four hours last night and got £16, which was great as they just go to bed when they are told! I prefer baby-sitting at night because once they are in bed you can sit around watching TV. I even do homework when baby-sitting because you have less things to distract you than in your own house.*'

Another pleasure for parents is seeing how their teenagers begin to appreciate the needs of other people, and develop an increasingly clear insight into what their parents consider right and wrong – even if teenagers, like David, don't always choose to change their ways because of these insights:

> '*As I get older I know more about what actually upsets my parents, like if I've been on the phone for ages, or if I've gone out without telling them. Other things we have arguments about are things to do with my friends. Stuff going wrong at school is another thing. Mum usually knows what's happened because I come home and tell her, and it's easier that way rather than a letter from school. Last week I skived off school after SATs with three friends, without telling the teachers. Lots of my friends do this, but the school found out and was going to write a letter home.*

When I got home that day, I just sat there for a time and then finally told Mum. She got very angry, but I don't think she got as angry as she would've if she had found out first from the school, or I had lied or something. She did say, "Oh no, I'm going to have to punish you and you know I hate that." In the end I was grounded for a bit, which in this case I know was justified.'

Nevertheless, parents with apparently close and easy relationships with their offspring have to accept that not only will they not be told the whole story, but that they don't even need to know the whole story. Sometimes it is also a question of both parents and offspring knowing that the other knows, but just not choosing to discuss it. David again:

'I'm absolutely sure that my parents don't know what we get up to at our age. I mean like when we were at dinner the other night and we were just having some random conversation and the subject of cannabis came up. They said, "You've never tried any of that, have you?" and we both said, "Yeah, yeah we have." My parents were a bit out of it because neither of them had ever tried anything. In some ways I think they would have rather not known, and maybe we were wrong in telling them, but normally we can discuss anything with them, and I think both Emma and I felt, "Well, why not?" At least it means we can now discuss it within the family, rather than just between ourselves.'

David, like most young people, does have his own ideas about parents in general, and how they might help themselves to help their teenagers.

'In general I think that parents should chill out a bit. After all, they're not going to whip their kids every night to keep them in shape. Neither are kids going to do

everything their parents say, especially as parents can't be around all of the time. Unless parents really scare their children into obeying them, they are likely to try most things. There is certainly a tendency to try the things which parents are warning them off, because if they say, "Don't do that", the thing must be good to try. There has to be a reason for not doing it and we want to find out why for ourselves.'

There is no such thing as a perfect parent: different teenagers need parenting in different ways, as even David is aware of:

'If there was one thing I could change about my parents . . . I am not sure what it would be. Sometimes I think they are too over-protective towards me, and sometimes I think they are too relaxed. Like one of my friends can do whatever he wants and I really wanted to do that for a while, but now I'm glad my parents care about where I am. My parents do tend to worry about me, if I am later back than I say I am going to be. That's the kind of thing that stresses them, but they've got respect for me, and are loving and caring, and that's what matters.'

There is no absolute gold standard for how teenagers should turn out, and the world continues to be made up of individuals. But there are certain things, which are outlined throughout this book, which should be helpful in making life easier and more enjoyable for everyone within families, and some of these are outlined below.

What may help parents keep the good times good!

- enjoy teenagers for what they are, not for what you want them to be

- make sure they know that when things get bad for them, you will be there and will go on loving and looking after them

- once they have been born, bringing children/teenagers/ young people up is the single most important professional job that anyone has to do in a lifetime, and one that does need time

- listen to what they have to say; respect their views and explore with them 'the territory between you being responsible for them and they being responsible for themselves'

- have respect for their lives and needs as seen by them, as well as as seen by you

- humour is the great lubricant between people, especially between generations

- don't always expect your advice to be followed (advice is advice, not an order); but do expect, and listen to, the reason given as to why it isn't being followed

- set rules, be consistent, but don't always expect the rules to be rigidly adhered to

- be aware of the fact that you are not being told everything that is going on in their lives, but don't feel you always have to challenge this. Accept that you and your teenager knowing that the other knows something doesn't necessarily mean that it must be discussed

- if you want them to share their lives with you, you must share how you feel about your life with them. Teenagers need to know what you think, even if they don't agree

What may help teenagers keep the good times coming!

- learn from what is good about your parents so that you can do it even better when you have teenagers of your own!

- ask your parents' advice about things that concern you, even if you don't take their advice. It at least makes them feel needed

- do the occasional thing which you know will please your parents, for example, just occasionally do the washing up, the same day and without being asked. It is a small sacrifice with a big return, and often saves having arguments about a whole lot of stuff which you are definitely not going to do!

- asking your parents if they want to use the phone before you use it will save hassle. You could even go as far as asking them if they want a contribution to the bill! But you may think that that is going over the top.

- sometimes parents do need to be told to 'chill out', but using more 'politically correct' words may go down better

- working to get some money, in addition to any allowance your parents give you, reassures both them and you about future financial independence!

3

The Daily Ups and Downs of Life With Teenagers: Parties, Alcohol, Smoking and 'Discussions'

ike the rest of life, living with teenagers has times which are terrific and full of rewards, and times of desperation and despair – and much of the time it is somewhere in between. Living with anyone – a partner, a parent, a relative, a friend – has these many different aspects; we are, after all, social animals whose daily diet is social interaction, both good and bad. New social interactions bring new experiences, and teenagers have to build on their previous experiences to deal with these. New social contacts will be handled in ways based on previous family experiences, but will also be developed more and more in terms of teenagers' own needs and preferences rather than those of their parents. At the same time, social interactions within the family – with parents, brothers and sisters – are continually changing.

Sammy Rendert is fourteen but appears at least a year older. She has two older brothers, is post-puberty, and is the daughter of Rosemary Rendert, a GP, and her husband Craig, who works in publishing.

'There are horrible things about being the youngest girl in a family. But the good things are when your older brothers are in a good mood and they spoil you. On my birthday I get lots of treats, but when they have their friends around they try to beat me up. A couple of weeks ago, my eighteen-year-old brother was having a dinner party and all his friends were here. I had a skirt on and was going out, and he decided to lift my skirt and show my bum to everyone just as I was leaving. It was dead embarrassing so I gave him a slap on his face. He was a bit drunk at the time.'

The relationship between brothers and sisters within a family changes as they get older, and the age at which they have more adult experiences, such as partying, drinking alcohol and smoking, will depend on where in the family they come. In Sammy's case, some of her experiences are the result of being the youngest in the family with two older brothers.

'My brothers have left home and live elsewhere most of the time. When I go and stay with them, they take me out to the pub, but my parents don't know that. I've been drunk a couple of times, though normally I don't drink much. I can't even remember what it was like, but I was definitely sick. Most of my friends my age have been drunk at one time or another, mainly at parties. The only time we drink is when we are at parties and there are lots of other people drinking. We don't go to pubs alone at our age because it's easy to see we're under age and we'd get asked for an ID. At the parties I go to, the boys tend to get a lot more drunk than the girls, and they drink anything and everything. I think the girls are a bit more sensible.'

Alcohol is the most common drug (mind-altering substance) used by young people, if you discount coffee and tea. Overall, the same number of girls and boys drink alcohol, but boys definitely drink more heavily. Nearly nine out of ten young people in the UK have tried alcohol by the age of thirteen, and by the age of fifteen almost six out of ten say that they have drunk alcohol in the previous week. A great deal of the drinking goes on in pubs and at parties, and the latter provide experiences which are considerably beyond any that their parents would have had when they were teenagers, and beyond what most parents wish to know about:

> *'I don't know about buying drink because I haven't tried. Most drink comes from parents' houses, at parties when the parents are away. These happen about every three months or so. Whether my parents let me go or not depends on whose party it is. They certainly want to know where I am going and what time I am going to be back.'*

Most teenagers sensibly try their first alcoholic drink at home, under the guidance of their parents. It is still not clear what represents 'sensible' drinking for adolescents. There is general acceptance that adult men should not exceed between 21 and 28 units per week and adult women between 14 and 21 units (a unit = a glass of wine, half a pint of beer, a shot of spirits). The safe level of drinking for adolescents should be less than this, depending on their age; but there is a tendency for young people to 'binge' drink, that is drink large amounts of alcohol at one sitting simply for the sake of getting drunk. This does lead to a number of teenagers ending up in Accident and Emergency Departments, either because they have had an accident while drunk, or because of alcoholic poisoning. By the age of twelve to thirteen years, just under one in ten teenagers have bought alcohol at an off-licence, and by the age of fourteen to fifteen, one in ten have bought alcohol in a pub. The most popular drinks for girls are wine and alcopops, followed by cider and then beer or lager. For boys, the most popular drink is beer or lager, followed by cider and alcopops. Low alcohol wines and beers do not seem to appeal to young people.

> *'I like partying, except for buying clothes for them with Mum, who is really irritating. I wish she wouldn't come shopping with me, she always wants me to wear straighter things than I want. The most recent party I went to was last night and was typically very rowdy, with every kind of music, though personally I like what is in the charts. My parents would have been horrified. Mostly when there is a party we say there is going to be a parent there, but that is usually not true.'*

Although most drinking in young people does not lead them into danger, one in ten have drunk more than the safe adult limit, and a quarter of thirteen to seventeen-year-olds get into arguments and fights after drinking alcohol. A thousand children under fifteen years of age are admitted to hospital each year with acute alcohol poisoning. The earlier young people start drinking alcohol, the more likely they are to use illegal drugs, but that doesn't mean that one leads to the other. It could just be that the same kind of personality likes the effects of alcohol as likes the effects of drugs.

The other exposure at parties is to smoking – both active and passive tobacco smoke. By the age of sixteen, one-third of young people will have smoked and continued to smoke, one-third will have smoked and given up and one-third will not have smoked at all. There is a remarkable leap in the number of young people, both boys and girls, who smoke between the ages of twelve and thirteen, and those who do so between fifteen and sixteen. At the younger age many are violently anti-smoking, and often trying to blackmail a smoking parent to stop. It is an age at which most say they will never smoke and they think it is disgusting. But then the new freedoms kick in, and the experimentation begins, with little appreciation, in the case of tobacco, of how addictive it is.

'What parents would be horrified by at parties is all the snogging and drinking, vomiting and smoking, both boys and girls. Most smoke because their friends do and they want to look cool. No one gets pressured into it, it's just that they want to experiment. There is no difficulty in buying cigarettes. No one ever asks your age. We did this trading standards project at school. A teacher took me and a friend, also aged fourteen, to a nearby town. We went round all the shops asking for cigarettes and everyone let us buy them. We weren't challenged once in about ten different shops.'

Teenagers are not ignorant of the theoretical information on the dangers of smoking. Half of young people think that cigarette advertising does have a definite effect on them, and young smokers are more likely to live in a family in which other members smoke, especially parents or an older brother or sister. The main reason young people give for trying cigarettes is curiosity, though the reasons for going on smoking include the belief that smoking puts you in a better mood and makes you act more confidently, and that smoking helps you lose weight. Nine out of ten adult smokers began smoking before the age of sixteen. However, if a young person is able to give up smoking before the age of twenty-six, it is unlikely that they will suffer any harmful health effects during the rest of their lives. At present, smoking ten cigarettes a day costs £578 per year, smoking twenty a day costs £1157 per year, smoking forty a day costs £2314 per year. A further factor is that the government, while decrying smoking, is raising £65 million in tax and £15 million in VAT from cigarettes sold to young people.

That parties are a potential area of conflict between parents and teenagers is shown by the fact that almost all young people that we interviewed were less than totally honest with their parents about what parties they went to. Sammy is no different when it comes to telling her parents what she gets up to:

'As far as honesty is concerned, it's so so. If the party is being given by people I know my mum and dad don't like, then I don't tell them. I just say that the party is being given by someone they do like and know will be sensible. The parties they don't like are ones given by my friends that they know are into drinking. It's drinking and drugs that my parents are really worried about, and they're afraid I'll get in with the wrong crowd. I hope they know that I am not that stupid. None of my friends do drugs, and it's not my scene either. I think parents had it different when they were young. Parties weren't so experimental. I think each generation gets to experiment younger and younger – with drink, with snogging, with drugs. My mum probably hadn't even tried drink by my age because it was much harder to get hold of.'

The idea of having a teenage party raises immediate anxiety for most parents. They feel under pressure to allow their house to be used by their teenager, while their teenager in turn can feel under pressure from peers to have a party or at least a 'gathering'. Such parties have a not unfounded reputation for trouble and damage! Neither side wants things to go wrong, and parents do usually understand how difficult it is for party-giving teenagers to stay in control. The kind of dilemmas parents face are: should the party be in their house or on neutral territory such as a local hall? Should adults be present or not? Should they be visible or not? Should they stipulate a finishing time? Should they allow people to bring drink or provide a limited quantity themselves?

'My parents were away over New Year's Eve. They wanted me to go with them, but I wanted to be with my own friends, not the children of theirs. They agreed I could have ten friends over, and they even left us some wine, beer and food. I guess I should have known better. It was agony. It wasn't my friends, but the gate-crashers who

*spoilt it for everyone. I spent the whole party worrying
and stopping them trashing the house.'*

Although young people do, from time to time, argue with
their parents, most of the time they find ways to avoid con-
frontation when they know that what they want to do will not
meet with parental approval.

*'The last argument I had with my parents was this
morning. Mum wanted me to go and buy some jam for
breakfast from the local shop, but I couldn't be bothered,
so we had a big argument. I didn't want any jam, anyhow.
Generally I get on well with Mum, and it's always over
stupid things that we argue. With my older brothers my
parents would always be arguing about them going to the
pub and what time they would be back. Sometimes I have
arguments with them about what time I will be back, but
Dad is more lenient than Mum so I try him first. I can get
round Mum by saying I'll be staying at a friend's house so
she doesn't have to worry, then she doesn't have to know
what time I got back. One of the best things about being a
teenager is getting to rebel, and rebellion includes getting
back later than my parents say I can. It's a way at getting
back at my mum if I am angry at her, because I know
that she will worry. I know it's not a nice thing to do,
but . . .'*

Teenagers' negotiations take into account the differences in
personality between their mother and father, which can be
exploited to the full:

*'I do play my parents off against one another. For
instance, Mum sometimes says, "Oh, I'm not sure about
that. I'll go and ask Dad whether that is OK by him."
Then she'll come back and say no, and I know she hasn't
spoken with Dad, so I'll go and ask him, and he'll say a*

*later time so it's OK. Time for getting home is the biggest
area of conflict, no doubt about it. I don't think my mum
had a social life when she was my age.'*

Their awareness of the differences in attitude to various
behaviours stretches beyond their own parents, and they are
keenly conscious of the advantages and disadvantages of the
stances different parents take:

*'Most of my friends' parents are less strict. That's good and
bad. It's good that they aren't so strict because then you
don't have so much pressure on you, but it's better that
your mum and dad are strict because then you won't get
into the wrong crowd. Most of those who are in the wrong
crowd want to hang around with people they think are
cool and stuff, but I don't think they actually like one
another much.'*

These issues do bring up again the question of 'control' by
parents: how best to maintain it, what works, what doesn't
work. It is a recurrent theme and there are no easy answers:

*'They ground me sometimes and the other thing they do is
stop my pocket money. Most of the time they stick by it
when they punish me, and I know that if I am grounded
for a week and I go out, then I will be grounded for
another week. It does stop me from going against them.
Going out is a regular argument with my parents,
because they don't like me going out on weekdays. We
sometimes argue about homework too, but Dad helps me
about that.'*

Arguments about homework are another recurring source of
anxiety and friction between parents and teenagers. The most
common after-school activity is watching television, followed
by homework, and then listening to tapes. Boys are three

times more likely to play computer games after school than girls. Girls tend to be more conscientious than boys about doing homework. Between the ages of eleven and fifteen, one in four to one in five boys do no homework at all, while only one in seven girls do no homework. The average number of hours fourteen to fifteen-year-old boys work is 1.2 hours per night, and girls work 1.5 hours per night. One in five girls and one in ten boys do up to three hours or more homework at the age of fifteen years.

> *'Being a teenager is good because you are more carefree. You don't have to go out to a job, all you have to do is go to school. After school you've just got homework, but most of it is not hard and you don't feel driven like I think you would if you had to earn money every day.'*

Sammy, like other teenagers interviewed for this book, thinks that parents must be understanding and spend time talking:

> *'The best thing about parents is when they are really understanding, when they are willing to spend time with you doing things that you want. Also, when they want to spend time with you and you don't because you are going out, and they just say, "OK, we can do it tomorrow" and don't get upset or anything. That's them understanding your needs and respecting them, and not insisting that their needs are greater than yours.'*

Any parent will have noted the remarkable ability of their teenagers to do a large number of activities at the same time! One thing worth noting is that the amount of time young people spend watching TV seems to be established at primary school age and doesn't alter much afterwards. At fifteen years of age, about half of young people watch up to two hours of TV a night and one in six watch for three hours. Sammy continues her observation on parents:

'The irritating things are their rules, like not going out on weekdays, obeying curfews and not drinking. Most of my friends' parents are the same, and often my parents and their parents talk to one another about what the rules should be. I don't like that because I think they will tell my parents some of the things I get up to. But I think my parents know more than they let on, and don't do anything about it because they know they have to trust me a bit, and that's right because we are, on the whole, pretty sensible.'

Sammy's parents live in a large semi-detached house just off a ring road. Most of the day-to-day 'caring' of Sammy is done by Rosemary, who accepts that as Sammy grows older there are things they used to enjoy doing together that will change:

'She was wonderful to go shopping with. When we could agree on something that she and I both liked for her it was a truly wonderful experience. She'd say, "Wow, I would like such and such from Gap but I can't quite afford it," and then I'd say, "Oh, it's gorgeous and would suit you – here, have this fiver to help out." It was a real bonding thing with the girls out together, but she hates me coming shopping with her now.'

Frequently the changes are not easy. The areas of friction change and will sometimes appear to parents as argument for argument's sake and difficult not to take personally, particularly if one or other parent feels in the firing line. Nor is it any easier with the youngest child in the family, as Rosemary has found:

'Most of my arguments with Sammy are about parties, her smoking and drinking, and her appearance – things like, "The heels are too high on those shoes." She gets angry with me about all sorts of things, and in a much more personal way than the boys did. The boys were angry with

the world at large when they were teenagers. "It's all wrong and unfair, and all grown-ups are horrible" – that kind of thing. But with Sammy, it's me. Whatever I do is wrong because it's me doing it. Not because I am a parent, but because it's me. That's the way it feels to me, anyway. It is really confrontational and difficult. I thought with Sammy being the third, I would be used to it by now and could avoid this kind of thing, but actually I find it much harder – probably because she's a girl and she knows how to get at me. She doesn't do it with her father, and he lets her get away with things more than he did with the boys, but I think that's because he's less involved.'

Parents may struggle to contain their irritation but teenagers are extremely good at sensing how to 'get at' a parent, consciously or unconsciously. It gives them a sense of their own emerging power if they can clearly see the effect they have.

'I do try not to get angry too often and try to preserve my anger for when I feel it's really needed, but it doesn't always work. We had a ridiculous argument about nothing this morning. I think it was really because of the party she'd been to last night, and her getting in later than she agreed she would, and me lying awake worrying about her; but what we actually argued about was her going out to buy something for breakfast this morning. I can't believe I was so stupid, and Craig got involved too. Why couldn't I have said what I really felt about her being late? Sometimes I try to turn things into jokes to steer things away from conflict, but Sammy won't allow me to steer them away. I think she needs the conflict: she's testing life and her own powers.'

Sometimes it is just a question of parents knowing how they should handle things but being too tired, irritated or distracted to manage the situation in a way that avoids conflict. It may in part be a reflection of the fact that many mothers are working professionally outside the home, as well as trying to play a major role in bringing up their children and still being responsible for most of the running of the household. Neither does it help if their own mothers were not attempting to do so much.

> *'It isn't her being wild. I just feel that she is cross with me which upsets me. It usually happens when I am tired. I come home, she gets at me, I get cross with her, and then I get cross with myself for having reacted. I really don't like getting angry and losing my temper, perhaps because when I was young I never saw my mother getting so cross. She was there for us all the time and she got by without losing her temper, so I feel that I am wrong to lose mine. I tend to bottle things up and then explode, which is not a sensible way of dealing with issues like Sammy smoking and drinking – particularly as it obviously doesn't work.'*

Parties, smoking and drinking are all part of teenage life. In spite of millions of pounds' worth of health education aimed specifically at teenagers, experimentation with smoking and drinking continues unabated. Parents should not feel they have failed if their own children are party to this experimentation. It is the norm. The best parents can do is state their views, and point out that cigarette smoking is highly addictive, even after a week or two of smoking, and is extremely difficult to give up. The pleasures of alcohol will be obvious to almost every teenager from seeing their parents drink, and rather than being hypocritical, open discussion about what is good and bad about drinking is infinitely more sensible.

However, parents have to accept that their offspring will, in the long term, need to make up their own minds from their own experiences. Back to Sammy again:

> *'If I was to give parents advice I would say, "Don't be so hard on your kids, especially if you know they won't be*

totally stupid and always do things which you are worried about." All parents have their doubts and sometimes they take them too far. If anything was going really wrong in my life, I could go and talk to my parents about it, but I don't think all parents are like that. I know that some of my close friends, when they are in deep trouble at school, are too afraid to tell their parents about it. One girl in particular is terrified of her parents because she knows how angry they get. They just can't control it and that is completely wrong.'

Some things which may help parents of adolescents to minimise stress:

- if you don't want conflict, don't have children – but by the time you read this it is probably too late!

- don't be too hard on your kids, especially if you know that they won't be totally stupid and do things which you are worried about

- negotiate ahead of time over routines like washing up and helping with the housework. If necessary, get a written agreement: 'Monday, Wednesday, Friday: washing up – Alice. Tuesday, Thursday, Saturday: washing up – Tom. Sunday: washing up – Dad and Mum.' Detail is often helpful: 'Table clearing, washing up and putting away!'

- remember what you were like at that age and how you regarded your parents' advice. Is there any more reason why your offspring should listen to your advice than you did to your parents'?

- realise that parties are an area of conflict. With parties in your own house always negotiate as to whether your

teenagers want you to be there or not, and accept that there
may well be a certain amount of damage

- be aware that with parties in other people's houses, it is reasonable to make some enquiries as to what is likely to be
  happening

- remember always to try to find something positive to praise
  first and then, and only then, see how it might have been
  done better!

- don't run your adolescents down in front of their friends
  and don't compare them unfavourably to their friends

Things that teenagers may find useful in reducing stress:

- remember that parents are grown-up adolescents with all
  the responsibility for you and very little control over you.
  Anyhow, that is the way they feel!

- parents get tired and like to sleep. A non-tired parent is an
  infinitely nicer person to negotiate with. Parents have to
  work during the day to earn the money to pay your phone
  bills, for the television and the video, so 2 a.m. discussions
  about noise tend not to be welcome

- get your friends to introduce themselves to your parents
  when they come into the house

- when you feel stressed with your parents, get out of the
  house and beat up on a football/basketball/baseball/cricket
  ball/tennis ball/softball

- say 'sorry' when you are wrong, loud and clear. With practice
  you'll be amazed how easy it is and what a wonderful effect

it has on your parents and their happiness and therefore, in the long run, on your happiness

- if you smoke and turn into a sixty fags a day person, remember that if you hadn't smoked, after ten years you could have afforded a bright red Ferrari at £48,000!

- remember when you have had too much to drink, you are more likely to have unprotected intercourse and four times more likely to have an accident. It takes about an hour to get rid of each unit of alcohol

4

Coping With Teenagers' Developing Sexuality and Sexual Relationships

Most young people feel that they invented sex for themselves, blissfully ignoring the results of a few hundred million years of evolution and the fact that almost everyone on earth is here because of it. The bizarre thing, given this evolutionary need for us to have sex in order for us (and our selfish genes) to exist, is how difficult many people still find it as a subject for open and easy discussion.

There are, however, many less sexual taboos for today's parents than when they themselves were teenagers. What hasn't changed is that most parents would prefer it if their teenagers did not start having sexual intercourse at a young age because of the risks of pregnancy, leading to an increased chance of failing to complete their education; because of the risk of sexually transmitted infections; and because of their child's general immaturity.

In spite of the fact that full sexual intercourse is occurring at a younger age, it actually normally occurs considerably later than most people imagine. If asked, over half of parents and young people think that the majority of all young people have had sexual intercourse by the age of sixteen. The facts are otherwise. Careful research has shown that approximately 28 per cent of men and 18 per cent of women had first sexual intercourse before the age of sixteen. This is an important fact. Girls need to know that they are in a huge majority if they have not had sex by the age of sixteen. It is also worth noting that although young people are starting to have sex at younger ages than in the past, they are marrying and having children later.

Sexual experience and sexual intercourse are two different things, but parents need to appreciate that sexual experience does begin at a young age:

'Alice is thirteen years old. She had been dating this boy for some months and they seemed to have a great relationship which I suspected was going too far as I kept finding them cuddling together! I did gently suggest to her that one thing tends to lead to another, but I couldn't be around the whole time to see that they at least kept three feet on the floor. One night one thing did lead to another and twenty-four hours later Alice told me that she thought she might be pregnant. I didn't panic, which was amazing, and calmly asked her what she meant. Her boyfriend Pete, she admitted, had "come" on her dress and that sticky stuff had come out on her. She'd gone to the school nurse next morning who had arranged for her to have the emergency contraceptive pills. Poor Alice had had to go to the local chemist to get them, where the old ladies there stared at her. When I asked her for more details it was obvious nothing had gone near her vagina, and I didn't want her to take the pills unless it was absolutely necessary. I was sad that she hadn't come to me first, as it could have saved her a great deal of stress, but she was proud of the way she handled it.'

Teenagers are frequently afraid of confiding facts about their sexual lives and other seriously worrying problems to their parents, especially if their parents blow up at them over relatively minor problems like 'not tidying your room'. This is compounded when the teenagers themselves think, or know, that they are to blame for what has happened. It is also difficult for parents to get it right. It is perfectly reasonable to get cross about the day-to-day irritations that teenagers constantly confront parents with, but your teenagers do need to know that you will be there for them and will help them at times of real crisis, and this should be discussed with them frequently and well in advance.

Alice, like most young people, was not rushing into having sexual intercourse, but gradually experimenting with her boyfriend.

'It was an accident, but I was terrified that Mum would say that Pete could never come home again. So I phoned my best friend Jane and it was she who suggested that I tell the school nurse about it. I've known Pete for about two years and he's thirteen too but about two months older than me. He'd been asking me out for ages but I didn't go at first as we were both running in the same crowd of good friends and that was really cool as none of us had paired off. Then he started going out with another girl, and at that stage I suddenly realised how much I liked him. He is an incredibly kind person and I can talk to him about anything. We are still very good friends even though he's been my boyfriend for seven months now. The first time we went out Pete knew that I hadn't kissed anyone before. He wasn't bothered, even though he had, but he said he enjoyed being with me and talking to me. What happened this time was we had been playing with the computer, playing music and talking to one another, and then we started touching. I was touching his willie, or he was rubbing himself against me and touching me at the same time, but we both had our clothes on.'

The age of first sexual experimentation is considerably younger than that of first sexual intercourse, with the mean age of first sexual experimentation for young people in the UK being between twelve and thirteen years and the mean age of first sexual intercourse being between sixteen and seventeen years.

When things went wrong, Alice used her common sense and she is glad she finally told her mother what had happened:

'I trusted Pete and it was something personal and nice that we both wanted to do. What made me freak was that he came on my dress. I had read in Bliss that you can get pregnant without actually having intercourse and that was what made me panic and get the emergency pills. Before taking them I phoned my friend Jane again and told her that I was quite scared. I had been reading about the ingredients in the pills and about the effects, and that the pills might make me sick. Jane thought I ought to tell my mum so I did and she was brilliant. She said, "From what you told me, I really doubt whether you could have got pregnant. Otherwise I would certainly say to take them." Luckily my period started two days later so Mum and I didn't have to worry for long and it was good that I didn't take the emergency pills. Mind you, if I had needed an abortion I wouldn't have had a problem with that.'

There are few subjects which raise such rabid differences of opinion in society as the question of abortion. In the UK the legal rules about abortion are based on the 1967 Abortion Act, and an abortion can only be done for certain reasons, in an approved place, and with the agreement of two doctors who have to sign a legal form. The commonest grounds for having an abortion are: 'when continuing a pregnancy is more risky to the physical or mental health of the pregnant woman than if the pregnancy was terminated.'

Both being pregnant and having an abortion are very safe, but in statistical terms, an abortion is slightly safer than a pregnancy, so this leaves a lot of leeway for sympathetic doctors to help.

When it comes to boys, their sexual experiences may differ considerably, but many go through a phase of wondering whether they may be homosexual.

'Before I had my first girlfriend, it was just wanking. It never seemed to be wrong or anything, just something I did when I felt like it – easy peasy. It seems like I've been doing that for as long as I can remember along with all my friends – though we don't talk about it much. There was a period when I did wonder whether I was gay or something because I was wanking all the time, and I thought that might mean I fancied men or something.'

However, only 4 per cent of men and 2 per cent of women report some kind of homosexual experience between the ages of sixteen and nineteen. Overall, around 6 per cent of men have sexual activity during their lifetime with someone of their own sex, and the rate is under 1 per cent for women. So most young men will end up heterosexual, and those that have homosexual feelings will hopefully go on to express, and feel at ease with, their homosexuality.

For most young men, sexual activity and being attracted to women progresses rapidly.

'I had my first proper relationship with a girl when I was thirteen. We had been fumbling around snogging, and when she was touching me and felt how worked up I was, she just took it out and played with me till I came. I first went the whole way with her when I was fourteen so it was a quick education! Ever since I've started having serious sex I've bought my own condoms, but I didn't go into the chemist when I was fourteen as it would have

been too embarrassing. I got them from the machines in the toilets of pubs. I'd have thought that they would have them in the school toilets but they don't. I do worry about getting my present girlfriend pregnant. I worry about her needs generally, and that includes the things she likes when we're having sex. I think how good sex is depends on who one is oneself and what the other person is like, and what they want from sex and what you want yourself.'

Girls tend to be better informed than boys at all ages, both about sex in general and about contraception, and this knowledge improves with age. But when young people of both sexes do have sexual intercourse, they need to be fully informed about using contraception. The two most commonly used methods of contraception among teenagers are condoms and/or the pill. The choices of contraception available are condoms, the combined pill, the progesterone only pill, the diaphragm or cap, spermicides, the female condom (Femidom), the safe period with fertility awareness, withdrawal, progesterone injections and the 'coil' or intra-uterine device (IUD). There are newer methods being developed but at the moment these are all variations on a theme rather than anything really revolutionary. It sounds as though there are a lot to choose from, but it's less than it seems and not all of them are ideal for young people.

Young people also need to know that they, like anybody else, can get emergency contraception from their own or any other GP, from a family planning clinic, from a hospital Emergency Department, or from a Brook Advisory Clinic. Young people will frequently feel embarrassed about getting contraception from their own GP, whom both they and their parents may already know. It's worth noting that emergency contraception can be effective up to seventy-two hours after the 'accident' took place but the sooner it is taken the better. The IUD or 'coil' can also be used as emergency contraception up to five days after unprotected intercourse. (See the Appendix for further details about various forms of contraception.)

Most parents are unaware of their teenagers' experimentations with sex, either because they don't want to know or because their children don't want to tell them.

'I was five when I was first told about sex. My mother locked me in the bathroom and explained it, though I can't remember what she said. I do have a younger brother, so I knew some of the differences as we used to share baths. I was thirteen when I had my first snog, which wasn't even by mutual agreement. My younger brother was part of a football team, and they used to go and practise down at the local gym and I would watch them. During a rest period their trainer, who was twenty-two and really immature, snogged me. I was so young it didn't occur to me to tell him to piss off. I progressed from snogging when I was fourteen. It was the first time I got really drunk and one of the boys at a party I was at, who must have been about fifteen and really manky, seemed to think, "Hey, wouldn't it be great to have her make me come", and that developed into me doing a hand job on him. At the time I was too far gone to think of it as anything but yucky, but I expect he was thinking "Wah-hey". I just got on and did it, it sort of just came naturally, but I do remember thinking, "Well, what's in this for me?" Then at sixteen I began to club. Clubbing frequently involves a swift snog, a swift grope and if the girl is willing all the way to full sex with minimum lead up. Often the sex happens outside in the car park or anywhere convenient, though you have to watch out for security video cameras. When I first had sexual intercourse, a whole group of us had gone to a rave party and we shared a biggish tent for the nights.'

Research shows that for about half of both men and women first intercourse took place with someone with whom they were in a steady relationship; and for one in three men and one in five women, with someone known to them for some time though not a steady relationship. The timing of first intercourse was considered well timed by three-quarters of young men and two-thirds of young women. For half of all men and women, curiosity was a factor in the loss of their virginity, and for the other half it was part of a natural progression in the course of the relationship. One in twenty men and women reported being slightly drunk as the main factor associated with their loss of virginity.

For many young people, their first experience of sexual intercourse is hardly an earth-moving experience:

'It was a fun time, because I hadn't realised that if you wanted to have sex at one of these things basically you got it without any hassle. We had this smaller tent, next to the big one, which someone who had been to these things before brought along and which anyone who "felt the need" could use. It was booked up every night several times over. Actually losing my virginity was a good laugh because the bloke was quite fit, but you have no idea how difficult it is to get clothes off in a two-person tent. I had this halter top on which was bright red and skin tight with no zip or buttons and looked like I had been poured into it. I was lying there thinking, "What's supposed to happen next?" and "What am I supposed to do?" and "Maybe I can have a cup of tea when it's over." It was a bit unsatisfactory but it didn't hurt – possibly because I had been riding bikes for years to school, but who knows whether bicycle seats make things easier when it comes to it! The sordid bit was that anyone who used the tent had to find their condom afterwards – not the most romantic thing. I didn't tell my parents as any intimate details of my sex life are just manky.'

Many parents are afraid that if they discuss the facts about sex with teenagers, or even if their school provides explicit sex education, it will encourage earlier sexual activity. The facts show the opposite. Research in this country and others clearly shows that the more informed a young person is about sexual matters, especially if the sex education is linked with teaching social skills, the more likely they are to delay the timing of when they first have sex, and the more likely they are, when they do have sex, to use contraception. This is important, because surveys show that up to 50 per cent of young people having sex for the first time do not use any contraception.

There is also the question of where young people want sex information from and where they actually get it. Among young women aged between eleven and twelve, one in two give parents as the main source of information about sex, one in five give school lessons, one in six TV or films, and one in ten friends. Among young women aged fifteen to sixteen, one in three give friends as the main source of information, one in four give parents, one in five magazines and books, and one in ten school lessons.

Among young men aged eleven to twelve, just over one in three give parents as the main source of information about sex, one in five give school lessons, one in five TV and films, and about one in six friends. Among young men aged fifteen to sixteen, one in three give friends as the main source of information, one in four give school lessons, one in five parents, and one in six TV and films.

Asked about what they would like to have as their main source of information about sex over one in two of all young people aged eleven to sixteen said parents, whereas one in four said school lessons. Very few gave friends, doctors, nurses, magazines, books, TV or films as their desired main source of information, but these scored higher when it came to learning about contraception.

Many parents feel uncomfortable talking about sex to their teenagers:

'With Sophie I have had an occasional talk about sex, but I have never actually sat down with her and talked about sex

and contraception direct – it was just too embarrassing for us both. I do know that she knows about sex because of her comments in overheard conversations with her friends. She certainly joins in conversations within the family about sex and sometimes we joke about who we fancy!'

(For parents who want to know, Brad Pitt and Tom Cruise are the men most young women aged sixteen to nineteen would like to go to bed with, whereas their mothers are more likely to be turned on by Robert Redford!)

It is no surprise that mothers and fathers still feel that young girls need more protection than boys when it comes to sexual experience.

'I do feel differently about sex when it comes to Sophie than when I was thinking about my son, and I am much more protective of Sophie. It's the old reason that she is the one that is going to get pregnant. But there is something more – a sort of feeling that it is OK for boys to go out and experiment and conquer, but not all right for a girl to experiment or be experimented on! It is a very sexist attitude and not one which I particularly like in myself. If Sophie started to have sex now at fourteen I would worry. I would be happier if she waited until she was over sixteen and, if I was honest, nearer eighteen. The reason is first because she would be more ready for it emotionally, and then because she and her partner would be more likely to use contraception and take precautions against sexually transmitted diseases. In fact they are actually quite judgemental about some of their friends around the age of fourteen who are having sex. Sophie doesn't think that someone of her age should have sex.'

Parents need to take into account that as children get older they inevitably begin to get more embarrassed talking about sex. It is best therefore to make an early start with discussions about the straightforward biology (when they are around five or six). The details, including information about contraception, can come later (about ten or eleven).

Furthermore, it is useful for parents to know that young people can get contraceptive advice and contraception from doctors and nurses at any age, without their parents knowing about it, as long as the doctor/nurse feels that the young person understands the issues sufficiently. However, it is also recommended that doctors and nurses always try to persuade the young person to talk to their parents about it.

Things that might help parents with their teenagers' sex scene:

- try to talk about sex and contraception when your children are young enough to be curious (ages seven to ten) but not too old to be embarrassed (from puberty onwards)

- if you find the subject of sex too embarrassing, in spite of what you must have done to create them, don't despair. If you cannot talk openly about sex, you are not alone; and most adults are not very good at talking to each other about it either

- try getting some good books about sex and contraception which you can 'discreetly' leave around

- find out what the school is teaching them about sex, contraception and sexually transmitted infections so that you are aware of the major gaps

- you can't dictate who they go out with, and too much disapproval may well keep the unwanted relationship going

- teenage magazines are a useful source of information about sex but do not be too shocked!

- education and ambition are the best contraception

- leave condoms around. They will probably insist that they want to buy their own but they'll probably disappear and it won't be the mice

Things that may help teenagers with sex:

- your parents must know something about sex if they made you, even if they can't talk about it

- most of sex is not about having sexual intercourse. Don't be in too much of a hurry – think of all the sexy things that you can do without having intercourse itself

- remember the main erogenous zone is the brain (even if you think otherwise) so use it as well as your other sex bits

- there are many different places you can go to for contraceptive advice, including emergency contraception: your family doctor, any other family doctor, a family planning clinic (look in the telephone book), the Brook clinic (look in the telephone book) and, if all else fails, your local casualty department

- remember the down sides to sex are pregnancy, sexually transmitted infections, disappointment, and emotional turmoil. OK, the up side is the pleasure

- even if your parents don't mind you sleeping with your partner at home, remember that the rest of the house may not necessarily want to hear you

- for teenagers, condoms have to be the best method of contraception. With or without the pill or another method, they stop pregnancies and sexually transmitted infections.

5

Blowing Minds: Teenage Exposure To and Experimentation With Illegal Drugs

Mind-altering substances have always been around within society and drug use is as old as civilisation itself. Opium, cocaine and heroin have been around for decades: for centuries if not millennia. What is new is the almost universal exposure of young people to the drug scene at a younger age and the advent of so-called 'designer' drugs. It is no use pretending that they are not fun; nor that they don't have, like most things in life, their dangers. One of the major dangers results from being arrested, owing to society's decision to make some 'mind-changing' substances illegal, while others, like alcohol, remain – at least after a certain age – legal.

Because drug taking is illegal and not discussed openly, it is extremely difficult to get a reasonable impression of what is actually happening on a day-to-day basis in the average young person's life. It will therefore be useful to look at one such person's experience. Andrew is seventeen and the son of Roger, a tax lawyer, and Olivia. He attends a private school, and his drug-taking history is complex but fairly typical of many young people nowadays.

'The first time I had anything was a joint made up with tobacco when I was nine years old. It didn't do anything for me because the nicotine had such a poisonous effect. It gave me a massive headache and made me feel sick. The first positive experience with marijuana was when I was thirteen. I tried it with my older sister and her mates – they were always hanging out smoking the weed. Once I did decide it was something I enjoyed – it took quite a while to do it properly – I was fourteen and began on it regularly.'

Although Andrew was younger than average when he started, young people's initiation into drugs is taking place at an earlier and earlier age. Cannabis use broken down by age clearly reveals how popular it is. Among twelve to thirteen-year-olds, approximately one in fifteen have tried cannabis in one form or another, rising to one in eight of thirteen to fourteen-year-olds, and one in three of fourteen to fifteen-year-olds.

'About 90 per cent of my friends do it too, and about 5 per cent of those that don't, did it in the past. We never actually smoked in school itself – either we came home during the day, or it was out in the fields, but quite a lot of it was in the street or wherever.'

In spite of the fact that more than three out of four young people agree 'that drugs harm your health', three out of four admit that most young people will try out drugs at some time. Andrew is no exception:

'The time I started smoking every day was when I was growing it at a friend's house and we had so much that we didn't really know what else to do with it. A lot of it was just curiosity, to see if we could keep it going because we were using really strong hybrids which had been specially developed. Being new at it, I thought it would all be really

complicated but it was dead simple. The problem was, that strength of weed really fries your head because this stuff is bred to contain massive amounts of the active stuff – THC, which is what does you in compared with normal weed. It's at least five times stronger. Generally, doing hash makes me tired, but it also makes me content with living, even doing the same things every day, over and over again. But on the whole it's totally mood dependent on what you feel like before you start to smoke.'

Most of the available cannabis is home grown, and 'hydroponics', or forced growing of cannabis using artificial light, occupies many a basement around the country. The more fancy hybrids of the cannabis plant, with names like 'skunk', are imported from Holland and elsewhere. Cannabis use, like other drug use, tends to fall off after people reach their early twenties, as jobs (if they're lucky enough to get one), marriages, children and mortgages do not allow such indulgences.

'My parents didn't seem to know what I was into, though I felt they must be aware. I mean, with the things I left lying around and the smell you'd have thought that it would have been obvious, but in fact they had no idea until I told them. At one stage I realised I was doing too much, but I couldn't stop myself. There was this teacher at school, who is a very, very strange character, absolutely fair and an intellectual – yeah – but definitely weird. When my work was going badly he asked about drugs immediately, because he said he could tell when I was stoned. He asked me what I had done so I told him, and when he got to know me better he said, "I think your parents ought to know. I'll tell them for you if you want." So he discussed it with them. My parents reacted quite well. We talked about it and they said not to worry, but they were most concerned about me getting caught, especially if the school threw me out.'

There has been much recent debate in the press and else-where as to whether young people who have been found with illegal drugs in school should be thrown out. Although public opinion may support school expulsion, individual parents, when faced with this sanction, feel very differently. Expelling young people may only help to increase their drug use at home!

Young people themselves are surprisingly punitive to those who use drugs at school. When twelve to nineteen-year-olds were asked what they thought should happen if someone was discovered to be using illegal drugs in school on a regular basis, over half said they should be expelled; one in three said they should be dealt with within the school situation; and just over one in ten said they should be suspended from school for a time. Expelling a teenager for using drugs in school needs to be thought of in terms of the fact that around half the school population will have used drugs, and should they be expelled as well, even though they were not 'caught'; and also in terms of the individual long-term damage expulsion will do to the rest of the child's life.

> 'For a time I went on to "acid" but the reason I did was not because I had any preference for it, but just that I got in with some hippy guys and that's what they "did". The first time I enjoyed it, but now I really, really hate it because it blows my head away totally. For some reason, people who have scientific minds like it more than other drugs, but my mind just does not cope with it and I get depressed, so I gave it up. Acid is the one thing I wish I had stayed away from, as it makes you see the world in a totally different way and it's not at all nice.'

Of other illegal drugs, just over one in ten of young people have tried amphetamines and just over one in ten have tried lysergic acid, but only four in a hundred admit to taking ecstasy – probably a considerable under-estimate. Andrew has tried a variety of illegal drugs, but there are some things he will not try:

'Then I moved on to speed, which is the best thing I've ever been into. Not for dancing particularly, but because you can have these conversations all night for hours and hours. It's like having a little computer screen in your mind which comes up with about eighty different things to say, all at the same time. It makes a million things you want to say seem intense and meaningful. I lost loads of weight using it though. I'll never do speed again – it's so difficult to get away from.

'I've tried ecstasy which I really liked. The first time was under perfect conditions, very relaxed – you don't want to plan to do it, the right time just comes along. I got it from one of my sister's friends who got hold of some very pure stuff, and they reckoned that if I was going to do it, it should be under optimal conditions. I really enjoyed that, though the whole process starts by you feeling sick – but that's just for a few seconds. Then all of a sudden it just flicks and your brain floods with a really good mood.

'If I was to say what the most dangerous thing about drugs is – well, getting caught, that's the first one. Personally I am not so worried about frying my head. I don't think I did anything which has done permanent damage – but the nearest is acid. What I like best, but don't do now, because I think it might fry my head, is ecstasy. It makes you a bit crap, lame and lazy – but you could say that about cannabis too.

'I did once take my absolutely best friend out, and we did all these drugs and he passed out – well, not just passed out, but severer than that, and we were miles from anywhere, near Skipton. He's a really sweet guy and has been my best friend for God knows how long, and there he was with his eyes totally turned up, and he flopped in my arms and fell on the ground. It was the first time I've seen

the person in a body just turn off, and I was shit scared
and saying to myself, "This just isn't happening", because I
was partly out of it myself anyway. Then he woke up with
this massive smile on his face saying, "All right, then?"
But that was all a bit freaky – to say the least. It made me
realise how bad some of these things are for you though.'

Experimenters with drugs are also likely to experiment with
other things in life, and are more likely to: smoke cigarettes;
use more alcohol; have more than four sexual partners in a
year; and start sex earlier. They are less likely to: wear a cycle
helmet if bicycling; and wear a seat belt in a car. This doesn't
mean that if a ten-year-old hates wearing seat belts you can
assume he's taking dope, but it does mean that if you know a
young person smokes cigarettes there is a high chance that
they will experiment with an illegal drug at some time or
other!

'I absolutely wouldn't want to do heroin. Injecting is the
only way to do it properly and I couldn't do that. I know
people who have done it and even they don't think it's good
for them. Anyhow the first thing you do is to puke. I'm
sure that in the long term most of the drugs fry your brain
a bit, and that also, in the long term, they can mess you
up because you can begin not to care about things like
school and work.'

The groups of young people who are at higher risk of becoming drug abusers are people with mental health problems;
members of families where there is conflict; members of families where there is already drug use; and children of single-
parent families.

'The thing about parents is that most of them can't even
conceive of what it's like because they haven't done it
themselves. They can say, "Yes, we understand", but it's

impossible to imagine what it's really like unless you've actually been there. The atmosphere is the thing, and you have to go there and do it to know. Raves are a thing in themselves. This one I go to regularly, the same people turn up to it every time, and that's the main reason for going to it.'

The reasons given by young people for taking drugs are revealing. Around half say they take illegal drugs for fun or curiosity; one in three say it's because their friends are doing it; and one in five think it's better than worrying about something else in their lives and it relieves anxiety.

'I've only been nicked once and I seriously intend not to get nicked again. It was a school day and I was cutting off to get ten E's for me and a friend because we both knew we could get some really high-quality stuff. This friend went off around the corner to collect the tabs. Now I never do drugs in public if I can possibly help it. Like I would never smoke a joint in the street if I had anything else on me. It just gets you into trouble. When this guy gets back with the ten E's I was sitting in this café. I wanted to go somewhere private to share them out, but he's in a hurry for a bus. I was like – we shouldn't do this here – but he had to give them to me so I grabbed them and put them in my pocket and turned around. Walking towards us is a plain-clothes cop and I'm watching in real slow motion, like in the movies, at him taking his wallet out. Inside was a CID card.'

Crime, drugs related or otherwise, is a very male occupation. Among young people, males are responsible for eight out of ten crimes where people are cautioned or arrested.

'Then the CID bloke says, "Can I see inside your pocket please?" and at that point it definitely entered our minds

should we run . . .? But it just wasn't going to happen that way and I prised my hand out of my pocket thinking, "Aaagh, I don't want to do this." I brought out this tube and he opens it and starts swearing, because he obviously hates the dealing thing. At that point I thought, "Right, extremely nice and polite total co-operation needed" kind of thing, but at the same time it was, "Oh my God, I'm in really freaking-out panic about this" and "I can't believe this is true – me being busted." We started pleading, "Please let us off, please don't take this up, please, we don't normally do this kind of thing," and he was just getting there when, oh hell, his mate comes along. I felt gutted, just totally gutted, 'cos it's not every day you get arrested! I thought I would never get done. I'd been in close shaves before but here it was me.

'*My parents were brilliant about it all in spite of their views, which were that they hated drugs. But they also thought that involvement with the police could seriously damage my life and that was bad and shouldn't happen. I mean, I've had friends whose careers have been totally mashed up through being nicked for having a very small amount of cannabis.*'

When male offenders are arrested, two of the main outcomes are being cautioned or found guilty – the outcome differing according to the type of offence, the age of the defendant, and the certainty of the police of a conviction. Among all offenders cautioned or found guilty relative to any crime, of those aged between ten and thirteen, nearly nine out of ten were cautioned; of those aged between fourteen and seventeen, nearly six out of ten were cautioned; and of those aged between eighteen and twenty, just over three out of ten were cautioned.

'*I wish now that I could make my parents less anxious about it – like not to think that my life has been ruined.*

But they are totally and utterly devastated by what has happened, especially with my dad being a lawyer and all that. They have such high expectations for me and I do want to keep all options open myself for my career. We also thought that I'd get expelled, but luckily there is no official link between private schools and the police. A state school would have found out straightaway. If my private school had found out, I would have been expelled instantly – no doubt about it.

'I do now regret doing drugs. It can alienate you from friends who don't do drugs and from those who only do hard-core drugs. Healthwise it doesn't do you much good and you can waste a lot of your time. It's too quick and easy a solution to feeling happy and giving you the impression that you're having fun. But working and doing well at work can make you feel good too.'

The use of drugs can, for many parents, come as a shock, as it did for Roger and Olivia when they were confronted with Andrew's drug taking. Roger has recently learnt a great deal about drug taking by teenagers from a parent's point of view.

'He's not fundamentally a hard case. I mean, I genuinely feel that he is quite fond of us and I don't think he has any deep-rooted aggressive or rejecting attitudes towards us. I believe that he trusts us and I would say that the basis of a relationship is there, but the cost is enormous, particularly through his experimentation with the drugs scene.

'He recently did something bloody silly and this has been the most acute anxiety-making event that we have had in the last year. He and a friend bought some ecstasy tablets, with the idea that they would each have five. When they were dividing them up in a café over a cappuccino, unbeknownst to them, two plain-clothes police officers were doing observation on some other

incident. It would've been hilariously funny if it hadn't been so serious. These officers, as they said later, had no choice but to arrest them. We had said to Andrew in the past, "We don't think you should use these substances. We know they don't do you any good. They interfere with your school work, the way you think about the world and how you react to us." '

What many parents may find reassuring is that of all the young people trying drugs, most will try just cannabis – infrequently, in small quantities, a few times, without problems and without contact with the law or the health services.

'The first thing I heard about it was a phone call from the police saying, "Your son is in the local police station and some officers are coming to search your house." I thought, "Oh Christ." So these characters came round and turned over my son's room. I had done a little search myself first, and flushed a minute amount of something down the loo. The next thing was panic on the way to the police station. Our son did look very pleased to see us, and our reaction was – I'm glad to say, because it wasn't what we felt – totally supportive. He said, "Christ, Mum, Dad, thanks for coming."

'What we had done immediately was to get a friend who is the best solicitor around to give us lots of very good and helpful advice. We were also helped by the fact that the arresting officers were actually CID and had other more important things to worry about. Once they found that it wasn't connected with some large-scale operation they were into, they lost interest.

'We were given a lecture about the police wanting to keep young people out of trouble, and "We don't think it is a good idea to have young men with a police record, but he must realise that he is in a very dangerous game," along with "Ecstasy is a class 'A' drug and ten tablets of it

are a lot." We asked whether it was going to be "possession" or "intention to supply", and that was the nasty bit. Our son admitted that he was very scared, and worried about loyalty to his friend. It was totally accidental that it looked as though the other boy was handing the tabs to our son. In the end, the other boy did get done for "intention to supply", because he was less co-operative and refused to answer questions. He had a very bad solicitor who told him to say nothing.

'Our son was co-operative, unaggressive, level headed, and gave a clear account of what he had been up to. We gave our middle-class story about what a promising lad he was and how this was one-off experimenting, and how we would make sure it never happened again.

'My feeling about it was that the police behaved in an exemplary manner, and I thought the man who did the cautioning was sensible; but I do think it is horribly contingent on which policeman you get and how they read the scene at that particular moment. My principal feeling about the law is that it is a waste of police time running around after cannabis users.

'I was afraid of four things for my son as far as drugs were concerned. The first was that the dope was making him muzzy in school. Secondly I was afraid that he might take some mind-bending stimulant at the weekends which wouldn't do him any good and would leave him flattened for the rest of the week. Thirdly I was afraid that he might get into trouble with the police, which of course he did. Lastly I was afraid that he might go to a rave or party with somebody driving who had been taking drugs, and be killed in a car accident.'

More and more people involved in accidents are now found to have cannaboids in their bloodstream, so Roger's worries are justified. Further, it does appear that regular cannabis users do have difficulty completing school work. Roger continues:

*'One thing I will say is thank goodness the school didn't
know. Two bits of weed in their pocket and they throw
them out, which is totally ridiculous. I was talking to the
head of another school and he said they'd lose half their
school population if they had that policy.*

*'We'd asked Andrew if he was still taking drugs and
he'd absolutely denied it. He'd say, "Oh no, no", and
wander off to do something else – scarcely a fruitful
conversation! It was a game of denial, probably brought
on by the fact that we didn't discuss drug taking fully,
after the conversation with his teacher, which was silly of
us.*

*'But for parents, it's not just knowing the facts about
drugs. You also have to get your feelings about them
under control. I'm not good about any kind of drug. I hate
them all, including medicinal drugs – anything which is
in any way chemical, or might leave me not so much in
control. I'm a member of the "let your mind alone" school.
I'm a control freak about my own head. I've discussed this
with my son now, who came back at me that my attitude
is a kind of cowardice really.'*

The most important fact about illegal drug use by young
people that parents need to know is that there are basically
three kinds of drug users. The first and by far the largest
group, representing over six out of ten young people, are
those who just experiment with drugs, usually cannabis and
only cannabis. They will do it three or four times and then
stop – '. . . been there, tried that, what's next on the varied
menu that life has to offer: sex, travel, music, religion?' The
next most common group representing around three out of
six drug users are the so-called 'social users' who will treat
drugs like having a drink down the pub – something you do
with friends on a moderately regular basis. These represent
about three in ten of the young people who try illegal drugs.
The final group are the ones to worry about. Around one in

forty illegal drug users will become drug abusers, 'addicts' or 'compulsive users', who frequently have other problems.

Roger's advice to other parents whose children are experimenting is eminently sensible:

> *'First you must try to keep your lines of communication open with your kids. Second, if it comes to the police being involved, if it is possible without absolutely abusing the law, stay on your child's side rather than on that of the police. While maintaining the role of mediator between your child and the police, remain extremely polite. Do not slag the police off and do point out to your child that they are just doing their job – but you also have to remain absolutely loyal to your child. The main thing about this particular episode for both us and him was that we all felt we had come through a very bad time – but all on the same side.'*

If one examines the figures for drug-related crimes as a proportion of all crimes for which young people are cautioned: of those who are aged between ten and thirteen, one in a hundred are drug-related offences; of those aged between fourteen and seventeen, one in twenty are drug-related offences; and of those aged between eighteen and twenty, one in four are drug-related offences.

The question Roger raises is whether even cautioning puts adolescents off:

> *'One of the troubles is that they think they know everything, even after such an experience, and go on doing silly things; and if you try to advise them, they get furious. You say, "Look, it was only last week that we were sitting in a police station and you were being cautioned," and all you get back is more fury. Although you have to be on their side, at the same time you have to hold your own views firm, while making sure that they*

*don't see their relations with the police as a war. It is a
very delicate balance. But if the crunch does come, they've
got to see you as being on their side or you will lose it
with them forever.*

*'The main thing that I would also say to parents is, "Do
not be frightened by the word 'drug'." I know that it gives
people an immediate picture of HIV needles and all that
scene; and certainly before all this happened I did believe
that if you started on the soft end you were bound to end
up on the hard end, and would end up hooked on heroin –
and that is so patently not true.'*

**A few things which might help parents if they are con-
cerned about their teenagers taking illegal drugs and don't
want to be ostriches:**

- discuss the simple end of drug facts with your child around
  the age of nine or earlier, and keep discussing them as they
  (and you) get older

- be at least a bit informed about the effects of drugs and
  why people take them (see the Appendix)

- believe the research that shows that if you provide young
  people with facts about drugs early it does delay them
  experimenting with drugs

- keep on talking about drugs in an honest way so that the
  lines of communication about what they are doing remain
  open

- discuss with them why you do not want them taking drugs
  in your house. You could be implicated which could mean
  you getting arrested, which would not be good for their
  source of financial support!

- do not think that your child (of either sex) will be different and will be the one not doing any experimenting with illegal drugs

- do not be rude and obstreperous to the police if your child does get arrested

- steer a course which supports your child (you have to go on living with them and they have the right to expect that support) but which at the same time aids the police in performing their duty: difficult but it pays off

What about young people themselves: does anything help?

- try to stay away from experimenting with illegal drugs for as long as possible

- try to be fully informed about the good and bad things about drugs (see the Appendix)

- keep your parents informed by providing them with the same information as you have, without scaring them stiff!

- take every possible precaution against getting arrested by discussing the illegal drug scene with your friends

- be absolutely clear as to what is considered 'drug dealing' as against 'possession'

- know what the legal penalties are for 'possession' and 'dealing' for all the various illegal drugs

- try to discuss your attitude to drug taking with your parents if you think they can manage to listen!

- do not take drugs in your parents' house as they may get arrested along with you, should you be so unlucky. If you are arrested you will need your parents to be on the outside to help you rather than sharing a cell with you!

- do not be rude to the police if you do get arrested as you will almost inevitably come off worse

- do not take drugs on your school premises as they may have to expel you if they find you out and that can seriously damage your future career if you want one

- if you do do drugs, keep out of the public eye and don't divide your ecstasy tablets between you and your mates in public. We all think we are invulnerable until we are caught

- try to stay well clear of anything that could be considered as 'dealing'

6

Parenting, Different Values and Conflicts

A continuing theme in the changing relationships between parents and their teenagers is that of trying to establish a new alliance based on mutual understanding of needs. The teenager is moving away from the dependence of a child into the independence and self-sufficiency of adulthood, and the parents are suffering from the loss of their child and loss of control. How this is handled by both sides will set the agenda as to the degree of conflict that may occur. Although, as outlined in this chapter, the frictions can be considerable, parents need to remain trustful that, in the long run, their wayward offspring will turn out all right. Jean and William Rankin have been married for eighteen years and are both architects. They are struggling to both control and let go of their two sons, Thomas and Kay, as they grow older. Jean explains some of the difficulties:

'Oh, dear God, why is it that our older son, aged seventeen, who can, with our consent, leave home, get married, claim income support and work full time, still

*behaves like a complete idiot, is totally dependent on us
day and night, and wreaks such havoc in our lives. If our
two sons turn out all right I shall be a very, very happy
person, but it is dealing with the problems now that
causes the agony. If only we knew what the future holds.
They say it's the agony and the ecstasy, but at the moment
it seems to be a great deal more of the agony: all the
responsibility but no control. It is particularly hard when
there is such a clear-cut clash between our values and
what our children's values seem to be.'*

Many parents have strong views about what they wish the
value system of their children to be and attempt to impose
it, without realising that this may have the opposite effect to
the one they desire, as their teenagers make obvious their
rejection of these values (and thus their parents) and fight
for self-identification. It is not that parents shouldn't
express and discuss their own values and why they have
them, but they should not expect their children to adopt
them automatically.

Jean again:

*'There is a dread that they will end up with very few
values that we would hold as important, or the wrong
values altogether: wanting to make a fast buck, not taking
responsibility for their own actions, having no sense of
responsibility for others, and no urge to contribute to
society. At the moment our boys will either come through
it and be terrific, and because they have rebelled they will
be stronger and independent in a more constructive way,
or they will spiral downwards and fall off the edge. It's the
not knowing what the outcome is going to be, our
impotence through it all, that is so difficult. Sometimes I
am seized by a sense of utter helplessness and the fear
that whatever we have tried to do and are doing will make
no difference.'*

One aspect of this is that parents themselves may be working on different agendas when bringing their children up, which will confuse their teenagers. William's and Jean's views are not always in sync; and for William, the worries are complex and to do with his own upbringing and his longing to be loved unconditionally, by his children at least:

> '*Many of my worries are the result of my own background. I grew up in a family with a very strong patriarchal father and a rather weak mother, and I rebelled when I was a teenager, though only within certain constraints. My loss is that I don't have, and never did have, a warm and close relationship with my parents. I didn't get unconditional love from my parents, and now I don't feel that I am getting it from my children either, and I desperately want it: unconditional love for what I am instead of all this strife and marking each other down. It probably boils down to respect. That's what I want. I want to be respected by them.*'

As a parent, there is a clear need to differentiate between your own needs and those of your children; not 'use' your children to supply something that was missing in your own childhood, but ensure rather that it isn't missing from theirs. To this end, Jean interrupts:

> '*You can't compare your relationship with your parents to our relationship with our children. We love our children very much, which is why you and I care so much and want the best for them. Things are particularly difficult at the moment, but I'm reasonably convinced that if we had had a boy and a girl instead of two boys, our experience might have been different. Girls are more empathetic. I would have found it easier to relate to a daughter. I can envisage sharing things with a girl, like going shopping together. Both of us could have*

done things with a daughter which we just haven't been
able to do with the boys. There is also the problem
nowadays that it seems they will be at home with us for
ever.'

In contemporary society there is an ever-present paradox, that whereas teenagers are seeking emotional and intellec-tual independence at an earlier and earlier age, they are having to be financially dependent on their parents for longer and longer. A third of young women are still living in the parental home at twenty-one to twenty-four, and men are even more homebound, with half of young men still living in the parental home at twenty-one to twenty-four.

Life can be extremely confusing for the contemporary young male, not least because of the role models offered by their parents. Jean again:

'We've provided them with a very rich but confusing
environment. William is always in the kitchen doing the
cooking, and is a gentle and emotional character who
hasn't shown enough interest in their passions, such as
football. In fact, we both object to their football obsession:
the logos, the kit, the whole huge commercial thing that
they are buying into; and at the same time they aren't
doing their homework or their chores around the house. It
might be better to let it go because it's healthy, it's a sport,
and they enjoy it. It's better than many of the other things
they get up to after school.'

Here is that dreaded question: 'What do young people get up to after school?' The facts are that, on average, almost half of young people spend up to two hours watching television, live or recorded, on each weekday (favourite for girls is *Neighbours* and *Home and Away*, and for boys, sports pro-grammes); over one in four young people spend no time at all doing homework, with about half of all children doing between one and two hours of homework on weekdays. The other main after-school activities are listening to audiotapes, meeting with friends and caring for pets.

William is also acutely aware of the 'non-male macho role' he presents to his children:

> 'Well, there is this male role thing. It is a bad time to be a male adolescent – extremely bad. The male identity has gone into crisis. Women have become a power, rightly after millennia of subjection. But it is tough and I wish someone could have told me about this years ago, given me some advance counselling so that I could have allowed for it when bringing my children up. What worries me now though is that I have not been a tough father figure. If I had been, and if we hadn't both been working parents, then perhaps everything would have been better. I have no interest in sport. Thomas is brilliant at football and I do take him around and support him in that, but I don't play myself and I wish I had been more sporting so that we had more in common.'

How to find the right way forward when conflict does occur? It often feels that there is no way out, and that each new attempt to be conciliatory by the parents is met with further rejection. Jean says she knows the way forward but not how to bring it about:

> 'At the moment I am the one who tells the boys what they should be doing, and all they do is scream back at me. Their father backs off and ends up in a corner holding his head in his hands, with the boys saying, "Look at you, Dad, you're a wimp." What's definitely needed now is for William to step in, and take over the dominant and responsible role. They need to have their dad be male and firm and say, "No, I don't want you to do that because of this and this, and I feel very strongly about it." '

Teenagers do not automatically follow in their parents' foot-steps, and certainly do not hold to the same ways of learning. Learning from books is held in great respect by many parents, including William.

'I work on the idea that you can talk with the boys and reason with them. Personally, I don't see my children's behaviour as grossly reprehensible but rather all part of growing up. What I find difficult is that their development doesn't seem to be mixed in with any kind of intellectual discovery. Most kids nowadays don't read books, they don't even read newspapers, so they don't know what is going on.

'How can they identify with – for or against – a whole bag of shifting cultural factors which are not bedded in anything traditional, with no religious orthodoxy, without definition of "this is what you are"? Young people are endlessly kicking against a wet paper bag. They don't have enough to rebel against. It's all a mess, it's always been a mess – it's just a different mess nowadays.

'I was told by my parents what to do. I sometimes think that parenting comes down to either being emotionally cold and directive, or showing your emotions which means that you can't be directive unless you're into using cunning guilt trips.'

Although this sets out an 'either/or' approach, in fact there are an endless number of variations on the ways to skin this par-ticular cat. Love, respect, trust, encouragement, guile, bribery and punishment all come into it. On a purely practical front, it is worth noting that when teenagers were asked when they should be expected to do various household chores they said they should be making their own bed and helping with the washing-up at ten years old.

Many of these issues come back to who has control and

how that control is exercised. How much responsibility should the parent hold and how much should be handed over?

'My line is that I've told them what I think and it's up to them to decide; they have to take the responsibility. At the same time, I have to admit that I do mind deeply when they decide not to do what I want them to do – especially when they sleep on in the morning and decide not to go into school. We threaten to withdraw certain privileges, like pocket money, and we stick with those – we withdrew Thomas's allowance for a month – but it doesn't seem to matter to them much. When I do spend the time and effort to get angry with them they respond, but I can't stand life being anger and shouting. They've got to decide somewhere along the line to do things for themselves. I try to talk to them as rational human beings as I want the warm and loving relationship between us that I didn't have myself as a child.'

Jean disagrees with William:

'I think you have to go on much longer being a parent, saying what you think about what they should do and what responsibilities they should take, even after they are mature. You can't just suddenly say, "Right, it is over to you, you have to take the responsibility for your lives now." We do try and state boundaries, in fact I use up all my energy doing it. The question for me is, "When do I give up and stop all this worrying? When do I let go?" Personally I don't know. What I do know is that the way we are reacting at the moment makes no difference whatsoever. They need consistency and they need firmness, and I've taken the lead on that, and the boys hate my guts for it because I am the baddy.'

This again brings into question what parents want. If, in the short term, life with teenagers appears hell, it is worth gazing at the horizon and trusting that, in the long run, the chances are that they will not turn into uncivilised savages bound only for a life of criminality!

'I admit that in seven to ten years' time our boys may be the most wonderful people, and we have to believe that, but at the moment it does feel as if we are risking an enormous amount with our liberal attitudes. They are pushing the boundaries to the absolute limits and are virtually falling over the edge, with the result that our anxiety levels keep us awake all night. Will it all have been worthwhile?'

The two final statements by William and Jean sum up the two opposing attitudes that are causing so much of the difficulty and conflict. From William:

'I would say that if they fall off the edge it's their own responsibility now. We've done what we can.'

and from Jean:

'And I would say to that, if I have done nothing else, I might just possibly have managed to stop them from falling off the edge.'

What about these areas of conflict from the teenagers' point of view? How do they size up the world and decide on how best to cope with the dilemmas that face them? As already suggested, many teenagers are a great deal more sophisticated and knowledgeable than their parents take them for. The problem is that although both parents and young people are, in most cases, behaving logically, they are using different logic seen from different perspectives – with both parties convinced that the road they are taking is the right one. The parents have experience to fall back on, while the teenagers are convinced that they can see what is right for them as individuals living in this age, now.

Jean and William's eldest son Thomas is seventeen:

'I definitely think that the kind of society that I'm growing up in is different from that of my parents. This society is not as rigid or straightforward as theirs was and the rules are not so obvious. Everything nowadays is mixed and confused, and added to that my parents are idealistic. Because they're so idealistic and have such high principles they look at things in a much more clear-cut, straightforward, "right and wrong" kind of way. I don't think there's ever been an age like it when everything has been so much up in the air.

'For example, I know that my dad does all the cooking and sometimes me and my brother call him a "wimp" but I don't think the new feminism has affected things much for us, and I don't have any worries about trying to be a "new man", though that might change when I get to twenty-five or thirty.'

It is true that gender issues do not rate high with young people, and where they do, the differences are fairly obvious. Looking at young people's main ambition in life by gender, although significantly more boys than girls see 'being well off' as important and significantly more girls than boys see 'being happy' as important, looking at the figures overall, 'being happy' is number one for them both – by far. There are differences. More young women than young men believe that 'one parent can bring up a child as well as two parents', but again, overall most men and women agree with the statement. Significantly more young males than females think that 'a man's job is to earn money' and 'a woman's job is to look after the home and the family'; but the overwhelming majority of both sexes disagree with both statements!

What does count with teenagers is that, in spite of all the conflicts, parents do make it abundantly clear that they will love, support, and care for their children, whatever else happens.

'The best thing my parents do is make it obvious that they really, really care about me and my brother Kay. I think we are probably on their minds most of the time and that comes across. They are always there and are always willing to help us out. I have a lot of friends who, when they were fifteen or sixteen, their parents weren't around most of the time, and it shows. There's another thing I like and that is even though I'm nearly eighteen, my parents are still trying to insist that we all eat together. We sit down and have a proper meal at seven o'clock in the evening on Saturday, when most parents would be disappearing off doing their own thing. Mind, sometimes I think that that's a bit pointless. I think you can stay a family in other ways, and this meal thing shouldn't have to be rigid. I do appreciate why my parents want it this way, but it isn't always reasonable in terms of my life-style. I do think though that on the whole, society has it right when we can do things like having sex and stuff like that.'

What young people can do legally at a specific age (see page 1) and what they would like to be able to do – actually coincide to a remarkable degree. At thirteen children can work part-time, and the most commonly cited age at which children think they would like to work part-time is fourteen. Young people can leave home at sixteen (with parental consent), and the age most commonly cited by children for wanting to be able to leave home is also sixteen. The same applies for the age of consent to sexual intercourse. Seventeen is the age for being able to drive a car, both officially and desired by young people. And the majority of young people do not want to be able to vote before eighteen years of age.

Teenagers can be acutely aware of the ambitions parents have for them, without necessarily feeling that they have to go along with their parents' desires:

> 'My parents do so much for us because of what they think we can achieve. That means they get worried about how we will do when we're older. It's about our school work basically, and about us achieving our potential in the long term. There's a conflict between their wanting us to do really well in life and our need to establish ourselves within our own social set up so that we feel happy with ourselves. Parents need to understand that their kids are going to have to have an independent world, and that as kids nowadays, they've got to learn how to fight, how to get on with people, and how to survive in the world.
>
> 'My parents do definitely listen to what I say when I want to discuss things with them, and they think about them too. Even when there's an argument they still take account of what I say. But a lot of the time I feel frustrated because they can be very uptight. Sometimes I wonder why they can't just live their own lives and let us get on with ours. They seem to be there the whole time, sitting on my back. I wish they'd just trust me a bit more, especially over school work. Personally I'm not so much worried about doing the exams as about putting in enough dedication to achieving what I know I can achieve.'

It is no surprise that educational achievements loom ever larger in parents' minds as children grow older, with society as a whole laying enormous emphasis on examination outcomes. There are significant gender differences here in adolescents, with half of all females now obtaining five or more GCSEs grades A–C compared with only four in ten males. One in five males and females get one or more A levels; just under nine out of ten sixteen-year-olds are still in full- or part-time education; seven out of ten seventeen-year-olds are still in full- or part-time education; and half of all eighteen-year-olds are still in full- or part-time education. But other achievements are also important for young people's self-esteem and, in the case of both males and females, this may be in the area of sports and other skills.

> *'One thing that really supported me was I was very keen on football and a lot of my friends were just amazing at it at fourteen and fifteen; but then we started going out and discovered other things that took us over, like drink, smoking and late nights. It's natural for kids to just drop in and out of houses the whole time, specially if you're living in a community where there are other young people. I come and go the whole time, which worries Mum. She wonders if I might be up to something. She used to search my pockets and look through my stuff, and I couldn't believe that.'*

For fourteen and fifteen-year-olds soccer is the commonest sport/activity for six out of ten boys outside school hours. Bicycling is the next most common activity for boys. Basketball is played by three out of ten boys. But of significance is that fourteen to fifteen-year-old girls are much less likely to take part in after-school games or activities, with only just over five out of ten taking part compared with over eight out of ten boys.

To sum up: although some conflict between parents and teenagers is inevitable, it is extremely variable from family to family. Without doubt, if two parents have very different opinions on how their children should be brought up, this will add to the confusion. However, parents do need to have clear values of their own which they discuss with their children and demonstrate in their daily lives. What parents should not expect is for these values to be instantly adopted by the children. It is highly likely that, when their children grow up, they will have similar feelings about life and how it should be lived, but it is something that they have to discover for themselves.

A further fact that will help parents is the finding that life for the average adolescent at the present time is not doom and gloom. When asked how satisfied they are with their life in general, only around one in twenty say 'not at all'; around one in ten boys and two in ten girls say 'not very'; one in five boys and girls are 'not sure'; around half the boys and girls say 'quite a lot'; and two in ten boys and one in ten girls say 'very much'.

Thomas has a last word of advice for parents:

'Kids grow up. I'm trying to give my parents the message that they've got to trust and respect me and also they've got to have an understanding of me socialising and wanting to be out late. But I'm not surprised that my parents worry because that's natural. In the long term, for me it is doing my work to the best of my ability and reckoning I am going to be OK. There is no kid that I know who doesn't get into conflict of some kind. I think my parents have got to see I have my own life and they've got to realise what kind of life that is. A lot of the conflict with my parents can't be avoided. We've just got to work it out.'

Things which can help parents avoid, or sensibly manage, conflicts and decrease their anxiety and stress levels:

● try (as far as possible) to agree in private about how you are going to handle conflicting situations, so that you don't end up arguing with one another in front of your teenagers!

● trust and respect your adolescent's viewpoint, even if you don't always agree with it. You are not losing control if you don't get your own way all the time

- when you don't agree with your teenager's point of view, clearly state your own viewpoint and, most essentially, explain why you hold it. Young people may be inexperienced but they are not illogical

- hang on to 'this is a short-term dread and things will be all right in the long run'. Almost everything does turn out all right in the long run – but the 'long run' may be long!

- avoid ultimatums. These almost inevitably mean that you will have to give in: 'If you smoke in my car, I will never let you borrow it again' – you will

- treat each of your adolescents as an individual, allowing them increasing privacy as they get older, and try to be fair. Adolescents have an extremely well-developed sense of fairness, which will not necessarily match your own.

- say 'sorry' when you're wrong, loud and clear: young people appreciate this as much as adults do!

- make it *obvious* how much you care about them and love them

And for the young person, when handling parents?

- for financial reasons, the chances are that you will need to be living at home until you are around twenty-five, so trying to ensure that these years are reasonably OK for yourself means making sure they are reasonably OK for your parents

- if they are really angry with you, let them scream, don't answer back, and discreetly remove yourself when they have finished – they'll feel much better for it

- try negotiating over the more routine areas of conflict, like what time you should be in by, how much homework you have to do each night, and at least try to stick to what you have agreed. Trust has to be earned, alas

- try to explain to your parents how you feel about the world and why you do what you do. A good discussion is infinitely less stressful for everyone than open conflict

- many of the activities you are trying out are things that parents have no experience of and are therefore afraid of – you could try educating them a bit!

7

Teenage Bullying: and What to Do About It

ullying and being bullied are certainly nothing new. Probably most of us have experienced it, or been accused of it, at one time or another during our lives. Although parents' attempts at controlling their children could sometimes be considered as bullying, it is not a term commonly used for interaction within families, except in extreme cases. Where it is commonly observed is at school, and one definition for being bullied used in recent studies is 'When another pupil or a group of pupils say or do something nasty or unpleasant to you, or tease you repetitively in a way that you do not like.' In a large study, when asked whether they had experienced bullying at school, about half young people aged twelve to fifteen years of both sexes had been bullied at some time during their time at school, and one in five had been bullied during the current year.

Bullying can take many forms. Even if it has a common aim – intimidation – the methods of achieving this differ, as Elizabeth Hunter explains. Elizabeth is a secretary and is married to Gordon, who works for Railtrack. Their son Jason is seventeen.

> *'The story starts eighteen months ago. Jason was fifteen and was put under a lot of pressure to be a witness against a sixth-former at his school, who the school had been trying to get thrown out for bullying. Jason had seen this guy Randy grab his friend Jake outside the school gates and force him into a car, and the school wanted Jason as a witness. Jason was sure that Randy would recognise him. He told his teacher that he wanted to help them, but was afraid that Randy would come after him.'*

Bullying in schools is difficult to deal with. Some schools practise zero tolerance, others, at the opposite extreme, cope by turning a blind eye to its existence.

> *'The school's response was that there was no way that could happen. "That only happens in films, it doesn't happen in real life," they had said. Jason was aware from talking to other sixth-formers what Randy was like and knew differently. I asked the deputy head what would happen if this guy did come after Jason and he said there would be no problem and they would sort it out.'*

When twelve to fifteen-year-olds in the UK were asked the question 'Do you ever feel afraid of going to school because of bullying?' two out of ten boys and three out of seven girls said 'sometimes', 'often', or 'very often'; and eight out of ten boys and seven out of ten girls said 'no'. When severe bullying is discovered at school, often the boy or girl responsible may be excluded, but this does not necessarily end the bullying, as Elizabeth describes:

> *'Anyway, they got on to Randy and he had to leave the school without Jason having to be any direct kind of*

witness. *But, unbelievably, someone in the school told Randy who the witnesses against him were going to be. There were five other young people of Jason's age, as well as Jason. I had one of their mums around here who was horrified that she had allowed her son to say anything. The school's response was, "Well, this never normally happens, but if there is any trouble we'll help you" – completely ironing out our anxieties.*

'*Immediately Randy was out of the school, his brother called Jason and said, "You were a witness against my brother so we want twenty quid out of you or we'll do you." Jason didn't want us to tell the school, but we did and the young deputy head came around. He was extremely good about it, and said he could go round and give the brothers a warning, but he didn't think it would help much. And the school couldn't do anything unless Jason made an official statement. We pointed out that Jason was already in trouble enough over all this, thanks to the school, and there was no way he was going to make a statement.*

'*We asked the deputy head what he would do if it was his son. "I'd go and break their legs," he said, and as he is responsible for PE and is a big guy, I dare say he would have. It was a bit ironic though, suggesting we take the law into our own hands!*'

When students were asked 'What do you think should happen to someone who keeps bullying another student in school?' three in ten said they should be expelled from school, three in ten that they should be temporarily suspended, and four in ten that they should be dealt with in some other way, but that they should stay in school. Breaking people's legs was not an option!

Elizabeth sought further help elsewhere, and later worried whether it was the right course of action:

'*I stupidly talked to one of my work colleagues, to get some informal advice, and he said, "Oh well, these family gangs around your area are very, very dangerous. They are linked with drugs so it might be worth considering paying the twenty quid." The school were incredibly against this and so were we, but Jason said that from his experience with his friends, when these guys said twenty quid, they meant twenty quid.'*

It is well recognised at all levels of society that giving in to blackmail in the long run does not work. The blackmailers inevitably come back for more, and it encourages them to blackmail others. Unfortunately, in this case, Jason's parents felt forced to give in:

'We finally agreed that Jason should pay the money in the hope that it would get them off our backs. We got him to insist on meeting them in the local high street at a specific time. My husband, some friends and I were stationed nearby and saw them take the money off Jason, quite OK without any force or anything. But then they marched him off to the "hole in the wall" machine of the local bank where they made Jason key in his number. Luckily he had nothing in his account. Then they said, "That's OK, Jason. You're in the clear now."

'At that stage Jason was working in a newspaper shop near here, and a week later Randy came in and said, "Right – I want another twenty quid." The good thing about it was that Jason learnt quickly that paying people money gets you nowhere. The school were furious and said they had told us not to pay, but we pointed out that we were only in this mess because they'd let Randy know who were going to be witnesses against him. Jason wanted to pay them off again but this time we positioned ourselves where they were going to meet and stopped Jason from going. When Randy and his brother appeared, Gordon, my husband, went up to them and said, "I know who you are and what you want." They* *tried to deny it, but we told them that we had already seen Jason hand over the money to them on the previous occasion, and that if they came anywhere near Jason again we'd go straight to the police. That saw them off at the time.*

  'It did affect our relationship with Jason though, because he wanted to give them the money and we didn't want him to. By that stage we'd adopted the school's point of view to try and stop Randy from intimidating other teenagers. It wasn't just boys either. He behaved the same way with girls in order to get them to have sex with him, although their parents didn't know at the time.'

Many people find it difficult to believe, but girls are just as likely to bully and be bullied as boys (though less often physical bullying); and the younger you are, the more likely you are to be bullied. A surprising fact for many people is that compared with the rest of Europe, bullying in schools in England, Scotland, Wales and Northern Ireland is relatively low. The highest rates of bullying on the international scene are in Belgium, followed by Germany, Lithuania and Russia. For most young people who are bullied in school in the UK, it is only likely to be once or twice a term, with a minority being bullied on a weekly basis.

Many parents, when they learn that their teenager is being bullied, will be torn between telling the school about it and following their own child's wishes, as Elizabeth explains:

'I think the other kids knew that their parents would go straight to the police, but we wanted to discuss it with Jason. I've changed my mind about whether it should be his decision or ours, because it's his life and we have to listen to what he says. We did encourage him to do what we thought was the right thing in the first place, but that turned out to be a mistake. He was actually very good about listening to what we said, but he did have his own

opinions as well and we should have respected them more.

'So Gordon saw them off, and we sort of forgot about it, but Jason gave up his job. It was an extremely good job and the man who ran the place was incredibly supportive. Jason was really afraid and avoided going out – it was like there was a rapist about. Gradually he did get more confident, but then unfortunately it started again. Randy rang up a month later asking for money, and we were right back to where we started. Jason was terrified Randy would come to the house, but we have a large dog so I wasn't too worried about that, but Jason wanted us to fit the house out with a burglar alarm as well. Gordon and I were totally supportive of what he wanted, because we shouldn't have allowed the school to play down the risk. We were really taken in and made things worse for Jason by not being aware enough and thinking it through. I began to wonder whether we should have sent him to an independent school instead.'

That might not have been much help. Research shows that overall a slightly higher proportion of young people get bullied at independent or voluntary schools than at local or state-maintained schools, though the rates and degree of bullying will vary enormously from school to school. Elizabeth continues to highlight the dilemma for young people, forced to choose between following courses of action suggested by their parents, based on their values, and dealing with the bullying situation themselves:

'We have to go along with Jason and give him as much support as we can. Randy hasn't come back at him again but we have about five sets of friends around here who are keeping an eye out for him.

'We do have all these other battles with Jason at the same time, over money and him staying out late now, and

*that's incredibly exhausting. The bullying has made me
and Gordon feel very vulnerable because we want to give
Jason as good a life as possible.'*

It is important to understand the impact bullying has on
young people, the quality of whose day-to-day life may be
completely ruined. Life can rapidly take on a nightmare quality, as Jason explains:

*'I had seen Randy talking to Jake, who's my best mate.
When I asked Jake about it, he first of all said it was
nothing, but he was visibly unhappy. Later he told me
Randy had threatened to get his friends to take him
apart if he didn't give him money. Jake talked to his
teacher, out of fear I think. I don't blame him. And 'cos I
had seen it happening, I got involved. I didn't want to
'cos Randy is known as a hard person, but I had to help
Jake, didn't I? The school got me to make a statement.
They said that no one else would know so there wouldn't
be any danger to me. I didn't talk to Mum and Dad about
it at first, not until the school got involved, 'cos at that
point I hadn't been bullied myself, nor have I ever bullied
anyone, but I knew it was going on. Mum and Dad
wanted me to help the school. They persuaded me it
would get things sorted. I wasn't convinced. I was kind
of pushed into it.'*

Although half of all young people have been bullied at one
time or another during their school lives, one in three young
people have also bullied someone else. One in five students
have been bullied in the past term, and one in ten have bullied someone else. There is a strong correlation between
those that have been bullied, and those that bully others.
Young people from single-parent and step-parent families
are more likely to have bullied others at school than those
from families with two natural parents. A high proportion of

bullies were also seen among young people who disliked their schools.

Jason's worst suspicions did alas come true:

> '*It was a couple of months before anything happened. This guy came up to me in the pub and said, "I know you made a statement against my brother." I told him that I had to, that the school made me do it. His response was, "You shouldn't have done that." From the way he said it, threatening like, I knew it wasn't going to stop there, and it didn't. They wanted money, and he'd threatened several others who had been involved. I just said no. The brother said that he and Randy would beat me up if I didn't pay. They took my wallet and found my pay check from the shop I work in. It was for fifty quid. They said, "We want that. You've got to cash it and then we'll collect it off you." I was lucky not to get beaten up at that point – it was real fear.*'

Bullies themselves do appear to have certain characteristics that might lead parents to worry more about their child being a bully than being bullied. In Norway they found that six out of ten known school bullies had committed a criminal offence by the age of twenty-four and that bullies were four times more likely than non-bullies to become criminals.

Being able to talk about it with their parents obviously does help young people greatly, even if they cannot agree on a distinct course of action:

> '*I did talk to my parents about it then. They said I shouldn't give them the money and I insisted, 'cos I thought that would lose them. So I met them down the High Street and gave them the twenty, but they said they wanted the whole fifty and took me to the bank. I had spent the rest already so there was nothing in there.*
> '*It was only a week before they wanted more. They*

*knew where I worked after school and at weekends, and
the brother came into the shop and said, "We want the rest
of the money." So I said, "Yeah, OK, whatever" and then
didn't turn up to give it to them. But my dad and some of
his friends turned up instead and faced up to them. I didn't
see them again for ages after that, but I did wonder
whether I should carry some form of protection with me
because I was scared.'*

A worrying modern trend is the increasing number of young
people who carry some kind of weapon to 'defend' themselves with. In one study in England, three out of ten boys
and two out of ten girls questioned did 'carry' something,
and of these, two out of ten boys who 'carried' said their protection was a 'weapon with a blade'. Around one in twenty
girls also said they carried a 'weapon with a blade'. A 'sound
alarm' was the commonest form of protection carried by
girls.The commonest feelings engendered by 'carrying' was
'safety' in girls and 'being in control' in boys. Reassuringly
though, like Jason, by far the majority – seven out of ten boys
and eight out of ten girls – say that they never carry anything.

Once intimidation has occurred, it is a difficult threat to
escape from:

*'Eventually I saw Randy again, after a few months, and he
was with his brother. I hoped he wouldn't recognise me but
he did and said, "Don't get your dad and his mates on us
again or we'll do you." Then he remembered that I was
one of the ones who had made a statement against him at
the school and said, "You're going to regret that for the
rest of your life. I'm going to get even on you. You're
always going to be looking behind your back." They took
my wallet again and walked me to the bank, and took
another twenty pounds. That was like the beginning of
last term.'*

Young people in England, when asked where they felt safe, gave interesting and disturbing replies. Just over eight out of ten young people felt safe in their home during the day, and seven out of ten at night. Seven out of ten felt safe at school, and only four out of ten felt safe on public transport. When a further group was asked how they rated the area they lived in for safety outside after dark: two in ten boys and girls rated it as 'poor' or 'very poor'; three in ten boys and girls rated it as 'adequate'; and five in ten boys and girls rated it as 'good' or 'very good'. What is of concern about these findings is the relatively large number of young people living in fear of violence, not only in their local area but even in their own homes. Girls appear to be more concerned about bullying in school, attention from 'weirdos', and sex-related attacks, while boys fear physical attacks.

When twelve to fifteen-year-olds were asked how often they were afraid of being physically attacked: one in ten boys and girls said 'often' or 'very often'; four in ten boys and over five in ten girls said 'sometimes'; and five in ten boys and three in ten girls said 'never'. Crime against young people is common and some studies have shown that as many as eight out of ten young people have been a victim of crime at one time or another in their lives.

Jason not only resents the bullying, but also the way it affects so many aspects of his social life.

'I don't like not doing the things that I normally do because of him being around and him knowing all the places I'm at. Going to school is fine, but I am limited about going into town because of him. I realise that there are loads of other people in the same position because of him too.'

So parents need to be aware of the fear their teenagers might have over being bullied, and how unsafe many feel within their daily lives – but without being overly protective. They need to discuss the issues and be aware if their son or daughter's behaviour suddenly changes in a way that suggests they are afraid. It is, however, a delicate balance because young people also need to learn to look after themselves, to learn that they can cope, even with physical aggression from others.

Jason's main suggestion for young people is:

'If I was to advise my friends about being bullied, I'd encourage them to tell other people about it and not give in to giving the bullies money. Some of my friends did finally tell their parents and they were very good about it. I don't think you should go to the police unless it's really serious. Bullying does go on a lot though and it is an area of conflict with my parents. I can't tell them exactly how the situation is because it'll worry them, but I wish I had talked to them more because they're definitely the most supportive.'

Some things to do if you are a teenager being bullied:

- share worries about what you see or what you feel with someone you trust. This may be a friend, parent, form tutor, teacher or other member of staff.

- try not to give in to threats. In most cases the threat will not be carried out, but when bullies know that you will give in to threats, they will tend to keep on threatening

- if you do tell a teacher, the teacher should decide with you what should be done

- be supportive to other pupils who are being bullied

- don't carry a weapon – it could escalate problems

Some things to do if you are the parent of a teenager who is being bullied:

- watch out for signs of distress in your children. They might be unwilling to go to school, complain of headaches and stomach aches, lose possessions, ask for extra pocket money, or come back with bruises. They are often reluctant to tell you what is happening in case you take the matter up with the school or the police, which they fear will make things worse

- ask and be interested in how your children have spent the day at school

- if your child *is* being bullied, try to get him or her to talk about it and tell a teacher

- try to work out strategies together of how to cope. Keep a record of what has happened and when, and work out ways to avoid the situations

- reassure them that they are unlikely to be the only victim

- advise them not to give in to the demands of the bully as this seldom works

- if your child is bullying others, try to talk about it and sort out ways to change their behaviour

8

Separation and Divorce: Effects on Teenagers When It Happens

Children and young people are, not surprisingly, confused, upset and extremely vulnerable when their parents decide to get separated or divorced. Their feeling of powerlessness in the world is increased as their life is threatened with changes which are beyond their control. Although most children will survive their parents' divorce without obvious damage, for many it is extremely traumatic; and in the short term children whose parents are separating are more likely to be unhappy, have low self-esteem, behavioural problems, and difficulties with their friendships. The longer term effects are dealt with in the next chapter.

In the UK at the present time, two out of five marriages will end in divorce, and one in four of these divorces will involve children aged between eleven and fifteen. The duration of marriage is also shortening, with one in ten couples now divorcing within five years, whereas twenty-five years ago it was one in ten divorcing within fifteen years.

During the acute phase of separation and divorce, the adults involved may themselves be so traumatised and upset that children's needs are put on the back burner while their parents slug it out at home, over the phone, with the lawyers, through the courts – determined, in one way or another and at all costs, to get what they consider to be just retribution against their partner. Love and hate are, as they say, two sides of the same coin.

In the past, many children have been used as helpless pawns in these murky battles, but this is beginning to change. Children don't ask to be born and once in the world they remain for ever the responsibility of *both* parents, whether they are living together or apart. The law, lawyers and society, in accepting this, as well as the inevitability that not all relationships are going to work, are continuing to look at ways to best serve the truly innocent party's interests – those of the children involved.

Even so, bitterness tends to be a paramount feeling for parents during these battles, one that Ruth Bull, a psychiatrist separating from her Conservative politician husband, is struggling to overcome. They live in the Home Counties and have three children: Noah aged twelve, Rosie aged fifteen and James aged seventeen.

> 'My situation is that Mark has been involved with this other woman for six months now, and left me two months ago. He isn't actually living with this other woman and the children have not met her yet. I've not been ready for that until recently, and to be honest I still hate the idea, but in the end it will be up to the children to make up their own minds about when it should happen. The trouble is I know that the children feel pressure from me to dislike her and will sense that they should only feed back bad news to me. I will have to try to resist that. I hope Mark will do the same on his part!'

Struggle as she does, Ruth's bitterness shows through, particularly when she sees how it is affecting their children.

'Noah was only just twelve at the time we told him about Mark and me splitting up. We did it on the day that we were actually physically going to separate. Noah was stunned and tearful. He immediately became very clinging and started sleeping in my bed; but he hasn't shown too many other signs of disturbance since. He does check up on me more often – asking whether I am all right, and he has become withdrawn and generally looks sad. He has difficulty expressing his feelings but is convinced our separation is not going to last because that is what he hopes.'

In all this confusion is both the child's inability to understand what is happening and why and also their inability to express their feelings about it all, other than wishing it wasn't happening and hoping it will come all right again as soon as possible and everything will return to 'normal'. Younger children's reactions can be initially violent and subsequently they can be 'clinging' and withdrawn.

'Only very recently did I explain that it is a permanent split. Noah's reaction was acute, violent but short lived. To begin with he was crying, screaming and wanting comfort, but I am more concerned now that he is withdrawn and doesn't speak much.'

Older children's reactions tend to be different. They frequently feel that it is their fault that their parents are separating, and that if only they had done this or that differently, behaved better, hadn't continually had arguments, then everything would be all right. They find it incredibly difficult to cope with their parents' unhappiness, which appears an added burden on top of their own feelings and anxieties – both about the separation of their parents and all the other stresses and strains of normal adolescence. 'It is not fair of you to do this to me.' It can sometimes be a relief to an older adolescent when their parents do finally separate, so that they can get on with their own life and stop feeling so sorry for them. At the same time, they may still hope that their parents can work it out and stay together – an ambivalence of feeling that anyone – child, adolescent or adult – would, and does, find difficult.

'My daughter, Rosie, was fifteen and was aware that something was wrong. She had asked if I was going through a bad menopause! It never crossed her mind that something was busting up between me and Mark. When we told her, she thought her father must be completely off his head and refused to believe it was happening. She's been talking a lot to her friends about it, but not so much to me. What I've found distressing is that during the months since Mark left, she has been intolerant of my unhappiness, hasn't known how to handle it, and has got angry and upset with me about it. I do understand her intolerance, but I could have done with a few more hugs. However, I know that I shall have to wait until she's ready. When I told her I was going to move ahead and be more positive about living my life without Mark, she said, "Good on you, Mum, you deserve a life on your own, without Dad," and was obviously both pleased and relieved.'

There are many explanations of why the divorce rate in the UK, which is the highest in Europe, is at the level it is at the present time. Adults may be disillusioned with many other aspects of their life, particularly in such a materialistically driven world, where the material goals that people are presented with by advertising and society are, for the majority, unattainable. Failing in one area of life puts added burdens on other areas. If your material world is not what you want it to be, then your relationship and emotional world ought to be. It may sometimes seem easier to change your partner than change your job!

There is another dilemma in the relationship between parents and children during separation. Parents, in their hurt, may be desperately seeking someone to sympathise with them, someone who will listen to their tales of woe concerning 'the other party', someone close, who will listen without criticism. This is frequently, alas, a son or daughter who does not want to take sides, has troubles enough of their own, and would rather not have to bear their parent's sadness.

> *'My oldest son James, who is seventeen, has been a wonderful help. He checks up on me and offers endless support whenever I am feeling down. He rings every day when he's away from home and gets quite disturbed if I disappear for any length of time without an explanation. He does, however, feel very uncomfortable if I am at all critical of Mark or his new woman. Otherwise, he's immensely sympathetic and on my side. It has made him have to grow up quickly, though.'*

Ruth cannot stay away from the question of 'whose fault it was' and how the children see this:

> *'The children don't see what has happened between me and Mark as my fault at all. They see it entirely as their father's decision and his fault. They see me as having done nothing wrong and nothing to deserve it. I've found that very supportive of them, but it would be hypocritical if I didn't realise that that's the way I have presented it. I do want them to continue to have a relationship with Mark and to keep some respect for him. But I have come to see that it is what you do that is important, not what you say.'*

Ruth is angry about an argument put forward by her husband, and all too frequently put forward by the parent who is going off with a new partner, that it won't have any effect on the children. This clearly demonstrates our very human ability to ignore the most obvious of facts when it suits us.

> *'Men often say that it will have no effect on the children when they leave. It's what they want to believe – but it just isn't true. It can't have "no effect" on the children. When we first told them, Mark said to me, "Well at least that's one thing that's not gone as badly as I'd expected," and I replied, "If they don't appear affected, that's because they don't believe it, or don't want to believe it, or they think so little of you that they are pleased you're going." Personally, I favoured the first explanation, but if they didn't believe it initially, they do now.'*

Of further concern is the fact that separating and divorcing does seem to have a cross-generational impact. Women and men who experienced divorce during childhood are more likely to experience the break-up of their own first cohabitation or marriage. But of more immediate concern are the feelings that the behaviour of their parents may generate, and the fears teenagers may have of losing contact with one or other parent (usually the father).

> *'I am unaware just how much the children have been damaged by it. I think it has dented both their respect for Mark and their sense of values, which is very far reaching. What I do know is that Mark, whose own parents divorced very acrimoniously when he was five, and I are trying very hard to keep communicating with one another so as not to cause any extra distress to the children.'*

In advising other parents from her own experiences, Ruth harks back to the bitterness that is generated, and how it is best to keep the children well clear of this.

'My advice to other parents would be to try to minimise the bitterness, especially in front of the children. Have your rows with your spouse out of the home so that the kids don't see or overhear them. And remember that it may take decades, if not years, to feel fully OK again. Encourage the kids to talk about it, but don't force them to. I did ask James, Rosie and Noah whether they discussed it among themselves and Noah said no, but James interrupted, "Hey, we talked about it just yesterday." I am glad if they talk to anyone about it, but best of all is discussing it with their peer group. Some of my friends offered themselves as confidants to them, which was kind and generous, but I knew the children wouldn't go for that, and they haven't. They've just got on with their lives.'

One almost universal immediate effect on children, of their parents separating or divorcing, is a fall-off in their academic work. The distraction and anxieties are just too great for them to continue to concentrate on school work. On the other hand, the continuity of their school life may be, for some teenagers, an extremely stabilising factor, when the rest of their world is falling apart.

'One of my concerns is whether they are failing academically because of Mark's and my troubles. Certainly James has failed some very important exams in the last few months, and it is difficult not to see a connection. But the children were determined to go to school every day, even during the worst times at home.'

After a separation comes the question of starting a new relationship. Some rush into new marriages as a salvation from unhappiness and confusion, a solution not generally recommended by counsellors, therapists and others. It provides for a too dependent new relationship, which is likely to fail when the urgent unhappiness and need for solace has passed. There is a saying: 'Avoid being the first new partner with someone whose relationship has just split up – it is bound to fail.' Cynically, one has to point out that someone has to be in this position! Most people would recommend that the partner left behind should try, if it is financially possible, to live independently during the acute phase of hurt and only try to form a more permanent relationship when the hurt has passed and self-esteem has been restored. The other thing that helps many people enormously through the acute period is their work.

> *'As for me starting on a new relationship, I've wanted to have privacy from the children over certain things, but there is fine line between what is private and what is secretive. I want to know what they're doing, but if I disappear without telling them what I am doing, they turn round and say, "But look at you, Mum!" I have tried to explain to them that for me this is a new venture. I have not been out with another man for twenty years, and I don't want to do it in the public eye. My children may mean well, but knowing that they are watching makes me very inhibited, and I think they understand that now. One thing that really helped me though has been my work. Another is that my friend Clarissa has been through it all and was totally supportive and someone I could gripe to whenever I felt like it.'*

Separation and divorce can affect teenagers in very different ways, which is not surprising given the variations in human nature, the different circumstances which can surround the situation and the way parents choose to handle it.

We decided not to interview Ruth and Mark's children because they were still so traumatised, but chose a number of children whose situation was less acute. The first of these was Jenny, who is fifteen and suffered among other things from losing and then re-establishing contact with her father. She demonstrates the resignation that many children feel nowadays, in the light of the fact that so many other young people are in the same situation.

'What I did find hard at school is that the other kids used to say, "My dad did this" or "My dad did that", but I didn't know what my dad was doing, because he doesn't live with us any more. I feel upset sometimes that we can't be together, and I've always had the longing hope that they will get back together. I did start seeing my dad again a couple of months ago, but he didn't talk much. It was OK though, and I did get along with him. When my parents were getting divorced I didn't really understand what was happening, why my father was staying behind when Mum and I left him. I don't really talk about it with my mum now. All my friends' parents are divorced so it's nothing special. Bits of information about them separating do leak out now and again, like recently I learnt my mum walked out on my dad. He does ring up now though, and wants to know what I've been up to. He tells me what he's up to, like what drawing he's just done or what house he's working on at the moment.'

Not all children are going to feel the same way as David, who is also fifteen. He expresses a quite different view, though he does understand that a lot of the burden of staying in contact with his father falls on him.

'I was thirteen when my parents split up. I don't remember feeling tremendously sad about it, because they both seemed quite happy. Before they separated I remember them arguing quite a lot, but afterwards they seemed to get on much better, and they don't appear to bear each other any grudge. I don't think about it much but I do make an effort to go and see my dad quite a lot. I *have to make an effort or otherwise it wouldn't happen very much. He lives by himself and I talk to him about different things than I talk to my mum about. I see Mum's new boyfriend as a good friend, as he is very enthusiastic about things which interest me, like clothes and films and things, and he's always very keen to help me with any of my work from school as well. There was a sort of sense of replacement when we first met. It wasn't difficult for me but I did worry about how my dad and my mum's boyfriend would relate to each other. Actually they seemed to get on with one another quite well. They've never really been in competition and that's been quite nice.'*

As already mentioned, children's first reaction to hearing about their parents getting divorced may be violent, and some young people may continue to feel anger at the world in general and their parents in particular. This can be particularly hard on the parent who has the day-to-day responsibility of looking after them. Clover lives with her mother and is fifteen.

'My first clear memory of anything awful in my life was last year, when Mum and Dad told me they were getting divorced. Mum said I just screamed as if someone had stuck a knife into me – but it was because I was so upset. Ever since then I seem to have been really angry with the world.'

This immediate distress which children feel when their parents separate or divorce usually settles, but there is still the likelihood of later problems that can occur many years afterwards, even when the children are adults. Talking to your children is vital, and explaining to them that because their parents no longer love one another it does not mean that they are not loved.

Getting teenagers to talk about their own feelings about the separation is also important. Jeff is sixteen and lives in Ireland with his mother. Not only does he wish that his parents would talk to him about it all, but he can't bring the subject up himself for fear of upsetting them. He also expresses his own feelings of continuing responsibility.

'My parents finally split up last year, after what seemed like endless fighting, silences – you name it. But they have never once spoken to me about it, or asked me how I'm feeling or how I'm coping. Most of the time I feel like screaming at them that I'm not OK and would they please just talk to me, but I don't want to upset either of them. Since the separation, my father has become distant, never bothering to call, but for some reason I keep making excuses for him. My mother acts as if it's some competition between them as to who loves me more. To be honest, I think they're just big children and I don't know why they can't sort out their differences in a civilised manner. I hate every second of being at home. If anything it's harder since the separation. I wish I could just be an ordinary unruly teenager, like my friends, but instead I have to think about how my mother would cope if I didn't ring home or if I snuck out to that party. I'm all she has now.'

Some parents find it difficult to show physical and emotional affection at the best of times, but this can be particularly hard on teenagers after their parents have separated and when there is only one parent to relate to. Jessie, who is fourteen, is particularly critical of her mother's ability to show affection to her new partner but not to her.

'My parents divorced last year and Mum thinks she's a good parent because she provides for us materially, but although I know she loves me and my sister she doesn't show it much. She won't offer a hug or a kiss, you have to

kiss her she's not really affectionate with us at all. She can be quite affectionate with my stepdad though and that makes me a little bit bitter sometimes. In my opinion, a parent should give emotional support and advice, but my mother doesn't. There's a distance between us, so I could never tell her anything personal. She has banned me from having a boyfriend during my GCSEs, but even before I had to sneak around if I was going out with someone – I just couldn't be sure of her reaction. But given Mum's coldness, I really need someone else's affection.'

The outcomes of separation and divorce are complex and have to be understood in the light of a number of different factors including: (a) the lessening stigma attached to divorce, (b) the effects of pre-divorce conflict, (c) the prejudices of those interpreting the research data and (d) the poorer financial status of the parents and their children after divorce. However, where there is evidence on the effects of separation and divorce, in no case does it indicate that there are benefits of divorce for children. So given the fact that divorce is going to continue, the main concentration of effort on the part of society and the individual needs to be on lessening the impact on the children involved. Some ways for parents to do this are given below.

Tips for parents about what to do and what not to do if they are getting divorced:

- don't fool yourself that divorce is good for children – the research shows that in the majority of cases the opposite is true

- if divorce is inevitable, there is a difference between a painful experience and a damaging one. Parents may not be able to stop the pain for their children but they should be able to minimise the damage.

- don't use your children as propaganda pawns in your marital battle

- don't download your own emotional packages on to your children and do not use them as emotional props. Confide in adult friends or find a good counsellor/family doctor

- although you stop being husband and wife when you get divorced, you don't stop being parents to your children

- do not make the other parent a hate object for your children (and mutually agree about this with your 'ex')

- both parents need to discuss, and together take responsibility for, the future relationships with your children

- maintain normal boundaries and rules, and avoid overcompensating with treats and presents

- same sex children as the rejected parent often feel rejected as well

- emotional hurt has to be acknowledged. If one parent does not turn up as promised, the other parent should acknowledge that this is painful but should not use the occasion to slag the other parent off

- there is evidence from the USA that if parents handle a divorce reasonably maturely then the children grow up to be more mature themselves

- if you manage half these things in the heat of a divorce, you are a near saint – but they do make a difference!

Tips for teenagers whose parents are getting divorced:

- keep on reminding yourself that the divorce is not your fault – even if you have been having arguments with your parents (this is normal)

- don't try to be a parent to your parent/s – they are the parents and need to behave as such

- realise that about half of all couples get divorced so you are not alone – try talking to your friends if you don't believe it!

- it is OK to go on as before – loving your parents, hating your parents, or just not liking them much!

- your view of your parents' marriage will be different from your parents' view of their marriage – and that's what growing up is all about

- don't expect your parents to tell you every detail of what is happening

- don't feel guilty if you want to get on with your life as a teenager – you may want to sort out how you feel about your parents later – and that is fine

9

Separation and Divorce: Effects on Teenagers After It Happens

here is a strange phenomenon that when people are happily married with children, the whole world seems to be full of similar happily married couples. However, when marital relationships break down, the world suddenly seems to populated by people with relationship difficulties.

Even the best relationships can be difficult at times, and separation and divorce are at one extreme of these difficulties. Although it is unreasonable to expect all married couples to stay together, it is not unreasonable for both parents to try to support the children through it all in the most untraumatic way possible – both in the short term and also in the long term.

The majority of children whose parents divorce do not have poor outcomes; but problems are more likely to occur with the children of divorced parents than with children whose parents stay together. Pre-divorce factors do in part explain the increased likelihood of children of divorced parents being unemployed, lacking qualifications and living in council housing. However, low income is less important than the divorce itself as a factor in why children of divorced parents differ from children of non-divorced parents in their personal relationships and behaviour as parents.

Although it is difficult to disentangle the proportion of problems due to associated financial problems, conflict prior to the separation, and the actual divorce – effects there undoubtedly are. What the long-term effects are and how they can best be mitigated, is the subject of this chapter.

Clarissa Dobson, a psychologist, has been divorced for ten years and is now living (on and off) with a new partner, Clay. Her own feelings of lack of self-confidence continue:

> *'What I have managed badly is being confident, or leading with confidence. I do manage and I do lead, but I don't do it with confidence. I don't have much serenity. It is just lurching from one moment to the next in panic, panic, panic. It is also particularly difficult having my middle child, Nicky, as a teenager in turmoil too.'*

Then there are the effects these feelings and others in the parent can have on the adolescent. The problems, how they get expressed, and their timing are legion and no two children will respond to these upsets in their lives in the same way. Some have virtually no problems at all, sail through the situation apparently oblivious to what is going on, and never look back. Others will appear all right at the time only to become deeply traumatised later. Some will appear deeply upset at the time but gradually adapt without further trouble, and others will continue to have problems over long periods of time. For instance, in one study, children whose parents divorced before they were six years old were, by the age of fifteen, twice as likely to be bed wetting than children whose parents were not divorced.

> *'The youngest one, William, he was a saga. He was only three when Tim finally left and he'd been very close to his*

father. He just seemed to shut down any feelings at the time. Much later he became very difficult in his behaviour. What I particularly remember was him soiling everything and then spreading it around his room. That was the most painful thing. He just put the stuff everywhere. When that persisted, I went to see a child psychiatrist with him, and when he was five, he had psychotherapy for about two years. He even started talking about killing himself. He quite liked going to the therapist but now he is adamant that it didn't help at all, even though he is easily the most coherent of the children when it comes to talking about his feelings, even to this day. It certainly helped me, him going to the psychiatrist, because I was seriously afraid that he might commit suicide.'

Both the gender of the child and their age when they suffered the break-up of their parents have a strong influence. Women from divorced families, who were over twenty when their parents broke up, were little different in terms of educational attainment, housing and income from other adults; whereas men from the same background were more often economically disadvantaged compared with contemporaries. Even so, both men and women whose parents broke up after they were twenty had an increased rate of break-up of their own relationships.

What can be particularly painful reminders of a previously happy time are the rituals that every family has, as Clarissa highlights:

'Birthdays have been very painful. Their father tends to ring up on these occasions, and no reference is made to the fact that he isn't actually here. Christmas is the worst, and we would all end up in tears when he rang at Christmas, so we asked him to ring up on Christmas Eve or Boxing Day instead.'

Often children may be unable to, or may not want to, discuss their anxieties with their parents and may try to communicate these concerns to other people. This can be hurtful to parents, who should feel pleased that they are at least able to express their feelings to someone. Clarissa explains:

'There were other sad things that I remember too. I remember William talking to the daughter of one of my friends. They live in Liverpool where my ex-husband lives. I remember vividly to this day hearing William saying, "My daddy's gone away. You live in Liverpool. Could you look out for my daddy, because you may see him there." It was as if he had lost his daddy and he wanted someone to find him again. That was a very painful episode.'

A problem for many parents is that they are so tied in to their own feelings of loss and anger that they may ignore the needs of their children and miss quite simple ways of helping them, which may not be immediately obvious.

'A thing that helped enormously was getting William a dog called Feather. Two friends suggested it, and it was an absolutely marvellous idea. William adores him, hugs him and strokes him, talks to him, and takes responsibility for him. I think he sees the dog as his own personal friend. Feather is always there for him and he is always there for Feather. Now I'm terrified that Feather may get lost. A cat, I'm sure, would have been just as good. William just needed something of his own to love.'

A problem with older teenagers is that having their parents separate may disillusion them about the validity of their own relationships. They can become over-sensitised to rejection and the possibility of getting hurt. This may lead them to avoid close relationships and be pessimistic about marriage for themselves. It can have the effect of very much wanting to be in charge of making and breaking relationships; but it can also mean that they feel totally devastated when they themselves are rejected (even more so than we all normally feel under such circumstances!).

It could be argued that much teenage behaviour that has been looked at is typical of any teenager, with or without divorced parents. It is therefore only through long-term studies of large numbers of teenagers, comparing those whose parents have divorced with those whose parents haven't, that the effects of divorce will be apparent. Thus Clarissa's daughter Julia, when she left school, began to behave in a way that might, or might not, be put down to her parents' divorce.

> *'She did tell me that it was only during her year off that she felt she was able to rebel, and that was her salvation. It was then she realised that she could be separate from all the trouble, that she wasn't responsible for what happened and didn't have to feel guilty. When she was away, a letter arrived from the local Boots the Chemist, saying that she hadn't paid the money she was supposed to pay. It turned out that she and her friends had shoplifted some stuff. Luckily the shop had decided just to charge them for what they had taken, but she hadn't managed to pay the money back yet. When she went to university I didn't hear from her for a long time, and she certainly didn't work as hard as she should have. I heard she drank quite a bit too, which she hadn't done before.'*

For parents, there is also their own guilt about the situation, their anger with their ex-partner, coupled with trying to protect against the worst by assuming the worst will happen.

> *'There were times when I felt they could all turn into complete delinquents. I used to catastrophise the situation the whole time, but we have survived. I was most worried that I would fall apart, not that they would; that I would*

*be unable to support them and bring them up. It's a feeling
of being totally responsible for everything that might
happen to them, when of course friends, school and other
things have an effect. I got it out of all proportion, and
somehow felt that because I was depressed, tearful and not
coping, everything was going to fall apart and get out of
control. In fact that didn't happen and they did really well
at school.'*

After a family break-up, the previous advantages that two
parents represented may become obvious to teenagers left in
the care of one, in terms of parental time and attention available to them, and in terms of them being financially worse off.

*'They don't seem to feel stigmatised but they do feel let
down. They feel that they've lost something they were
entitled to – the security and the care of their father. As a
result, whenever they have any challenges in life they fall
apart a bit and get angry that their father is not there for
them. It often expresses itself by the younger two getting
very angry with me, which is actually very unfair,
particularly as I am no longer in a financial position to be
able to offer them the things they had before we were
divorced.'*

The financial disadvantages for these teenagers tend to continue, because children from separated families are more likely
to live in poor housing and be less well off when they are
adults themselves. Other research indicates that they tend to
leave school and home younger, become sexually active earlier, get pregnant or be a parent at an earlier age, need more
medical treatment, perform less well at school, use cigarettes
and drugs more. This is how it averages out. It obviously does-
n't apply to all teenagers of divorced parents as they grow up.
But even women who were older than twenty when their parents divorced are more likely to experience break-up of their

own partnerships by the time they are thirty-three than their contemporaries whose parents have not separated.

The parent left looking after the teenager may also fear that their child will want to go and live with the absent parent, which Clarissa is certainly sensitive to.

'Another thing I found very difficult was them seeing my ex-husband, because I thought they would be seduced by his new life and want to go and live with him. I was falling apart and thought I had become a bad mother and a tearful depressive, and there he was, happy and smiling and not appearing to be the slightest bit worried about the whole thing. I felt an unattractive misery, and I had continual financial worry.'

For help in this situation people need to use whatever supports are available for meeting other people and not getting isolated. It can be extremely claustrophobic to rely on your children for company, and is certainly not good for them!

'When I am with other people, the hurt dissipates and we all manage to forget our troubles for a time. One needs to lean on other people, talk to other people, because one finds even in families that haven't broken up, that they've been through even worse experiences. I thought our situation was unique, but of course it wasn't.'

Clarissa's main advice to others is:

'Don't catastrophise. Things can turn out all right in the long run, even if the long-term effects are difficult to predict. Don't worry too much about the things that I worried about – that my children would become delinquent, get into drugs, get pregnant, leave home. As a family we actually became very close and talked about our feelings much more than when their father was

around. Before that it was just practical talk about where we were going on holiday, who was using the car, where we should go and eat. We didn't discuss our feelings at all. Now they tease me a bit and say, "Oh do stop going on about all that psychological stuff." But I did honestly used to think, in my darkest moments, that we wouldn't survive. I remember reading about a woman in the same situation who drove her car and her children into a river and thinking I understood why she had done that. For a time, I thought it was an impossible situation to survive, but we did and they are very close to me now and to one another. However, I do think it has affected how they see their own long-term relationships – that's the main scar.'

This may seem very one-sided and only from a woman's point of view; and certainly men do see the present system being stacked in favour of women, when it is the woman who leaves with a new partner, as Clarissa's new partner, Clay, explains.

'I felt incredibly angry and upset to begin with. Normally everything is slanted to women's advantage. They get the money, they get the children, they get the house. But for me, it has been wonderful, because the two older children decided to stay with me and the judge accepted that I should have "care and control". I have brought them up since they were nine and thirteen. It seems to me to be civilised and correct that the care and upbringing of children should be shared when there is no real fault on either side. Of course, where there is violence or physical or sexual abuse involved, that makes it a different ball game.'

For some men it can be an enlightening experience which they would not otherwise have had.

'Bringing them up has been a combination of being extremely hard work, hugely educational and enormous

*fun. OK, so I can't hide the fact that we've had our
screaming matches, and they probably, from time to time,
had to go to school with flu, or worse. But they have been
such wonderful company and all four of them are such a
pleasure now that I feel really proud that, in spite of our
divorce, my ex-wife and I have managed to produce these
four who – and I know I am biased – are such outstanding
people. I always wanted my children to be, in some way,
better people than I am, and that is what they appear to
me to be.'*

All the research indicates that if parents can keep in contact
with one another in a reasonably civilised way after a divorce
the outcome for the teenagers is considerably improved.
Living near to each other, so that the children have easy contact with both of their separated parents when they wish to, is
also of benefit.

*'What has helped enormously is that my ex-wife and I
have kept in contact and have managed to keep some kind
of friendship and respect for one another. Initially though it
was difficult. We very much share the children's lives and
they come and go from both our households as they want
to, though now they are older that is quite intermittent. I
also think that they have been very supportive to one
another, they are all good friends. It was remaining in
contact with my ex-wife, having birthdays all together,
making sure that arrangements over weekends, Christmas,
New Year were well worked out so that the children and
both of us parents knew what the plans were and no one
got disappointed, that has made all the difference. Any
rows I have had with my ex-wife, and there are bound to be
some, have been over the phone, out of the hearing of the
children. We also have an absolute agreement not to slag
the other person off to the children. That has not been hard
for me because I think my ex-wife is a lovely person. If*

that sounds too good to be true, well, OK so there are some
reservations, but they are kept well in check!'

So what is it like from the children's point of view? First it is
a relatively common experience, as around 44,000 children
aged eleven to fifteen are involved in divorces each year. As
already suggested, the experience will be extremely variable,
but will also very much depend on their relationship with
their step-parent – if there is one.

'My parents split up when I was five. I don't remember
having minded at the time but apparently I started at my
nursery beating up on other children, stealing their
tricycles and pulling them apart, and hitting them against
a tree. I certainly don't mind about it now because there
are a lot of advantages, like you have extra friends and
know more people.' (Oliver aged fourteen)

'I was really upset. My parents split up when I was about
eight and I remember that I had just seen a film about
some children who were really unhappy when their
parents split up, and then, a week later, my parents did. I
do think that on the whole, it's been all right. My parents
don't hate each other. They keep in touch and they help
each other out every now and then. Certainly if I had to
give advice to parents who are splitting up and want to
help their kids and probably themselves as well, I would
say to them, "Don't hate each other, because it's much
worse for the children." ' (Andrew aged thirteen)

It is worth repeating here that most children, regardless of
their parenting background, survive into adulthood without
psychological problems.

'I live with my mum and stepdad. Whenever they argue
they blame me for starting it. I love my mum but since

she's been with him *she's really nasty to me but nice to my brother.' (Grace aged fifteen)*

All families have some conflict within them. By the age of sixteen, 23 per cent of young people brought up by birth parents reported conflict with their parents, compared with 33 per cent of those brought up in a stepfamily, and 50 per cent of those brought up by a lone parent.

'The most strenuous time in my life occurred when my mum and dad took their separation legally through the courts. It was during this time that my dad brought his new girlfriend to live with him. He never really told me their situation so I had to confront him. He admitted his relationship with the girl and her two children from a previous marriage. I felt let down by my dad and overcome with hatred towards his new girlfriend. I visited my dad at his expensive house that he shared with his new family. I resented Angela so much and, as she was in the house most of the time, I spent most of my time outside where I met new friends. I resented my dad also, because of how he paid so much attention to his new family.' (Rebecca aged sixteen)

Overall, children brought up by two birth parents until the age of sixteen have higher levels of 'life satisfaction', fewer psychological problems and less conflict at all ages than those brought up in disrupted families. The amount of trauma caused to children during the course of separation, divorce and the years after varies in degree from child to child. When divorce is inevitable, one of the main determinants as to how much suffering the children have to undergo is how well both parents devote themselves to avoiding causing their children the same trauma as they are causing each other, whoever is seen to be to blame.

The effect on children after separation/divorce is less if parents cope with, and recover from, the effects themselves.

Some long-term things which may help parents decrease the pain and damage to children after divorce:

- maintain communication with your 'ex' even if this is incredibly difficult. It can be done and is of enormous benefit to the children and to you

- try to set up a mutual agreement not to slag off the other partner

- ensure there is contact between the children and the partner the children do not live with. This has to be the responsibility of both partners

- do not, at any stage, off-load your feelings of pain about the situation on to your children. They have problems enough of their own and it can be very damaging

- live geographically close to one another if possible, as research shows that this gives a better outcome for the children, probably because it allows easier access to both parents

- keep as many stabilities as possible after divorce: the same house, the same school, contact with the same group of friends

- behave as a couple on family occasions such as weddings, birthdays, graduations, and do not insist that new partners come too

Some long-term things which may help young people when their parents get divorced:

- don't allow your parents to draw you in to taking sides

Young people need two parents and you have the right of access to both

- don't feel guilty about making sure that your own needs as an individual and a teenager are attended to

- don't feel that you have to please everyone (both parents) all the time. Just because your parents are divorced it doesn't mean that you personally have to think of their needs more than if they were together

- you did not ask to be born, and you are your parents' responsibility (both of them). That responsibility should come before their own needs (but it won't always!)

- having divorced parents doesn't mean that you can blackmail them by playing one off against another. This will just cause more trouble for you in the long run

- realise that you are not alone and that thousands of other young people are in the same position. Ask them how they are managing

- having one person outside the family with whom you can discuss your most intimate feelings and thoughts is hugely helpful – see if you can find someone you can trust

10

Being a Step-Parent to a Teenager

The term step-parent has alas, like the term 'mother-in-law', almost mythical overtones within our society of incompatibility, difficulty, even wickedness. This is a pity, not only because the role of step-parent is a relatively common one today – but also because it is difficult enough to cope with it even half well, without being 'bad-mouthed' in advance.

It is equally difficult for the step-child, having to relate to a third parent who may seem to be supplanting a real, biological parent. Further, the teenager and the new step-parent can seem to be in competition for love of the same person – confusing and challenging if you are a young person desperate for attention and security to support you during adolescent challenges of self-identification in the outside world.

No wonder the stage seems to be set for operatic or maybe pantomime dramas between a teenager and a step-parent. Stepchildren have had to face many changes: the initial separation of their parents, living with one parent or the other, one or more new family set-ups with or without stepbrothers and sisters. But the 'step' relationship is one which can, like divorce, be handled better or worse.

Tony Bream is an example of someone who appears to manage it well. He has not been married before and teaches art at a local college of further education. He met Tara Jackson some years ago and they subsequently got married. Tara had been married before and had two children by her first marriage: Shane aged seventeen and David aged thirteen. Part of Tony's 'managing' is that he recognised the possible pitfalls, even if he was not totally prepared for all of them!

> *'When they moved in I can remember there being three of them and one of me. I remember the boys having a smell about them, probably due to boys not washing enough. Their pants seemed to be an item in my washing. Then there is the reputation that stepfathers have. One has to be careful in the present culture – we don't get a good press – but Tara was brilliant at handling that. The boys were very tolerant of the situation at the time. Maybe they will have a breakdown at thirty and demand explanations we haven't given, but they are not seeking them at the moment. I think it's good that Tara and I haven't had any children of our own because Dave and Shane haven't lost their primacy. I think they try to normalise things as much as possible, but they would still like their mum and dad to have a reconciliation.'*

That the factors surrounding separation and the subsequent new family structures have a profound effect is shown by the fact that teenagers who have lost a parent due to death do better in the long run than teenagers from stepfamilies.

For some people the role of step-parent begins well and continues well; with some it can begin with all sorts of difficulties but gradually settles down; and with others it starts badly and continues that way. For Tony and Tara, it is the first of these, but Tony still recognises the vulnerability of his situation and how he has had to adapt as his stepchildren get older, just as if he was their biological parent.

> *'My stepchildren are easier now they have grown up and are becoming thinking, perceptive, self-reliant young adults. OK, so they were sweet when they were younger, when you had to tuck in their shirts and do up their shoelaces and deal with their curiosity. Listening to how they talked when we walked to school together was fascinating. We laughed a lot together, especially at the stage when David had only one adjective and one noun and when we passed a dog he would say, "Strange dog". I saw the dog the other day. All these years on and I still thought "Strange dog", and realised both how much time had passed and also how attached I am to them both.'*

Whereas divorce seems to have a worse effect on younger children, they seem to do better in stepfamilies, possibly because they can adapt more easily to a new family structure. Conversely, there is a higher risk of a poor outcome for children in stepfamilies compared with those in lone-parent families if the children involved are older.

There does seem to be a subtle way for step-parents to avoid trying to be a substitute for the absent parent, but rather gently supplement the absent parent instead. So Tony can be both irritated and amused by some of his stepsons' behaviour, as any moderately objective adult might be: father, stepfather or friend.

> *'I don't suppose that a stepfather's attitudes are all that different from a father's over some things – like I get annoyed by their laziness and selfishness. I cannot understand why, when we have two television sets in the house, they both have to watch the same one and argue over which programme we are going to watch. There are*

three sofas in the lounge and they both want to sit on the same one in the same place. They kick each other and squabble, which is exceedingly annoying, but then I didn't have any brothers or sisters and Tara tells me that I am not in tune with the rivalry between brothers and sisters. I wish that Shane, who is so clever at school, at seventeen could just occasionally manage to take a plate off the table after a meal and put it in the dishwasher. My own childhood was very different and regulated by rules. But from them, just a tiny bit more co-operation would be great.'

There is another set of feelings that emerge from the role of stepfather: someone who knows the children well, has invested affection, care and time in their upbringing, and yet still doesn't necessarily infringe on the role of their real father. It is a relationship which any close friend of the family might have.

'I do have these fears for them which are no different from those a natural father would have. At the moment mine are that Shane will have a terrible car crash when one of his less responsible friends is driving them home from the pub. Before it was that they would be run over on the road if the lollipop lady wasn't there one day! Shane got beaten up at the bus stop the other day, which seems to happen to young men these days. I'm sure I would have different fears if I had teenage stepdaughters instead. I also worry because Shane is getting near that age when he is going to leave home and he'll have to make out in the outside world. So I worry whether we've adequately prepared him for that and whether we've done enough about his education.'

To a certain extent these fears about education are well founded, because stepchildren tend to leave school earlier and with fewer qualifications. This statistic is based on averages so not all stepchildren do worse; but if you take all stepchildren, on average they do worse at school.

Again like the real parent, step-parents may want their stepchildren to grow up with a different set of values from the ones they were imbued with by their own parents.

'I'd like the boys to have a different attitude to girls from mine when I was their age. Mine was based on inadequate knowledge of the similarities and differences between males and females. I think this generation are much more in tune with one another and not driven just by seduction. The sexual imperative doesn't seem to be as strong. That doesn't mean that we were any more successful at seduction. I just want to make sure they aren't hostile to women. I do try and talk to them about it but I know that Shane thinks I talk to him too much about things that he considers are sensitive and he gets embarrassed. He has said to me on occasion, "Just because your parents didn't talk to you, doesn't mean you should feel you have talk to me about these things." '

Step-parents have to be just as sensitive, if not more so, when it comes to the tricky question of having more children.

'One thing I've tried to discuss with them was, "What do you think about Mum and me having children of our own together?" Their response was, "Do we really have to talk about this when all we want to do is just enjoy our meal?" '

One thing that is obvious is that it makes it very much easier for the teenager if it is made absolutely clear to them what the agreed and well-defined role of each parent/step-parent is. These roles are much easier to define if there are no other stepchildren or biological children involved, no stepbrothers and sisters or half-brothers and sisters. Shane thinks things would have been much more difficult if Tony had had children.

> 'It's a huge advantage, because Tony can devote all his time to us. If we had had to put up with his children in the house, I think there would've been a problem. There's just not enough room, and I don't mind fighting my brother over the sofa, or the TV or whatever, but it would have upset all that if we'd had to learn to live with bloody stepbrothers or sisters.'

Another reason why this relationship works well is that Tara picks out the positive aspects of Tony's role as stepfather and sees them as a definite plus, as well as still managing to maintain a respectable relationship with her ex-husband (over most things!).

> 'The good thing about the two boys having a stepfather is that they have three grown-ups to relate to, and three contributing adults in a financial sense. There are also three of you to do a pincer movement on an issue, if you have to. Like if I don't think Shane is working very hard, Tony will hear about it because I will ask him for support, but I will also ring up their natural dad and say, "Look, I want you to say the right things as I don't think there is much work going on here." Their dad and I seem to agree on all the important points, except on the financial side – him contributing enough. The boys have increasingly expensive tastes!'

There is a way of managing the delicate three-way relationship between your new partner, their children, and yourself, which Tara thinks Tony does well, though he has the added advantage of being relatively well off and able to support the whole family.

*'Tony acts as a mixed support, being their mate but not at
the expense of supporting me. He never undermines me,
but if I have been particularly beastly to the boys he will
go and talk to them about it. I have to say that Tony really
enjoys the boys, and is even glad that they are not his.
And the boys have had financial security, which lots of
children in a similar position don't have.'*

It doesn't stop there. There is also the children's relationship
with their biological father which has to be managed, and
here again, like Clarissa in the previous chapter, Tara does
have fears about her sons preferring to go and live with him.
This is a recurring worry among divorced parents as children
grow up and develop their own independence.

*'It used to be an issue when they were small and they
went to see their father, but it isn't now because they
make up their own minds about what they want to do.
The younger one, David, hasn't been for ages; Shane goes
about once a month, which I think is par for the course.
What they tend to do with their father is go out shopping
or to the cinema, rather than staying overnight. I
certainly wouldn't have liked it if they had gone to live
with him, which is the danger you run if there are two
households they can choose between. The fear is always
there, that if you have a big row with your children they
will throw up their hands and say, "I'm off to live with
Dad." '*

In reconstituted families where things go wrong, some of
the major problems appear to revolve around stepchildren
mixing in with natural children, which can upset the delicate
balance of a household. When a marriage breaks up, school
takes on increased importance for teenagers. If children have
to move schools, this can be yet another disaster to be coped
with.

How well the role of step-parent can be managed is reflected upon by David, aged thirteen. He explains some of the factors which go to make up his relationship with his father and his stepfather.

'*Tony, my stepdad, is very generous and he's very open about things – sort of easy to talk to, maybe that's why he teaches students. I don't really know if I think of him as my dad or my stepdad. Maybe I just think of him as Tony and that's it. My actual dad, I call him "Dad", I don't really know how I feel about, though I have thought about this a bit. I kind of don't see him as such a major person in my life, but he's there and I do see him from time to time. Sometimes it's because I want to see him and sometimes it's because he takes me out for a meal or a film. Other times it feels as if I have to go and see him, but more and more I am open with him about it and can say that I've got to go out with my friends from school, or something like that, and he doesn't mind.*'

On the down side is the sad fact that after a divorce, two in three fathers lose contact with the children in the family they left. Maintaining contact is something that all the adults involved have to work hard at if it is to succeed. The parent doing the main caring for the teenager has to encourage and make opportunities for their son/daughter to visit the absent parent, and overcome their fears that the children will want to live with the absent parent if they have too much exposure to them. The step-parent has to be understanding of their partner's fears about letting the children go, and the absent parent has to arrange their life to include the children in it, which may not always be easy, as observed by David.

'*The worst thing about my dad is that he is so disorganised. Often it is difficult to fix to do something with him, like go out to the cinema. He never seems to quite know what he's doing and he's always cancelling things at the last minute, and that lets me down. My mum has to plan meticulously ahead of time, my dad is just so vague. I can't understand how they ever managed to live together.'*

Another very sensitive area is step-parents disciplining their stepchildren. This is fraught with implications which teenagers may be quick to exploit with all parties involved, if not handled carefully. Shane is quick to pick up on this but chooses not to use it to his own ends.

'Basically, when it comes to disciplining me, it falls on Mum, because my stepdad doesn't feel he can put his foot down very strongly. Mum does appeal to him over some decisions where she feels she might be being over-protective of us. The last time that happened was over a holiday I was planning with a friend who was going to drive. Mum appealed to Tony over that and they agreed I couldn't go. On the whole, he's more lenient than Mum is, and does see things from my point of view, but I don't play them off against one another. That just wouldn't seem right.'

Nor does Shane think Tony always gets it right – nobody ever could.

'The worse thing about Tony is that he sometimes gets involved in things which it's not really his place to in my eyes. One time it was about what I spent my money on. It's my money and if I want to buy a music centre, that's my business and he hasn't the right to interfere. He also niggles occasionally about things I don't worry much about, like who uses what towels in the bathroom.'

It is no good denying though that there are advantages for teenagers in having divorced parents, in that they can have two sets of parents and two households to exploit. If they manage the situation well (and they are often experts), they can get more presents at Christmas and birthdays, more holidays, more parties and, on occasion, more sympathy. David has a clear idea though as to who, in his family, is mainly responsible for making things work to his satisfaction, and he also has some down-to-earth advice.

> *'In the long run it seems to have worked out really well because Mum has it so organised. The main thing is if parents can be tolerant of one another after they've got divorced, and try and understand what the other parent is trying to do, it does make life so much easier for the kids.'*

There is also always the question of whether a problem arising between teenagers and their step-parent is a teenage 'thing' or a step 'thing'. In most cases it is going to be a combination of the two – the stresses and strains of adolescence added to by being in a stepfamily. Doreen James works in a travel firm and has a son called Peter, aged twenty-four, from a previous marriage which ended many years ago. Five years ago she started a relationship with Jim Hinde, who has two daughters, Janet aged fifteen and Christine aged eighteen. Things did not run smoothly for her as she explains.

> *'Teens is when it gets difficult. One thing about being a step-parent is that natural parents have difficulties with their children in one way or another, but it is very easy if you are a step-parent to be made to believe that that is why you are having trouble. It may actually be just the trouble that all adults have with adolescents, though the 'step' part may be added in on top of that. For instance, during the summer, I was driven to distraction by the mess my two stepdaughters kept their rooms in, with*

*tangled heaps of wet towels, bathing costumes, knickers,
T-shirts. It got so bad there was a very definite smell that
came out of them of unwashed clothes. Sometimes, when
they were off at the beach, I would make a raid, take all
their dirty clothes and wash them. They would get back
and say, "Oh great" and yet, within no time at all, their
rooms were in the same old smelly mess again. I felt "Hey,
this is my holiday too, you know." I work really hard the
rest of the year and there is no recognition of it
whatsoever.'*

Doreen also had to deal with the lingering suspicion in her
stepdaughters' minds that she was in some way responsible
for breaking up their natural family.

*'When Janet and Christine first came to stay they were
ten and thirteen. They didn't know me and I didn't know
them. I was very keen to be acceptable to them and that,
not surprisingly, wasn't reciprocated, because they had
each other and they got on very well together. Another
difficulty was that besides a sort of wariness of me, there
was a feeling that whatever the actual history of my
relationship with Jim (and I had nothing whatsoever to do
with the break-up of their parents' marriage), the fact
that I was the woman who was not their mother but who
was now living with their father meant I was
automatically regarded with a lot of hostility. I was seen
as the stumbling block to their parents living together
again.'*

To make a step relationship work, it is essential for the new
partner to realise that the biological parent is going to have to
devote time to their children. Although Doreen has insight
into the fact that Jim is torn between the needs of his children
and her own needs when they are together, she is not altogether sympathetic and is inclined to feel left out and jealous.

There is also no question that teenagers play on this, albeit not necessarily consciously.

'Also because Jim doesn't have them all the time, he is very keen that the time he is with them is very good, and quite right too. The first summer that Jim and I were together, I felt very left out because he was doing things with his children all the time. He would say, "If you want to come and join us on the beach, you would be very welcome." Why wasn't that taken for granted? It did hurt and make me feel left out. I also felt that perhaps I should let them have time on their own together, but I felt excluded and that there was a deliberate attempt on the part of my stepchildren to break us up as a couple. If I just play my role as a housekeeper, there is no trouble, but if it is obvious that we are in bed together and we don't want to be disturbed, there is trouble – and that is inevitable. Another thing is, I can't be critical of Jim in front of them, as the two girls get furious at me if I say the slightest thing against him and will sulk for days.'

These are all added problems for second marriages, and not surprisingly second marriages are even more likely to end in divorce than first marriages. Sex is a very sensitive area. Teenagers do not, in any way, like the idea of a parent having sex with a new partner.

'I mean take the new sexual relationship. It musn't be shoved in the children's faces, that would be awful, but it needs to be dealt with straightforwardly and not hidden. Initially the girls made snide and hurtful remarks if Jim showed me any affection when we were together. The first summer they came to stay, Jim and I didn't sleep in the same room which I found difficult because it was not acknowledging the reality of the situation. I thought both

*my son and Jim's daughters were old enough to deal with
it, but his ex-wife insisted that we didn't share a bedroom
as it would be upsetting for the girls. There was one night
when he came to "visit" me in my room, and the younger
girl got up and wanted her father, and it was very
awkward. There was a huge amount of guilt when we
were discovered.'*

Doreen is torn between putting down the major part of her
problems to 'teen' factors or to 'step' factors.

*'If I wonder whether there are any problems specific to
having a step relationship, I think they are mostly
problems which exist in any family, but they are given a
kind of extra poignancy by the fact that these teenagers
are not your own flesh and blood. Therefore you take it
harder and feel more upset and hard done by.'*

The real agony comes for teenagers where the new relationship has been handled badly and clearly demonstrates their
helplessness in the face of their parents' decisions – even if
they can observe with 'gritted teeth' humour, as Polly
Campbell does, who is sixteen.

*'My stepdad is the last person you'd ever want to live with.
He's a bit of a control freak – the remote control, that is.
He's one of those obsessive channel-hoppers who likes to
have the remote securely in his hand. He nearly went
insane the time my mother hid the remote in the back of
her trousers. He was searching all over the living room and
even had us going out to the car to check it wasn't there.
The remote had only been missing for about ten minutes
but I think he'd started to get withdrawal symptoms. If his
hand is resting on a firm surface, you can see his fingers
twitching slightly like he's pressing buttons. It's funny
really. But he likes to control what we watch. He'll switch*

*over to the news or the history channel, or something
equally boring, when you're in the middle of a really good
film or the programme you've been waiting all week to
watch. If you complain he'll say, "Well, who paid for the
TV?" and/or send you off to clean the kitchen.'*

Polly clearly understands the relationship between herself and
her stepfather, which has all but broken down completely.

*'I don't love my stepdad and he doesn't love me. In fact I
don't even like him and I can't see that ever changing.
Everything I say at the moment has a "tone" or "attitude".
I can't even sneeze without being accused of having an
attitude.'*

It is clear that continuing conflict between warring parents,
whether 'step' or 'biological', both before and after the break-
up of a marriage, is stressful for children and may explain
why they have a higher incidence of behavioural problems,
particularly aggressiveness and anxiety. When it comes down
to it, many of the problems are to do with the three- or four-
way relationships everyone is having to handle. The adults in
the situation are meant to be (but certainly not always are)
the more mature, and are, after all, the parties responsible for
the readjustments which the teenagers are going through. It is
not as if the teenagers asked their parents to get divorced and
remarried. Doreen recognises this.

*'I think if you don't like your stepchildren, you rationalise
it by saying, "Oh well, that's because she's a stepchild,"
but the fact is that if you try, you can find something to
like in almost any child. You need to look for the good
things, and if you have a basic liking for children you will
like your "steps" whatever – just as you like your own
children, in spite of what they do sometimes. If you can't
find anything to like in your stepchild, that's your*

*problem, not the child's. It is inevitable that the stepchild
will give you a hard time sometime, but your own children
will do that anyhow.'*

Step-parenting is an extremely hard role to play. It has to be
worked at, but it is down to the parents, not the teenagers, to
make it succeed.

Things which may help step-parents:

- do not attempt to be a substitute parent to your stepchild

- accept that being a step-parent is a difficult relationship to
  get right

- children from divorced parents appear to do better if their
  parents do not marry a new partner

- allow the natural parent time alone with their child(ren);
  the relationship is unlikely to work if you don't allow free
  access between your new partner and their children

- do not compete with the natural parent in trying to be the
  better parent

- however bad the original marriage, you may have to accept
  being resented by the step-children

- stepfamilies can be difficult for the natural parent and the
  step-parent; the new partner may feel excluded by the natural parent, and the natural parent may feel threatened by
  the step-parent's relationship with the stepchildren

- you do not necessarily have to like your stepchildren, but
  if your partner has teenage children, you will have to do

more than just tolerate them, and adapt to their needs to a certain extent

- bear in mind, for the children's sake, that second marriages have a higher breakdown rate than first marriages

- however good you are as a step-parent, the stepchildren may not want to acknowledge the new relationship

- less is demanded from children of their stepfathers than of their stepmothers, so stepfathers can often be more of a 'friend'

- if you both have children from previous marriages, acknowledge the difficulty that the children from the two families may have in being friends with one another

- try to be as fair as possible with treats and punishments between stepchildren and your own children – equality makes everything easier

Tips for stepchildren:

- remember, and keep on remembering, that your parents separating or divorcing is not, was not, your fault

- you do not have to love, or even like, your step-parent, but you do have to try to behave yourself and live with him/her

- being totally 'impossible' and making everyone feel bad is unlikely to make you feel any better, and is unlikely to make the step-parent disappear

- try to see your step-parent's point of view and realise it is difficult for your step as well as for you

- try not to make your relationship with your natural parent exclusive of their new partner; allow your parent to have some time alone with their new partner, and expect time alone with your natural parent in return

- if your step-parent is making you feel uncomfortable, tell someone

- if you feel low and depressed seek help; talk to a friend, another adult, someone at school, your natural parent

11

Teenagers With Depression and Teenagers Who Harm Themselves

There is a wide spectrum of feelings in young people (and adults!) between feeling 'happy' and feeling 'very depressed' normally covered by such terms as being 'anxious', 'worried', 'miserable', 'down', 'fed up', 'under the weather', 'shitty', 'low', 'pathetic' and so on. The very range of terms indicates how common and how normal this is. We all have to deal with adverse situations in our lives and some of us deal with them better than others. Factors which help or hinder with this coping are self-esteem, self-confidence, and satisfaction with life, which all seem to be interdependent and difficult to disentangle.

Some worry in our lives is not only normal and inevitable but is actually beneficial. If we didn't worry about our families, the environment, our health, the future, we might not be helpful to others, reliable in the way we work, mindful of what is going on around us and of other people's feelings. The downside is that too much worry distracts and disables us. It makes us feel helpless and overwhelmed.

Looking at the main worries for young men and women:

young men worry most about how they look, family problems, problems with friends, career problems and unemployment; and young women about the way they look, problems with friends, family problems and health problems.

Donna, who is seventeen, explains her feelings about her looks.

> *'It seems to me that all other women are really quite beautiful, whereas since thirteen I have always been a pudgy child. My older brothers spent all their time calling me "fat" and "little fatness" – even though Mum tried to stop them. Dad spent years saying to me, "Well, you and I are the fatties of the family – never mind." All my friends at the school I went to were well groomed, beautiful and fashionable.'*

There are a number of factors which seem to influence how much young people worry. For instance, young people who live with both their biological parents are less likely to be worriers; young people who get on well with their mother and father and can talk to them are less likely to be worriers; young people who report not being able to trust adults are more likely to be worriers.

Low 'self-esteem', or not feeling good about oneself, is another factor which increases worry, but it is not clear whether worrying gnaws away at self-esteem, or whether low self-esteem makes one more vulnerable to anxieties. Maybe the two are totally interdependent. It is worth noting here that self-esteem improves with age in both young men and young women but is generally lower among girls. Donna again:

> *'Basically from the time I was twelve until I was sixteen I felt absolutely awful. It was a complete nightmare. I spent all of those years thinking, "I am really fat", "I am really unattractive", "I am really unpopular", "I am worth absolutely nothing", "What have I to live for?" kind of*

thing. It was fine for the first couple of hours after getting out of bed, until I had to go to school and start seeing people. After that it just went from bad to worse. I would lock myself in my room for hours and cry – it was just horrible.'

There has recently been a gradual realisation that so-called 'moodiness' in teenagers may, in some cases, be frank depression. If asked, nine out of ten young people say they feel 'generally happy about their life at present' and three out of ten young people go on to say that they feel 'very happy about their life at present'. But this does not exclude the possibility of young people feeling depressed or fed up at other times than 'at present'. In fact, most teenagers will feel sad, depressed or anxious at some time. About ten in every hundred young people (more girls than boys) will be frankly depressed, but only two to three in every hundred will have such bad depression that they need psychiatric help (severe depression is twice as common in girls than in boys).

A group of over 600 fourteen to seventeen-year-olds were asked how often they felt 'fed up'. Nearly one in ten felt fed up or depressed every day; one in four at least once a week; and only one in thirty girls and one in fifteen boys said that they never felt fed up or depressed.

Depression can last for a considerable time. For many young people sad feelings are there, but are inexplicable and difficult at the time to express. The causes may be more obvious in retrospect, as they were for Donna.

'I felt completely inferior because I never ever fitted into a group at school, which was a very cliquey place. You had to be in a group or you were a complete loser. Maybe if I had been with a different set of people I might have fitted in but I was just a kind of hanger-on. There was no one around who I could talk to about how I felt, on a

*really intimate basis, not even Mum or Dad. I get on OK
with them but I felt they wouldn't understand how I felt
deep down inside me. OK, I did have friends, but I didn't
really feel close to them, and in some ways they were part
of the problem. They seemed so absolutely fine, so
together, so pristine, ultra popular, ultra pretty. They just
saw me as miserable and depressed. I didn't cope at all
during that period. The slightest thing would knock me
flat. It didn't occur to me that I could control it and I had
no wish to.'*

A strange factor about being human is that most of us get the
impression that 'everyone else is all right' when we are feeling
lousy. However, if you ask people about feelings of lack of
self-confidence from time to time, they are virtually universal.
It is true that some people have more of these feelings than
others, and also that some hide their feelings of inadequacy
more effectively than others.

Young people's feelings can be very fragile and it doesn't
take much to push them into feeling not wanted by things
that may never occur to parents.

*'I'd just got back from being away with friends because
Mum and Dad wanted to go on holiday by themselves. I
went into our house and it was all quiet and gloomy and
there didn't seem to be anyone around. I went upstairs and
knocked on my parents' bedroom door and they were
there, and just said "Hi" and "Did you have a nice time?"
I had expected them to be really pleased to see me and to
say, "Come in and tell us all about it," but they didn't. I
felt incredibly rejected and I thought, "They don't want
me, and they don't need me." '*

Somewhere during the course of growing up, we all have to
deal with anxiety and stress. Part of developing independence
as a teenager is no longer having your parents' total protection

on a day-to-day basis against the vicissitudes of life. These have to be faced and dealt with by the teenager, and the teenager has to learn to survive them in a way that is not damaging but an actual learning experience. The best way for parents to help their teenagers through this is to build up their children's self-confidence by praising them when they do manage by themselves rather than running them down when they don't. Something that has been shown to help relieve anxiety and stress is exercise (and it does not matter what sort). Hard exercise makes the body release endorphins which seem to help it relax and they counteract the chemicals released when the body is stressed.

When the feelings of depression and lack of self-confidence become extreme, a teenager may have suicidal feelings or even attempt suicide, if only to call attention to a problem that they cannot express to adults in any other way.

'The lowest point of my life was at school on the playing field. I was just so low and then someone the other side of the field yelled something at me which I will never ever repeat, and that just tipped me over. I took some aspirin when hiding in the corner of the field thinking, "I just don't want to be here, I can't take it any longer, I can't take seeing anyone else." But there was a bloke in my English class who had seen me sitting at the edge of the field and seen the other person yell at me. When I didn't come into English, he excused himself and came to find me. He sat down and started talking to me, and took the bottle of aspirin away, saying, "You don't want to be doing this – what's the point?" He was so sensitive and so kind that I have credited him with saving my life. None of my friends would have been able to talk to me the way he did or would have thought to.'

Some of these episodes may not ever reach the attention of an adult, and even when a parent or friend does know about them, they may be so transient and non-life threatening that medical help is not needed. It is therefore likely that such episodes of 'self-harm' are more common in young people than is usually acknowledged.

> *'This bloke took me to the school lavatories and showed me how to make myself sick, which I had never been able to do before. It was only about twenty minutes after taking the tablets so they more or less came up whole, which was great as I didn't want the fuss of telling anyone else. No one else knows about it to this day.'*

The term 'self-harm' covers episodes which appear to be suicide attempts and those that are obviously not, but are designed to draw attention to the young person's needs. Deliberate self-harm is associated with upsets in family relationships, behavioural problems, poverty, fatherless families and unsupported mothers of adolescent children. Around one in two actual suicides in young people occur where the young person comes from a home where there has been parental separation or divorce. Self-harm also includes so-called 'cutting' activity, a relatively common behaviour in girls where they scratch or cut their arms with scissors, knives, razor blades or pins. It appears to arise out of quite complex feelings which Donna describes.

> *'When I felt the worst anguish, totally acute pain, but couldn't express my fear and self-hatred, I started to scratch myself on my arms, and scratched and scratched until blood came, and doing that over a couple of hours really released my feelings. It kept me going through a time I wouldn't have been able to cope with otherwise. After that I began to cut myself very lightly on my arms, first with a pair of scissors which didn't work, and then with a razor blade which did. This became more and more frequent as a way of coping with my feelings.'*

Jane, who is fifteen years old, has also cut herself in the past and describes the complexity of the feelings leading to hurting herself:

'I did cut myself when I was fourteen. I can remember exactly what my sister said just before it happened. We were sitting watching TV and it was just before I had some exams, though not important ones. We were arguing about who should work where and I said to her, "You know I am going to blame you if I fail my exams?" and she said, "Oh, you need an excuse for being a failure, do you?" I just went right out to the kitchen and got a big carving knife out of the knife holder. Then I went into the dining room where I knew no one would be and cut my arms – not at the wrist but higher up. Mum and Dad were at home, and I only did it to draw blood. I didn't want to die. I wanted to make some kind of statement about the way I felt. I didn't have to go to hospital or anything.

'I think that cutting is really to do with hating oneself. Sometimes now I do scratch myself, which feels the same as cutting. It's an overwhelming feeling of anger and frustration which has to be let out somehow. It's letting emotions out – that's what cutting is, definitely. It is just trying to take away one's feelings by cutting oneself. There seems to be no other way. I can't cry or anything, and yelling and screaming draws too much attention to those feelings. Once you've done the cutting, then you've let them out and it's over with, so it is effective in a way.'

Cutting and actual attempted suicide do occur together in many young girls as Donna has demonstrated, and the same is true of Jane.

'I didn't know what my attempts at harming myself were about. I think I was totally confused. Maybe I didn't want to live, but it couldn't have been that because I survived.

Looking back on it, I think it was more a cry for help. The first time was when I was fourteen and then a couple of times when I was fifteen. I took about forty paracetamol when I was fourteen.'

Over eight out of ten young people who deliberately self-harm do so by self-poisoning, and usually by taking an overdose of tablets. One in ten self-injure and about one in ten use a combination of both methods. Most common among the tablets used is paracetamol, then a mixture of other drugs, followed by antidepressants, tranquillisers and sedatives. Of those who self-injure, nine out of ten young people use self-cutting or asphyxiation. The remaining methods of self-injury are mainly jumping and hanging.

Overall, there is growing evidence in young people of a link between depression, antisocial behaviour, substance abuse and suicidal risk. But exactly where stress comes into all this is difficult to define. High levels of stress cause us anxiety. Too much anxiety and we feel that we can no longer cope with our situation. This is something that everyone knows about and has experienced. We could probably all do with some lessons in stress management, for although we are experts at stress, we are not experts at how to deal with it.

Other relative factors are stresses within the family which may detract from attention being paid to the needs of the teenager, who may, at the same time, be having a hard time struggling with her own life and feelings.

'I had been arguing with my parents and my sister before I went away. Part of it is my sister Susan being so intellectually clever, which makes me feel that I don't match up. She'd just got eleven As for GCSEs! Also Dad was ill around that time and I didn't bat an eyelid – just kept on with my life as normal, totally self-interested and selfish. The entry in my diary on the day Dad went into hospital was "Went shopping". I was also into a bit of a

*sexual relationship, which added to my confusion. He was
a guy who was meant to be looking after me from time to
time. I started getting really depressed then and began to
think that my mum, dad and sister would be better off
without me.'*

Repetition of deliberate self-harm is very high, with a follow-
up estimate of nearly one in two trying again within two
years. Among those who succeed in committing suicide, the
rate of 'repeating' is about twenty times higher than among
those only deliberately self-harming without actually killing
themselves.

Parents should not feel that they have, in any way, failed if
there is a need to seek help elsewhere, as Jane did – from
friends, doctors or teachers.

*'Mum was really good all the way through it, but I just
needed more support than Mum and Dad were able to give
me. I was a black hole of need. I think that parents should
keep an eye out when young people hurt themselves like I
did. I expected my parents to know how sensitive I was
feeling without actually telling them. I could have gone
over the edge at any moment if I hadn't taken myself off to
the doctor. I have to say that if I had a child like me, I
don't know what I would do.'*

Jane's advice to other parents whose children appear to be distressed is:

*'You have to take anything that someone who is doing
what I did seriously. You have to ask your kids about it as
well. You have to say, "Look, do you feel as though you
don't want to go on any more?" and you have to realise
that probably most of us teenagers have times when we
just don't know what to do with our emotions. Parents
need to talk about it and say, "If you do feel like that, just*

come and say so"; or have some kind of code so that they can recognise when you're in distress if you're in company. You just need the reassurance that you are worthwhile, that they do love you and care about you, and that what you are going through is temporary and is not going to last.

'Mum was good at getting the guilt thing right though. She made me aware of how selfish I was being and how it would affect everyone else if I were to die. I was feeling, "Well, everyone would be better off if I wasn't here." I didn't have the capability to understand what a nightmare it would be for them, and how much they would miss me. Mum was very good at explaining. I think people my age just don't have the experience to know what effect it would have on others, but also we are just totally preoccupied with ourselves and how we feel. You're just so selfish at that age, just absolutely self-centred and immersed in what you're going through and what you're feeling. But you've got to realise that you are not the only one involved in the equation. It must have been totally shocking and difficult for my parents, but I'm glad we all came through it with the aid of counselling. I had individual counselling and then we also had some as a family. They were both useful though.'

In summary, up to the age of twenty-four, it is estimated that over the year around two in every hundred males and as many as ten in every hundred females will deliberately self-harm. Women tend to attempt suicide or cut themselves, but the number of suicides in young women is relatively low compared with men. The reasons for young women self-harming are complex and are related to self-esteem, self-confidence and how they see themselves in relation to those around them. Self-harm that ends in death is more common in men and is dealt with further in Chapter 15.

One thing that should reassure parents and young people is that most of us, as we grow older, do grow better at learning how to cope with worries, anxieties and depression, as Donna found:

> 'That was before I learnt to like my own company, and be perfectly happy in it, which is how I feel now I am seventeen. I can't even remember the last time I felt depressed, and if I do feel it coming on, I just say to myself, "Oh, for God's sake stop feeling sorry for yourself and get out and do something." But this is something you have to train yourself to do. Maybe you have to reach rock bottom first.'

Things that may help parents with teenagers who are anxious, stressed or depressed:

● find time to talk about emotions and feelings with your children, both boys and girls

● moodiness, bad temper, headaches, feeling tired all the time, feeling unable to face people, sleeping problems, being disorganised and finding it difficult to finish things, may be part of being normal but if they are interfering with a young person's life it may mean they are depressed, stressed or anxious

● some stress is good for us and helps us do things and achieve; too much gets in the way and makes us less efficient

● seek help if the problem has lasted longer than you would expect and/or other people have commented on it

● realise that you being stressed can have an effect, and can cause stress for your teenager

- find out what is making your teenager stressed – words of support are more valuable than criticisms

- if you think (or know) the problem is school related, talk to the school and find out if they are aware of problems your son or daughter might be reluctant to let you know about, like bullying or work difficulties

Things that may help teenagers who are stressed or anxious:

- 80 per cent of worries are not worth worrying about as they are unimportant or very unlikely to happen. When you start worrying, ask yourself how important the worry really is and will it still be important in five years time?

- write down your main worries, then work out for each one whether you can do something about it

- try distractions like talking to a friend, going out for a walk, sending an e-mail

- have a special fifteen-minute worry time each day. Collect up all the worries and only allow yourself to think about them during that fifteen minutes. Then try getting rid of them by imagining you are putting each one in a box and throwing it away

- do some exercise: run, swim, cycle, skip – this reduces the stress by releasing hormones called endorphins

- time management is often the problem with exam and work stress, so work out what you are actually doing with your time by filling in a weekly timetable. See how much time you are attending lessons, chatting, watching *Neighbours*, eating, sleeping, arguing, studying and so on

Tips for parents to improve your teenagers' self-esteem:

- make them feel valued for being them

- show them that their opinions matter and are worth hearing

- respect them and listen to them even if you don't always agree with them

- do not complain about them not doing anything and then not allow them to do things

- give them responsibility and opportunities to do things and achieve, even if they do not always do them as well as you would do them yourself

- concentrate on the good things they have done, rather than always seeing the negative side and telling them they are wrong

12

How and What Teenagers Eat

ood in our society is synonymous with caring and the giving of love. As a result, it represents an ever-sensitive area of potential conflict, with both parents and their children being acutely aware of its potential for control from birth onwards.

Parents may worry that their teenage children are not getting enough of the right nourishment because of their preference for junk foods. They may get irritated by constant grazing and/or munching in front of the TV rather than sitting down for a meal; and get exasperated by their teenage boys and their friends when they find the fridge has been emptied of the week's food. They may also be anxious that their daughters are developing an eating disorder if they go on a diet or skip a meal.

Modern life, with varying work schedules, single-parent families and flexi-working hours, means that fewer families actually sit down for regular meals together; and when they do, teenagers complain that they do not always want to conform to routines and rituals which do not fit into their own timetables.

However, research involving teenagers keeping food diaries shows that most teenagers are getting enough food. Most are adequately nourished, despite skipping meals, especially breakfast – even though snacks may provide up to 30 per cent of the energy they need. Jan, who is the mother of three children, Julia, Samantha and James, expresses her frustration.

> '*What I find incredibly stressful is trying to shop at lunchtime, and then rushing home from work to cook everyone a specially chosen meal, only to find that half the family is going to be somewhere else for supper and they haven't bothered to tell me beforehand. My fury is partly because they have been so off-hand and partly because I don't have control over what they're eating.*'

Junk food can provide many of the nutrients but on its own may be deficient in some of the vitamins found in fresh fruit and vegetables. Although it is important to try to get a balance of different types of food and nutrients, there is no correct diet; and even the experts always seem to be changing their minds. There is a general consensus, however, that for long-term good health, the ideal is to eat a variety of foods, avoid too much fatty and fried foods, and eat plenty of fresh fruit and vegetables.

Different cultures eat different foods, prepared in different ways, as Julia, Jan's eldest, explains.

> '*I don't know why my parents are always on to me about eating more veg. The veg I do eat is boring enough without having any more of it. Frankly, I think what I eat is fine – all sorts of different stuff. I also love eating with my friend Raj, because his family likes these really hot curries, which I can barely manage without exploding but he thinks are mild!*'

Girls are more aware of diet and health foods than boys, who are more interested in quantity. Girls eat more fruit and salads. Four out of ten girls prefer to drink low-fat milk compared to three out of ten boys. Boys eat more chips than girls, but crisps are eaten on most days by four out of ten boys and girls.

Shopping with teenage girls often means your trolley is filled with so-called 'low-fat' foods. Food labelling has improved but still can and does cause confusion. 'Low-fat' means different things for different foods as there is no law to say how low 'low fat' has to be. A low-fat yoghurt may have 0.5 per cent fat, whereas low-fat butter substitute may still have 40 per cent fat. 'Low calorie' can only be used if there are less than 40 Kcal in 100 gm of the food. 'Reduced calorie' has to contain less than three-quarters of the calories of similar foods. 'Light' or 'lite' is meaningless and can refer to taste, calories, alcoholic strength, or colour. Stork Light butter substitute has 60 per cent fat, whereas Kerrygold Light spread has 39 per cent fat. 'No added sugar' usually means no added sucrose. But beware! There are other types of sugars which are bad for the teeth and no lower in calories, such as glucose, dextrose, fructose, honey and syrup. Not everyone agrees with this approach, as Jan's husband Jake makes clear.

> *'I love my food and I'll eat anything, but it drives me mad when Jan and I are out shopping and she has to look at what every food contains. My own attitude is that if one gets a bit of everything, as well as fruit and salad and stuff which everyone knows one has to have, then what the hell does it matter when it comes to tiny differences. It takes all the pleasure away from cooking if you have to spend your time worrying about what's in it.'*

Food requirements change during the teen years but girls in their early teens tend to want to lose weight, while boys want to put it on. Only about one in five boys and one in six girls can be considered seriously overweight by national weight guidelines (see height/weight chart in the Appendix) but there are many who are over-weight due to eating too much and taking too little exercise. Growth spurts occur around the age of twelve in girls and fourteen in boys. When this rapid growth is happening boys need on average between 2800 and 3000 calories a day, and girls need 2400 calories. These requirements will be affected by how active they are. You use about 1 Kcal per minute just to stay alive. Walking slowly uses 3 Kcal per minute but if you get up speed it is 5 Kcal per minute. Walking upstairs uses 9 Kcal per minute, cycling 5 to 7.4 Kcal per minute, running 7.5 Kcal per minute.

If your son or daughter is very overweight and needs to shed a few pounds, the easiest way is to cut down on the fat content of the meals you are all having, and encourage them to take more exercise, even if it is only cycling or walking to school. Remember, fat has many more calories in it per gram than other foods. One gram of fat contains nine calories, one gram of carbohydrate contains only four calories. Try semi-skimmed or skimmed milk, grill rather than fry foods, stir-fry vegetables because you hardly need any oil, eat more fish and less chips, eat more pasta, cut down on meat, and eat more vegetables and fruit (this will be cheaper as well). Use pure sunflower, soya or olive oil rather than butter or cooking fat. Beware of things labelled 'vegetable oils', which are actually high in saturated fats. If eating fats, eat unsaturated rather than saturated fats. Saturated fats increase the cholesterol in your blood and therefore the risks of heart disease later in life.

unsats	sats
sunflower oil	meats
olive oil	butter
soft margarine	full-cream milk
nuts	cream
fish	eggs

About one in five teenage girls and one in ten teenage boys are vegetarian, which can be quite a problem for parents, especially if no one else in the family is. There has, however, been a general trend away from meat eating in the population as a whole, thanks to BSE and the evidence that a fish-eating 'vegetarian' diet is probably the healthiest diet around. If you are cooking vegetarian meals, you may need to check that you are including all the different types of foods – especially if you are feeding a picky vegetarian who's not so keen on vegetables! The iron from vegetable foods is less well absorbed than that from meat foods, so provide foods with a high iron content like beans, lentils, chickpeas, eggs, nuts, cocoa, curry powder, wheatgerm, dried fruit and green vegetables; and you may need iron tablets which you can buy at any chemist. The other vitamin that vegetarians may become short of, especially vegans who don't eat any animal products (including milk and eggs), is B12; so they will need to take a supplement like 'Barmene'. Vegetarians get their proteins from nuts, beans, lentils, chickpeas, rice and peas, as well as milk, cheese and eggs.

Most of us are going to eat what we want when we want it, and on the whole that's the way it should be, giving in to those instant wants – chocolate biscuits, cream, whatever. But what you eat as a teenager does affect your health when you are older, so there are a couple of areas of eating that it is worth putting a little extra effort into. Too much saturated fat when young is linked to adult heart disease and possibly breast cancer, and too little calcium is linked to having 'thin' bones which break easily (osteoporosis) when you are older.

Things that parents may find useful to know about their teenager's diet:

- unless your adolescents look obviously too fat or too thin, don't worry too much about how and what they are eating – let their individual appetite dictate how much they eat

- if you do want to put energy into changing their diet, then try to get them to eat more fruit and vegetables by making these easily available

- involve them in decisions about what to buy in the way of vegetables and fruit and get them involved in the shopping and cooking – should you be so lucky that they are interested!

- if your adolescents have decided on being vegetarian and cutting out meat, fish and milk or milk products (butter, cheese), they just may get deficient in protein, calcium, iron and some vitamins. Try supplying them with multivitamin pills with calcium (especially B vitamins), and buy lots of foods made from soya

- it is a myth that fast foods have to harm your health. They may not be four-star restaurant eating, but they can, and do, provide a good mixed diet. Suggest an occasional tomato in exchange for chips

- stock your grazing lands (fridge and cupboards) with masses of low-fat, high-taste, tempting snacks – if you can find them – rather than crisps, chocolate and biscuits

- if you are lucky enough to have a physically energetic sportsperson as an offspring (they do just happen by occasionally), they will not necessarily need any special food – just a bit more of it. Don't be fooled into buying highly expensive powdered protein supplements – these are just not necessary

Things that teenagers may find useful if they want to think about what they eat:

- you have to eat enough to stay alive, which, at an absolute minimum of sitting twenty-four hours a day watching TV, needs 1700 Kcal for women and 2000 Kcal for men, for them to stay the same weight

- given that most people don't spend twenty-four hours a day watching TV, but walk about, go to raves, have sex and grow, women need at least 2500 Kcal a day and men need 3000 Kcal

- one or two things that you eat now will have some long-term effects – especially if you overpig on fats and eat too little calcium (especially girls)!

- if you are overweight you are doing one or both of the following: eating too much and not exercising enough

- if you want to lose weight, eat less, especially fats because fats have far more calories for the same weight than sugars, and exercise more – that's all there is to it!

- make sure that there are lots of your favourite foods in the fridge so that you can do healthier grazing

13

When Teenagers Eat Too Little
or Too Much

or most of us, food represents a necessity of life, a social occasion, a pleasure and/or a recurrent tiresome chore. However, sometimes problems with food take on a different dimension and can be symptomatic of other problems.

This was the case in the Weller family. Karen Weller is now eighteen but was much younger when things first began to go wrong. She was living with her mother Jane, a drug representative, and her father Ken, who runs a sports centre. She has younger twin brothers, Mark and Hugo, now aged fourteen. Jane and Ken are churchgoers and, although not particularly sociable, they are extremely involved with the local community as it relates to the church and are supportive of new families who move into the area.

Karen explains:

'I first realised things were wrong when I was twelve. I was developing earlier than the rest of my friends, getting breasts and that kind of thing, and had just started my periods. There were various incidents from my childhood

179

which had made me think I wasn't worth much and that I wouldn't be loved unless I was still a child, and that made me really scared to grow up.

'I got the impression from my parents that it was good to be busy and do things for other people but not to receive comfort and help oneself, and certainly not as an adult. So it didn't occur to me to talk to somebody when I found I was lonely, scared, and very unhappy.

'I was involved with sport, and my parents were working, so it was a very busy household. Then my dad's father became ill with Alzheimer's disease and came to live with us and there was even less opportunity to talk to my parents. I started to feel very ashamed and embarrassed about my body. I was keen on doing gymnastics but wasn't very good at it because I was one of the biggest there, which heightened my feelings of embarrassment. Eventually I reached the point at which something snapped and I wasn't able to cope any more. It was then that I decided to lose weight.

'I remember being upstairs in my room and crying, and my mum coming up and saying, "What's the matter?" I said, "I want to lose weight. I don't like myself as I am." I expected her to be quite scornful and say, "Oh don't be so silly," but she was supportive and said, "OK, if you want to, then I'll help you." That was a big relief because I was able to share with somebody else what I hadn't been able to share for months.'

It is important to realise that dieting in young women is fairly normal. Whether this is a good thing is debatable, but only a very small percentage of those who do diet go on to have eating problems. Approximately seventy in every hundred young women will diet at one time or another, but only about one in a hundred will go on to have a diagnosis of anorexia, and four in a hundred a diagnosis of bulimia and binge-eating problems. It appears that dieting in 'vulnerable young people' can act as a trigger to specific eating problems. Girls who are perfectionists, lack self-esteem and self-confidence, are obsessional and very competitive, seem to be more at risk of developing an eating disorder.

Karen is typical of many young women.

'I don't think I was overweight, though I wasn't slim. Gym was after school and I wanted to go but dreaded it at the same time. All my family is so active. My mum was very fit at that time and was out working a lot, my brothers were into football, and my father's job was sport. I did start to lose weight, but I was trying to solve the wrong problem. I was trying to return to being a child so that I could be loved again. I didn't realise I could be loved as an adult and didn't need to earn that love.

'When I went back to school after the summer, I had lost a huge amount of weight. I was getting too thin and people noticed. My mum talked to me about it and said, "Karen, you're losing too much weight." But my family were not very good at talking to one another at that time because my grandpa was dying. That put a lot of pressure on the family so I was trying to be quiet and good, and staying out of the way.'

Young women often hide their eating problem and suffer alone. They deny there is a problem and don't seek help because they feel ashamed. They convince themselves that it will get better on its own (which it sometimes does) and are frightened that being treated will cause them to gain weight. Many young people, more girls than boys, will have some type of eating disorder but these will not be severe enough to fall under the heading of anorexia or bulimia.

Anorexia and bulimia are different entities, though there is an overlap and one may lead to the other. Young people with either problem are obsessed with dieting, their size and their shape – especially the size and shape of their thighs and tummies. Anorexics tend to be in their early or mid-teens. The problem is more common among fashion models, young people who are trained in sports and trained dancers. Excessive exercise, two to three hours a day, is often linked with anorexia. Anorexics make 'not eating' an obsession. They starve themselves on very strict diets and consequently lose their appetite. They avoid all fattening foods, a minority abuse laxatives, and some make themselves vomit. Girls' periods stop and their skin gets covered in fine downy hair. Anorexics also often become withdrawn, depressed and secretive. The long-term outlook for young people with anorexia is that five out of ten recover, three out of ten improve without being completely cured and may develop bulimia, while two out of ten carry on having severe problems. An associated problem is osteoporosis (thinning of the bones which can lead to fractures) which may affect them when they are older.

The hype about eating disorders and the concentration on the worst cases of anorexia mean that parents tend to panic when they realise or are told their child has an eating problem. Although dieting is something most of us have tried (usually unsuccessfully!) at one time or another, the idea of being so obsessed with food that you will not eat and actually starve is very difficult to comprehend. Karen's parents were supportive but still found it hard to understand.

'My family certainly didn't understand the rules I had set for myself about how much exercise I did and what kind of food I ate – not surprisingly, because I never actually talked to them about it. I was still eating three meals a day but I cut down how much I ate at each meal. I cut down on cakes, then on puddings, and then on anything high in fat like a flan. I was still eating with the family. What I was doing was very much built into the family routine because I didn't want to disrupt anything. I just wanted to be left alone. I did notice though that my

brothers started treating me as fragile and my friends weren't sure what to do. My best friend at school stayed with me, and would walk with me when I was obsessively walking round the playground. She would cover up for me when I was eating hardly any school lunch, and she would try to listen and understand, though she found it really hard.

'Until I got down to around six stone I felt quite fit, especially given how much exercise I was taking. I did feel empty, but I didn't take any notice of that. My mum was so worried because of my periods stopping she took me off to see my GP, but he wasn't much help. She then took me to another one, who told us I had anorexia. This meant nothing to me.

'Once I was under six stone I felt tired, empty, lethargic and I wasn't sleeping. I had grown very anxious and unhappy, frightened and guilty, whenever I ate, and a lot of the time in between. I was getting really desperate and so was my mum. I actually saw her cry when I had to go into hospital for treatment. She had never shown much emotion before – any hurt or negative emotions – and that really struck me, seeing how much love she really had for me. This was the first thing that broke through all the fear surrounding my feelings.

'I had to stay in hospital for several months and when I came out I asked Mum if she would help control what I was eating. I was 5 stone 10 pounds at that stage. The only way I could cope with eating was to block my feelings out and go quite numb, which took so much energy I couldn't keep it up for long. What helped most was seeing that my mum cared for me. Up until then I hadn't really felt that love from either of my parents.

'The anorexia did get better, firstly because I felt that I wanted to be better for my mum, and then because I wanted to be the best person I could, and I realised that wasn't going to happen if I was desperately underweight.

*It was also because I was part of a Christian family,
which hadn't made any difference to me until I became
really scared. Then I started praying and found that I had
an awareness that I was praying to somebody. I was
starting to trust in some kind of God and I found that
trusting did give me some peace. I wanted to be the person
God wanted me to be and that helped a lot.'*

Bulimia is more common than anorexia, and only one in three bulimics will have had a history of anorexia. Bulimia also occurs more commonly in older teenagers. Bulimics try to diet, fail, lose control and then overeat and binge on vast amounts of high-calorie foods. Afterwards they vomit and/or take laxatives to try to get rid of the food they have binged. They usually feel anxious, depressed and guilty and they hate themselves. Some try to relieve the tension they feel after bingeing by 'cutting' themselves (see Chapter 11). Bulimics tend not to lose weight; most have a normal weight for their height. However, there can be more general body changes as well as tiredness, dizziness, tummy pains and lethargy. Periods stop in around 80 per cent of girls with bulimia, returning only when the bulimia stops. The long-term outlook for young people with bulimia is that five out of ten are completely cured, three out of ten continue to have some problems, and two out of ten have full-blown recurrences.

Karen was one of those anorexics who did go on to have problems with bulimia.

*'At first it was just eating a little bit extra, but because I
had been rigidly controlling it, I noticed, and then I would
compensate and it became more and more extreme.
Bingeing and losing control – that's an anorexic's worst
nightmare! I went out and bought cake and biscuits and
binged, and that made me more guilty and stressed until I
learnt how to make myself sick. I became totally unable to
control my feelings.*

'My weight would go up a few pounds and then down a few pounds. I had eating bouts followed by starving. I classified things as "safe foods" to binge on because they were low fat – things like bread, potatoes, cottage cheese, fish – but I would eat too much of them. It was chaotic eating.'

In retrospect, parents will often say they were worried that their child had an eating problem but did not know how to cope with it. As with all things that happen to one's children, parents tend to blame themselves. This is accentuated by the fact that there is evidence that mothers with eating disorders do have an effect on their children's eating habits.

Jane Weller, Karen's mother, is typical of many mothers who largely blame themselves for not having noticed the problem earlier. She is also cross with herself for not having taken immediate action when she did recognise what was going on because she was so busy working.

'Karen changed to another school when she was twelve and it was then that things started to go wrong. She's always been average academically and I think she feels much less able than she actually is. The new school was far more sporting. We were all eating what I considered a fairly healthy diet, and the eating problem didn't show itself at first, but I have to admit that I am a vegetarian, and won't normally eat even butter.

'The first time I thought something was definitely wrong was on Karen's thirteenth birthday. I looked at her and thought, "She's very, very thin." I started to read books about eating problems but there weren't very many. I was also very preoccupied at the time. My husband's father had come to stay. He had Alzheimer's and was dying. I was trying to look after him and do a full-time job.

'I finally took Karen to the family doctor, partly because her periods had stopped. She'd started when she

*was just twelve, and they had become very regular, but
when she took up all that sport, they stopped. The doctor
said, "Don't worry, dear, they'll start again soon." I was
there and I heard him say it.*

*'Everything seemed to happen together. She was
exercising at home as well as going down to the gym two
or three times a week. Her periods had stopped, she was
eating less and less and was extremely thin; and there I
was holding on to this belief that it would all go away. I
was completely wrong and I let it go on far too long
without doing something about it.'*

The milder cases of eating disorders resolve without any formal
treatment or acknowledgement that there is or has been a problem. Even when there is acknowledgement by the parents and
the young person, it can be very difficult to find the right support and treatment. Few GPs have experience of how to deal
with eating disorders and hospital facilities are often limited and
patchy in what they offer. Where you live will often determine
what help is available and how soon it can be accessed.

The Weller family were typical in the difficulty they had in
getting help:

*'In the end Karen did become very depressed and we got
another GP to refer her to the local adolescent psychiatric
unit, which was miles and miles away. It was a very
worrying month before she was seen. I was furious at the
delay, and at our GP for not having recognised earlier
that something was very wrong.*

*'Karen was finally referred on for in-patient treatment
at a special place for people with eating disorders. By this
time she was extremely depressed and I felt guilty and
somehow totally helpless. I'm sure everyone thought I was
a bad mother; but I had failed to see how serious it had
got because I was living with Karen's problem on a day-to-
day basis.'*

As well as having to cope with a child with an eating disorder, parents are often faced with the strong message given by the outside world that it is their fault. This is an added stress whenever the behaviour of a child becomes abnormal, even if nothing is actually said. Many parents say they feel that they are being blamed, though this is probably partly their own feeling of guilt and failure. Talking to friends whom you trust can help, and often you will find that the friend knows someone else who has been through the same experience.

Having a child in the family with an eating disorder puts stress on the rest of the family. Jane just touches on this.

> '*Karen's problems have affected my relationship with my husband Ken because I have had to give so much attention to her. He didn't take much part in her eating problems himself, except occasionally encouraging her with a remark like, "Why don't you have some butter on your bread?" He also did try to tell me something was wrong, at a time when I was trying to ignore the fact, but at that point we chose not to talk about it.*'

There is no one reason for the overall increase in the number of young people with eating disorders. The current idealisation in women's and teenage magazines which makes us fight against biology must be in part responsible. Although the main worries concern extreme anorexia or bulimia, anyone who is unhappily preoccupied with dieting and weight watching might be said to have an eating disorder. After going through the experience as a parent, Jane would say to other people who are worried about their children having anorexia:

> '*Get as much help as you can, as early as you can, and look out for signs that do not directly appear to indicate anorexia: changes in eating patterns and exercising to a point which seems extreme. The most difficult thing is to know when to take action, but don't always assume that*

*things will sort themselves out. I waited too long because
I couldn't be objective enough to say to myself, "Right,
this has gone far enough. We need help." Another thing –
if your own GP doesn't seem to be providing what you
need, change to another one. GPs are human like
everyone else and they are not always brilliant at
everything.'*

Six years on from the start of her illness, and now better,
though still vulnerable, Karen also has advice for parents:

*'I think parents should talk to their child and offer
support, but never force them to eat. When I was forced to
eat, I couldn't cope with other things. Parents should value
a person for who they are and show the child that they do.
Parents who get anxious and focus on the eating problem
will isolate that person and make the problem even worse.
The individual has to feel that they are valued and loved
for who they are, so that they don't need an eating
disorder. Feeling unloved and having an eating disorder go
together. Once somebody can learn to love themselves,
then they can see themselves coming out of the eating
disorder. They shouldn't be comforted by the eating
disorder because then the eating disorder becomes the safe
and comfortable place to be, and the incentive is to stay
there!'*

**Tips for parents who think their child has an eating disor-
der: (There is much overlap between anorexia and bulimia
and these tips apply to both)**

- refusing to sit and have meals with the family may be an
early sign to look out for, along with demanding to eat different foods from the rest of the family, especially (in
anorexia) those not containing any fat

- watch out for the disappearance of food from the fridge and money to fund the binges (if bulimia is the problem)

- look out for the regular smell of sick in the bathroom, especially after meals

- the earlier a young person with an eating problem gets help (especially one with anorexia) the less likely it is to become a major problem. The first port of call for help is your GP, but at least talk to a friend or a counsellor, and try to admit there may be or is a problem

- if your teenager agrees to see the doctor, the consultation will be confidential, but it may be helpful to let the doctor know about your concerns or fears – even if the communication cannot be two-way

- try to arrange to have regular meals where all the family sit down together, and try to make sure that you keep eating normally yourself

- don't force high-calorie foods, be supportive but firm, and continue to show affection

- try to avoid making your teenager feel guilty

- contact the Eating Disorders Association: First Floor, Wensum House, 103 Prince of Wales Road, Norwich, Norfolk NR1 1DW. General Helpline: 01603 621414. Youth Helpline for those aged eighteen years and younger: 01603 765050. 4–6 p.m. Monday to Friday. Website: www.gurney.org.uk/eda/

- read Palmer, R. L., *Anorexia: a Guide for Sufferers and Their Families*, Penguin, 1989 and/or Fairburn, C. G., *Overcoming Binge Eating*, Guilford Press, New York, 1995

Tips for teenagers who have or think they have an eating disorder:

- talk to someone – your mother, your father, a friend or a teacher

- realise it is just like having any other illness, pneumonia or diabetes, and there is treatment and help available

- get help sooner rather than later – the longer you leave it the more difficult it is to treat (this is particularly true for anorexia)

- see your family doctor. If you don't want to tell your parents, make your own appointment and be seen alone. Your parents will not be told unless you agree

- contact the Eating Disorders Association Youth Helpline to get more information: 01603 765050. 4–6 p.m. Monday to Friday. Website: www.gurney.org.uk/eda/

Tips for teenagers who have bulimia:

- bulimia is a series of vicious circles which need breaking

- dieting is the main problem as it imposes strict rules which make you feel good and in control; but as soon as you break a rule, even in a small way by eating a biscuit or a piece of chocolate, you overreact, give up all rules for the day and binge

- bingeing makes you feel bloated, full, fat and ugly which leads to you vomiting to make you feel better

- vomiting also makes you feel bad about yourself which leads to low self-esteem, which leads to extreme concern

about shape and weight, which leads on to more strict dieting, which makes you feel hungry, which in turn makes
you want to binge, thus setting up another vicious circle

- vomiting is not a good way to get thin. Vomiting, even
immediately after a binge, only gets rid of 50 per cent of
the calories. The average binge is 2000 calories or more, so
even after vomiting, 1000 calories will still be absorbed, so
bulimics do not, in fact, tend to lose weight

- stopping the bingeing and vomiting and eating normal
meals does not cause massive weight gain. Those who have
recovered from their bulimia tend to stay at their normal
weight

- people with bulimia judge their self-worth and whole being
in relation to shape and weight. Loss of control and bingeing causes shame because of the loss of will-power. This
produces guilt and embarrassment, which then feeds back
into feelings of low esteem and helps keep the eating problem going

Tips to stop bulimia:

- stop dieting and realise that you are unlikely to get better
unless you do. Easier said than done, but you need to
realise that you have to accept that your weight is your
weight, partly influenced by your genes and partly by what
you eat and do

- keep a regular food diary of all you eat and drink, how you
feel, when you vomit, when you take laxatives

- eat at least one meal a day with the family or other people
– do not get too hungry. Plan a snack between the meals

but try not to graze. If you do, you are more likely to binge as you will feel you have broken the rules

- only weigh weekly – not daily or hourly – and you will see that you do not really put on weight. Daily weighing is a bad idea as everyone's weight fluctuates a bit, and it will only make you panic and start dieting again

- list the foods you think of as forbidden, such as cake or chocolate, then try having a little of them in a planned way

- list alternatives to do other than bingeing – ring a friend, have walk, feed the cat – and look at the list and do one of them when you feel a binge coming on

- there is a danger that when you feel better and think you will never binge again, you probably will – especially when you are stressed or unhappy. Do not think of a lapse as complete failure, but restart the self-help strategies before the pattern gets re-established

- a danger time is when you feel completely better and think you can try to lose weight again by dieting. DON'T – this will just set the whole cycle off again

- there are occasional times when it is perfectly OK to be greedy – like at a party or at Christmas – and that is not an eating disorder!

14
Teenagers With Long-Term Health Problems

arge surveys carried out in the UK have found that around one in five males and females aged five to fifteen rate themselves as having a health problem which sometimes interferes with their day-to-day life. In the same age group, one in ten males and females report having restricted physical activity owing to a long-standing health problem.

It is worth noting that as far as severe illness/admission to hospital is concerned the commonest reason for admission of male adolescents is trauma, and for female adolescents it is termination of pregnancy.

The commonest long-standing illnesses among adolescents are asthma, which occurs in approximately one in ten, diabetes which occurs in between two and three per thousand, cerebral palsy affecting two per thousand, and epilepsy affecting around five per thousand. Each of these illnesses brings particular problems, and how these problems express themselves depends on the severity of the illness and the characteristics of the individual and the family. But there are common issues for parents and teenagers who have to cope with illness during the adolescent years.

It is vitally important, however, for all those caring for and coping with a teenager with a chronic illness to remember that they are teenagers first, with all the delightful and challenging elements of a normal teenager, and that the illness is secondary.

One teenager with a chronic illness is Beth Hewitt, who is fifteen. She lives with her parents, Liz, who works as a cashier in a local supermarket, and Alan, who is a tax officer. Also in the family are an older brother Jake, aged eighteen, and a sister Jessica, aged twenty. Beth tells how she was first diagnosed with diabetes two years ago.

> *'It all started with me being basically tired. I was taking caffeine pills in huge doses in order to stay on my feet. I thought it was because I wasn't getting enough sleep. I was just totally knackered all the time and I was literally falling asleep everywhere. I was also drinking about four litres of water a day, taking a two-litre bottle of water with me to school which I'd finish by lunchtime. I had no energy at all.*
>
> *'I went to the doctor with my mum and he did a urine test and a blood test. That showed high sugar, so I was sent up to the hospital. I'd gone to the doctor and said, "Mum's stupid. She thinks I might be diabetic," and I was laughing. What was annoying was having to admit that she was right!'*

Diabetes can run in families and occurs because the body does not produce enough insulin (at the moment we don't know why) which controls the sugar levels in the body. Young people with diabetes need to have insulin injections for the rest of their lives to control the condition. While diabetes is developing, it is common to feel generally tired and unwell, be constantly thirsty, and need to pee a lot. Although it is never pleasant to find one has an illness, discovering a reason for feeling unwell can be a comfort, as it was for Beth after her diabetes was diagnosed.

'In a way it was a relief, because then I did know what was wrong with me. I was starting to get ridiculously worried as to whether I had cancer of the lymph glands or something. I was worried because of sleeping such a lot. At first I remember crying with shock because it was going to involve the rest of my life, and that was really freaky. But it's not as bad as I thought it would be. Not like my friend at the clinic who has it, whose parents control her absolutely. They just command her whole life, tell her when she should have her hair cut, and what it should look like, and things like that. It's appalling and she gets very depressed about it, but it's not such a big deal for me.

'I was off school for a week, though I didn't actually stay in hospital overnight. I went up there for a few hours during the day while they showed me how to do the injections. I've always hated injections, but it is totally different when you are giving them to yourself. If I hit a particularly sensitive spot on my skin, I stop, and don't do it there but try somewhere else. I learnt how to do it after three times, and I've done it myself from the age of thirteen, so I've never been unconscious or anything with low blood sugar. I'm not really frightened of that happening because even at night I wake up if I begin to go low, and I always have something with me to take. I think Mum is more worried about all that than I am.

'I am now on four injections a day, which the nurse says I can alter according to how I want to eat. It's better for my body if I eat regularly and I shouldn't really miss any meals out, but I do change the regime at weekends to suit myself. This worries my mum, but the nurse has told us that the only injection that matters is the Insulatard in

*the evening. The rest I fit around when I want to, as long
as I have snacks and things, which I think I manage quite
well. My individual blood sugars are quite erratic but my
other blood tests are OK, which is a good way of
managing things. On that front, therefore, I think I am
dealing with it quite well.'*

Every chronic illness has its own particular set of problems.
With epilepsy, it is the fear of having a fit in front of one's
friends or while doing something potentially dangerous such
as cycling or swimming. With asthma it may be the fear of
having to stop in the middle of a sporting event as one feels
one is going to suffocate, or the nuisance of always having to
have a supply of inhalers. With diabetes it is the fear of the
blood sugar going too high or too low and the need to eat
meals regularly.

Blood sugar is more difficult to control in the teenage years,
partly due to the hormone changes associated with puberty,
partly due to what adolescents do – such as drinking, sport,
raves – and partly because teenagers are less likely to adhere
rigidly to the diet and to the routine of the insulin injections.
We know that good control of diabetes does improve the
chances of young people not getting complications when they
are older, such as blindness and heart disease, so it is important to manage the blood sugar levels. This can cause
difficulties between the teenager and their parents. Beth again:

*'Mum and Dad always worry about whether I have my
glucose tabs and glucagon with me (an injection which
has to be given if the blood sugar falls very low). I
suppose they think that I am instantaneously going to die
or something. But when they go away for a couple of
days, it's never a problem. It's not like I can't manage
without them, but they definitely worry. It's all the books
Mum reads about it, knowing all the facts and listening to
what the doctors and nurses say, but she doesn't know the*

practicalities. If you're not diabetic I don't think you can know, frankly.

'It is difficult not to get angry with my parents. They worry too much and say useless things like, "Oh, I wish I could take it away from you." That just pisses me off because they obviously can't. I think that if you are a diabetic, you have to have some understanding of where your parents are coming from, and the worries they have for you, but if you are not diabetic yourself, you can't really tell someone what to do. Everyone has their own ways of living, their own attitudes and needs; each person is an individual and has to adapt accordingly. It would be so much easier if Mum and Dad were more relaxed and did not take everything the books and the doctors say totally literally. The one person who has been really great is my aunt in Edinburgh. She's got a daughter with eating problems which she finds really difficult, but she's very good at telling my mum to chill out about my diabetes.*

'I think my parents have calmed down a great deal. At the beginning the doctor said that half my diet had to be carbohydrate, so they were cramming carbohydrates into me. This made me put on a lot of weight which I have found really difficult to lose. Now they leave it all to me a bit more. They are getting more confident because as yet nothing ghastly has happened. Also, the nurse at the clinic reassured them that I knew what I was doing and that I really was doing all right. It must be very tough for parents watching their child grow up fast and not being able to do more for them. It is my life, and when they tell me I am doing something wrong it drives me up the wall because I have to tell them, "But you don't know what's right for me." They are good when I ask for help. It's when they give you help you don't ask for which is deeply annoying.*

'Getting low blood sugars at annoying times is difficult. When it happens, Mum tends to say, "I told you so – you did this, this and this wrong." Sometimes I feel like saying*

*to her, "Oh yeah, go on, rub my face in it." Going to the
edge of hypoglycaemia (low blood sugar) is really
unpleasant, but it does warn me what is going to happen.
It also shows that sugars are not up in the sky – in some
ways that's reassuring.'*

People are often scared of illness in others, especially when
there is the threat of funny behaviour and unconsciousness,
both of which can occur with diabetes and epilepsy. But being
open about the illness usually helps to disperse the fear,
demystify the disease, and makes others realise the person is
still a person and not a disease. Beth has had no problem in
being totally upfront about her illness.

*'My friends just totally accept that I have to inject myself,
but they do seem to think that I am amazing to be talking
to them and whacking a needle into myself at the same
time. Interestingly they don't seem to think they could ever
do it, but they would if they had to.*

*'It doesn't interfere with my life because I don't let it. I
suppose theoretically if one didn't tell anyone about it, it
would be far more difficult. Personally, I find just
integrating it into my everyday life is best. If people are
going to be friends with me, they just have to accept I'm
going to whack a needle into myself every so often – in
front of them – and not be fussy about it. It's just
something which happens. I'm an outgoing person by
nature, but I guess if someone is not outgoing then they
are going to find it harder. The other day we were in the
shopping centre for lunch, and I just sat on some steps and
gave myself an injection because I couldn't be bothered to
go to some rather unhygienic loo belonging to a
restaurant or something. I do get some funny looks,
though. No doubt people think I'm whacking heroin into
myself instead of insulin, but that's their problem. I'm not
going to go out of my way to make a big inconvenience to*

myself, to do something which basically keeps me alive. That's letting it ruin your life and I'm not going to let it.

'*My diabetic friend is completely different. She is terrified of stepping the slightest bit out of line. I asked her the other day whether she ever got pissed and she replied that she had had a sip of someone else's champagne last week. That was like the most daring thing she's ever done. The worry is that it's not her choice, it's her parents' choice. If you offer her a drink she'll say, "Oh, my parents won't let me." I got drunk before and after I was diagnosed, but even when drinking I can tell when I'm going hypo. I'm careful up to a point, probably more careful than I would've been otherwise, I have to admit. It's like being more aware than more careful. Why should I be the only one not drinking? I don't have to get paralytic, but I quite like being a bit pissed and I soon learnt how to manage it.*

'*It doesn't stop me doing anything really. I've started going to aerobic classes and that's not a problem. I just have some coke nearby and drink it like everyone else drinks water. My message would be: live a normal life but be prepared. The other message is: be in charge yourself, don't rely on other people because that just fucks everything up. You can't rely on your parents to be there all the time to do your injections. You have to take charge. It's just not convenient otherwise, and it's much easier injecting yourself.*

'*I'm glad I got it when I did. If I had to choose any time, I think I would have chosen to get it at thirteen. I would have found it difficult having it younger, and I would find it really difficult if one of my children got it, like when they were a baby, because you wouldn't be able to tell if they were going hypo. I would be constantly checking their blood, and they would end up with grottily pricked fingers, like I have myself at the moment. I'm not especially worried about my children getting it, because I guess by the time I have children they are likely to have some easier way of dealing with diabetes, not just injections. I hope so! I wouldn't want my children to go through it any younger than me, but I suppose me being a diabetic would make it easier for them. It would freak me having to give my child injections.*

'Diabetes is rather like having asthma or epilepsy or something, but injections instead of puffers or pills.'

Liz finds the increased anxiety of her daughter having diabetes fairly difficult to cope with, on top of managing Beth's normal teenage demands. She remembers very vividly the sequence of events leading up to her daughter's illness.

'I took her to our family doctor because I noticed that she was drinking a huge amount and I was beginning to think she might have diabetes like my cousin. Beth marched into the doctor's surgery saying, "My mum thinks I've got diabetes." The doctor did the tests and said, "Your mother is absolutely right – you have." He came right out and told us and the full realisation that I had been right really struck me.

'I was totally shocked. I felt as though I had been hit very hard with a wet towel. I was numb. I really didn't know what diabetes was all about, in spite of my cousin. The numbness lasted a fortnight and then was replaced by a period of being very weepy. I felt I was in mourning for the health of my child. It would have been good to have another mother to talk to who had been through it all. You do hear terrible things – coma, sudden death. I hadn't got a clue how I was going to handle it.

'The hospital was great – they didn't admit Beth, which was less traumatic. The diabetic nurse was terrific too and showed Beth how to do her injections. She was given a book about diabetes which I like, but which she absolutely hates me reading. She does everything her

*way – the injections, managing her diet and all that – but
she hates people reminding her about it. She thinks she
knows better than the book. I find it useful, but somehow
it does divorce things from the person, and it doesn't say
much about providing psychological support.'*

There are conflicts for parents. They want to manage and
control their child's illness as this makes them feel better, but
they also want to be relieved of the burden. It is particularly
difficult to deal with the normal teenage risk-taking behaviours that young people with a disability also want to join in.
This is in part because those with a chronic illness are often
more immature than their peers. Decisions will have been
made for them and they are more likely to have been cosseted
and protected by parents. They may also have had fewer
opportunities to be independent, especially if they have a
physical disability.

*'I know it's wrong, but I can't help getting more worried
about Beth than I did about my other children. Like last
week she came home covered with vomit. She said that
another girl had been sick over her at the party, but I
could smell alcohol on her breath. I said, "Now come on,
Beth – you're drunk." I spent the night in bed with her
because she was afraid she might have drunk so much
that she would become unconscious. With her brother and
sister I just got cross when they got drunk, rather than
worried out of my mind.'*

Chronic illness in teenagers can undoubtedly be an added
burden for parents and young people, during puberty and
afterwards. Some teenagers deal with it by becoming more
extreme in their behaviour, more moody, more aggressive,
and seeking to experiment with the extremes. Parents naturally feel more protective, and are less willing to give them
their independence.

Some tips that parents might find helpful:

- it is important to remember that a teenager with diabetes or any other chronic illness is, first and foremost, a person and not a disease, and should always be treated as normally as possible

- most young people who have a chronic disorder or disability cope with adolescence as well or as badly as any other teenager

- young people with a chronic illness or physical disability are more vulnerable than their peers during adolescence in terms of emotional and behavioural development

- there are fewer positive role models for young people with disabilities

- make an early start in encouraging and allowing young people to be in charge of their illness, to be responsible for their own medication. Get them to arrange their own doctors' and hospital appointments, and let them take part in the choices about their illness

- listen to their views about how they want to manage their illness and do not make assumptions, or bypass them, in discussions about treatment and care

- to begin with, they may not manage their disease or problem as well as you would, but they need to take control and this has to be balanced against the safety of their care

- you are likely to find it more difficult to relinquish control and the caring role if someone has been very dependent during their childhood years

- a small number of teenagers with a chronic disability find adolescence and the transition from being looked after to being in charge of their illness very difficult and they may try to opt out of medical care

- young people with a disability will want the privacy that other teenagers want and must have with regard to relationships

- a teenager with a disability will need the advice and help all other teenagers need, about sex, drugs and contraception

- be aware of the help offered by voluntary organisations and self-help groups: the British Diabetic Association, the National Society for Epilepsy, the Cystic Fibrosis Trust and the Council for Disabled Children

For things which may help teenagers, see the tips in *all* the other chapters

15

Teenage Suicide

There is no one explanation for the rise in deaths due to young male suicide in the UK in the early and mid-1990s. Between the mid-1970s and the mid-1990s the successful suicide rate among young men aged sixteen to twenty-four almost doubled, a rise which was also seen in almost every European country except Germany. Increasing unemployment, increasing drug and alcohol abuse, family breakdown, media influences and changes in gender roles may all have played a part.

However, since 1996 there is evidence that this suicide rate has begun to fall again, not drastically but there is sufficient evidence of a definite downturn – again without any obvious explanation. Have young men begun to find their place in society again? Is there a moving away from materialism towards values that young men can more readily identify with? We do not have clear answers, but sadly male teenagers, and to a much lesser extent female teenagers, do still kill themselves, as is recounted in the following story by Felicity Green about her fourteen-year-old son, James.

Felicity has worked as a community nurse and she is married to Tom, who works as an insurance broker. They have a daughter, Jane, aged sixteen.

'James was a brilliant person but was very sensitive all his life. He had told us that there was a problem at his school. Some of the children in James's class had complained to the head teacher that a certain geography teacher just wasn't able to communicate the work. The head teacher's response was that things would sort themselves out and he made the children apologise to the person concerned. James refused to apologise as he was sure that he was in the right.

'When I say he was sensitive, when something happened – like our cat was run over recently – he was extremely upset and it went very deep. He wrote about that in an essay for school, which seemed to me to be mature, but I don't think we really understood how bad he was feeling. He was also intensely hung up about the way he looked. Everything had to be just right – with all the right clothes and the right trainers – and his hair had to look just right. He was very self-conscious. If we were shopping, we would have to go to ten or twelve shops to get the right pair of jeans – he was a perfectionist. In the end it was he who suggested that he should have his own allowance so he could choose what he wanted. It was a great way out and the first time he spent it all. He was only twelve but he soon learned. He was sensitive in other ways too. He always remembered everyone's birthday and would do a card. At Christmas he had to do the Christmas decorations and again everything had to be just right. I was amazed by how understanding he was about how groups at school worked – how people behaved and why. Maybe that was part of him being so sensitive.

'But while he was outwardly articulate and physically very advanced, part of the problem was that emotionally *he hadn't developed so well. He was insecure and wounded because he was finding things difficult in his life. One thing in particular was communicating with other people. He was very shy with people he didn't know and didn't trust. Two friends who had moved school with him were very important, but one had gone back to Australia and the other had moved to a private school. James had said that he was finding it difficult to make new friends.*

'*James pushed himself incredibly hard at his new school though. There was one time when he was playing football and he twisted his ankle. The referee told him to go off, but he absolutely refused and went on playing. It was obviously agony, but he wouldn't give up as he wanted to be part of the team – it meant so much to him. He was screaming in pain that night, but he had to do his best. Physically, he challenged everything.*

'*It all happened at a time when he had had his exams and was in a relatively relaxed mood on a Thursday, a month ago. On the way home in the bus, a girl who he was very infatuated with dropped him in front of all his friends, in the harshest possible way. This girl was sitting at the back of the bus with all her friends and she just walked off the bus past James and said, so the whole bus could hear, "I don't want to be your girlfriend any more." He was devastated, not least because of the embarrassment, but all the same he asked his older sister Jane not to tell us, as he felt it was just between him and his friends.*

'*I think it was all part of him being teased at school. People hid his books and he got punished, but it's difficult to tell if one could call it actual bullying. There might have been some much more serious stuff going on. James was very, very angry that Thursday night after the incident on the bus, and although we had a normal supper together he beat up on Jane, verbally and physically – so*

*badly that we had to separate them. On Friday evening
and Saturday he was quiet and just watched videos. We
weren't too happy about this but if that's what he wanted
to do, that was fine.*

'He blew up over the slightest thing during that
weekend, like him coming in from the garden with his
gum boots on and when I told him to take them off he just
exploded and called me a "silly old cow". Jane made some
remark about his language, and he stomped out of the
house with nothing on his feet and disappeared. When he
appeared again after a couple of hours, all covered in
mud, we were really angry and concerned. It wasn't an
easy time.*

'After that he became quite calm though, and managed
to explain some of the things which were making him
unhappy. He didn't have any social life outside school. The
school didn't have enough sports facilities. James was very
keen on sports like football. I think he found things easiest
when he was getting on with his mates in the football
team. He also said that he didn't like his room any more
and wanted to change it.*

'There was another row on the Sunday. He wouldn't
come for a walk with the rest of us, and when we got back
he had eaten the entire chocolate pudding which I had
made for lunch. Before long, he was sick as a dog
everywhere. This didn't help things.*

'On Monday, his friends from school said later that he
seemed very depressed. He came back from school
clutching his geography exam results, which were not as
good as he had expected, and he was obviously worried
and demoralised about that. It wasn't an issue for me,
though it was for him. Things seemed fairly normal at
supper, and later on in the evening I talked to him about
football and about a project he hadn't handed in because
he wanted to get an 'A'. He didn't think it was good
enough yet and it was a month overdue already. He was*

busy at his desk and it wasn't a frightfully fruitful conversation – but that was the last time I ever talked to him.

'*I went downstairs and watched a* Cutting Edge *programme on the TV. When that finished I went up to say goodnight to James and to Jane. Jane said she'd tried to say goodnight to James but he hadn't replied. I'd heard a bang while I was watching telly, but I didn't know what it was. James seemed to be in the bathroom but I couldn't understand why he was being so long. There was a catch on the door which I broke by pushing hard against it. James was just lying there with a plastic bag on his head. He seemed to have vomited and the bag was tied around his neck with a piece of string.*

'*I desperately pulled the bag open and tried to resuscitate him and screamed to Jane. She called the GP but his line was engaged so she dialled 999 to get an ambulance. Then she came back and tried shaking James and shouting in his ear. The ambulance finally arrived but they said it was too late, and when the GP came he said the same. It was a terrible experience – unbelievable.*'

The most common cause of death for young people is accidents, mainly road traffic accidents, and the second most common cause is suicide. Deaths due to suicide in children under the age of twelve are rare, and are relatively unusual in those under fifteen.

There appear to be two main types of suicidal behaviour: (a) where young people deliberately set out to kill themselves and (b) where young people deliberately harm themselves but without the intention of actually killing themselves. Although most young people who deliberately self-harm fall within one or the other of these groups, there will be some young people who set out to kill themselves and fail, and others who accidentally kill themselves when they did not intend to do so.

When adolescents who have attempted suicide are asked 'why?' around one in three give 'a wish to die' as the main reason, and the other two in three give reasons like 'a wish to escape', 'to express hostility', 'to make someone feel guilty', or 'to gain attention'.

Once a teenager has died, whether by committing suicide or through an accident, the main focus of attention has to turn to helping all those who are in any way involved to grieve, and then to begin on the slow path to recovery.

'Tom, my husband, was not there when it happened. He had stayed late at work and I had to call him on his mobile. He came home immediately but he minded very, very much that he wasn't there. He had been tired at the weekend and hadn't spent much time with James.

'We absolutely don't know why it happened. James had seemed normal at supper and was telling us jokes, even though his friends said he had been low at school. I thought he was over his distress at the weekend and yet he just went upstairs and died, all alone.

'What helped afterwards was seeing a psychiatrist who offered to help. Talking to him did make us feel better, but Jane didn't want to come. There wasn't anything I feel we could have done differently. We were worried about James's inability to communicate his feelings, but that had always been a problem. Perhaps I should have made more effort to find someone he could off-load his worries on to, if he couldn't do it to Tom and me. Children need some sort of 'granny' substitute. It could be a close friend, and it doesn't always have to be something important to talk about – it could just be the colour they want their curtains.

'Another thing I feel concerned about is whether drugs were involved at all. I just don't know whether James had ever taken any drugs. There had been a scare at the school because two children aged fourteen had been found with drugs, but the coroner didn't do any tests for that.

'We all coped in different ways. My husband has thrown himself into work because he's a workaholic anyway. I keep myself busy all the time too. Our friends were wonderful. Some came and stayed on three or four successive weekends and we talked and talked. I talked to Relate and I went to a local support group for parents whose children had died. That was very helpful. I've just joined a Parents Association for the Prevention of Young Suicide (PAPYRUS), an organisation that was formed to make people aware of the problem, especially the mental health problems which young people have to face nowadays.

'Jane was supported brilliantly by her school and by her friends. She had a week off, but when she did go back the teachers and everyone talked to her about it. James's school contacted CRUSE who organised sessions where the children were encouraged to express how they felt about James's death. Though the school did seem to concentrate on helping the girls. They seemed to assume that the boys would be able to cope better themselves.

'Some people were not so helpful, in particular some members of the local mental health team; and there was a totally untrained counsellor whom unfortunately our GP had never met. You have to pick and choose around until you find someone who understands, who is sympathetic and who you can talk to.

'The key point I tell other parents, to help prevent this from happening, is keeping lines of communication open to your children. All the time, whatever you are doing, talk to your children about their feelings, and your own for that matter. It is so easy not to talk about feelings when leading a busy life. Our family was together a great deal, but what with school, the football matches, going away at weekends, and getting the house in order, we had so little time for conversation. It's all to do with trust and communication and if, as a parent, you cannot always *offer this yourself, then try to make sure children have some kind of "granny" figure around.*

'Another thing is to ask young people whether they have ever thought of killing themselves and what they think that means. Many girls think of killing themselves when they get teased or pushed out of a group. Young people can be brutal to each other and may not know how much emotional pain they inflict. This happens in life to all of us on occasion, and you have to learn to cope. You can't be cushioned against emotional hurts all the time. Maybe we have all had thoughts about killing ourselves. I certainly did when I was young.

'But what makes the difference to someone like James who actually gets pushed over the edge into doing it? Maybe it was lack of confidence and lack of interpersonal skills which made him so vulnerable. James needed an emotional first-aid kit. We are taught what to do when someone starts to choke physically, but when it comes to the emotions we have nothing to guide us, especially boys. Some adolescent behaviour is totally irrational and impulsive. Studies of suicide attempts in young people show that suicide is often a very impulsive gesture.'

Felicity mentioned her worries about whether drugs might have played a part in James's death. Drug misuse is on the increase, even among relatively young people of thirteen and fourteen; and is associated with around one in ten episodes of attempted suicide in both sexes. Suicides associated with alcohol misuse are also on the increase, with four in ten episodes of attempted suicide in males and three in ten in females being attributed to this cause.

The families of people who have committed suicide are often faced with a continuing need to search for an explanation as to why it happened and whether it could have been prevented, and with recurring images of the death itself. Self-blame is

common, but you have to remember that it is not always possible to differentiate in teenagers between stress, anxiety and
depression. There is much interaction between them and so
there are many different ways in which young people react to
these different feelings. They may become moody, complain
of headaches or stomach aches, feel tired all the time, cut
themselves off because they feel unable to face people, have
sleeping problems, get totally disorganised and find it difficult
to finish things. Much of that would be considered 'normal' in
adults as well as in adolescents! It is change in a young
person's behaviour which should alert you to something
being wrong.

When disaster does happen, families require all the support
they can get – from professionals, from friends and relations,
from their children's friends and from the school. We all need
to care about and support others at these times, however
rarely they happen. We need to overcome our instinct 'to stay
away because I didn't know how to help'.

Finally a quick reference to 'media influences'. There are a
number of research studies which indicate that when a young
person commits suicide, if it is highly publicised in the
papers, on the radio and on television, there is a subsequent
rise in both the number of suicides by young people and in
suicides carried out in the same way. It has therefore been
suggested that it would be wise for the media not to spread
such news across their front pages or in their high-profile
news bulletins.

Some things which may help parents if they think their teenager is suicidal:

- mistrust the belief that someone who talks about suicide
  won't do it – it is just not true

- if you have any fear that your teenager is suicidal, talk to
  your family doctor about it urgently

- value yourself and your teenager for what you are, not what you wish you were

- listen to teenagers and show them that their opinions matter and are worth being heard

- give them responsibility and praise them when they take it rather than damning them when they don't

- share your concerns about your teenager with others: partners, friends, teachers, relations – most will have, or have had, the same problems somewhere down the line

Advice to young people on what to do if a friend appears suicidal:

- if someone close to you seems distressed, try to get them to discuss how they are feeling

- remember that the statement that someone who talks about suicide won't do it is just not true

- if a friend says they think they would be better off if they were dead, you need to take it seriously and do something quickly

- get them to talk to you further about this feeling, and then persuade them to get more help from their parents, a teacher, a doctor, or anyone else they feel they could confide in

- although normally you would respect someone's wish when they ask you not to tell anyone else about how they are feeling, in the case of someone telling you that they feel they may kill themselves, then you do need to tell someone: your parents, a teacher or some other adult close to you

● this may seem deceitful but you have to judge whether it is better that your friend actually commits suicide or whether you should be helping your friend not commit suicide by helping them to get help

(adapted from Hawton, Keith, 'Suicide and Attempted Suicide in Young People', in Macfarlane, Aidan (ed.), *Adolescent Medicine*, Royal College of Physicians of London, 1996)

If you know someone whose child has committed suicide remember:

● there is still a stigma attached to suicide which makes the bereaved family feel isolated and even suicidal themselves, especially if friends feel too embarrassed to mention it

● there is a strong need to talk about the suicide, learn how to deal with other people's reaction to it, feel better about themselves, and get the suicide in perspective

● if you know someone whose child has committed suicide:

　– don't pretend it hasn't happened
　– talk about it with the parents
　– refer to the child by his/her name in a straightforward manner
　– listen rather than commenting – they will want to off-load their own emotions rather than listen to yours
　– keep in contact with the parents after the acute period

16

Teenagers As Parents

n the list of parents' worst fears, the kind that wake you up at 2 a.m., the fear that your fourteen or fifteen-year-old has got pregnant, or is getting pregnant at that very minute, must rank high. Not surprising, given that the UK has one of the highest teenage pregnancy rates in Europe with, in 1996, almost one in a hundred girls aged thirteen to fifteen becoming pregnant. The teenage pregnancy rate in the UK is twice that in Germany, four times that in France, and seven times that in the Netherlands.

Teenagers that do get pregnant are likely to have had low educational attainments, come from families with financial problems, have had emotional problems themselves, and be the children of teenage mothers. More than half the girls with all these characteristics will get pregnant as teenagers.

Getting pregnant may be careless or may be a positive choice. Going ahead and having the baby may be an ethical choice, may be necessity because of discovering the pregnancy late, or may be because the girl really wants the child.

Whatever the reason, about half the girls who get pregnant under the age of sixteen will decide to have their baby.

Sian Sibert works as a secretary in a publishing firm in Leicester. Her father is a vicar and her mother has never worked.

'I was fifteen when I got pregnant. It was definitely not planned and the baby was by my first boyfriend. All hell broke loose with my parents.

'I ignored it till I was twenty weeks pregnant, and then my friends told me that I must see a doctor, because they were sure of it. I was too but I had tried to pretend it wasn't happening. I got up in the mornings, had my Weetabix for breakfast, threw up and went to school. I was fifteen and about to take GCSEs. Mum said to me at breakfast one morning, "You're not pregnant are you?" and I said, "Oh, I doubt it" and went off to school. That was the end of that conversation. I was disappointed because I had hoped it would come out then and that she would have pressed me a bit harder about it.

'So I did go to the doctor and had it confirmed. I went home and told Mum because the doctor wanted to see us together. Mum burst into tears and said, "What will your father say, and what will all my friends say?" My boyfriend was eighteen and working.

'My father said I would have to go away and have the baby adopted and then I could come back. There was no question of my keeping it, or of me having an abortion, as far as he was concerned. As I was about twenty weeks pregnant at that stage, the doctor had said that an abortion might just be possible.'

In England in 1996 there were 3645 abortions carried out on girls aged fifteen or under. Most abortions are carried out very early during the pregnancy. In England and Wales, 90 per cent are done before thirteen weeks, and only 2 per cent at twenty or more weeks. There is a higher rate of late abortions in young teenagers because they often deny that they are pregnant or are too frightened to seek help. The main message about getting an abortion is to get help as early as possible. For most women in early pregnancy there are usually grounds for getting an abortion if they want one, but it should not be assumed that all young teenagers who get pregnant will want one. This was the case for Sian.

'My father's reaction made me dig my heels in, and I insisted that I was going to have it. Mum said, "Well, it's your baby, you'll have to look after it," and that was the end of that conversation. After that, things were very difficult at home. I was banned from seeing my boyfriend, although I considered we were a couple. I felt very angry, because I felt I wasn't being supported by anyone.

'The whole thing of having Josh was so lonely, especially the labour. My mum didn't even offer to stay. It was a thirteen-hour labour which seemed like forever, and I cried my eyes out. But I absolutely loved Josh when he was born because he looked exactly like his dad. It was an automatic response and he seemed a perfect baby to me. What was even more hurtful was that when my mother did come in to visit me, she took one look at Josh and said, "Oh my God, he looks just like his father." I thought, "Thanks Mum, don't ask about me, will you?" That was a moment when I did consider adoption.'

Adoption does still remain an option, but compared to twenty to thirty years ago this option is less often taken. The adoption laws have been redrafted to make the whole process easier, but at present only six in one hundred babies are adopted under the age of one year. If a young person does want her baby adopted, this can be arranged through the social worker at the hospital where the child is delivered.

'I went back to school and did my GCSEs a week after I had the baby – which was totally daunting, as no one knew what to say to me. In the end, I didn't go into the sixth form, but I don't know whether I would have anyhow, baby or no baby.

'I do think that my parents should have supported me more. It was not being able to talk to them that upset me. I didn't understand what was happening to me, what was happening to my body. It was an adult thing and I felt grown up at the time, but looking back, and having a teenage son myself now, and looking at him and his girlfriend – I realise that I was only a child when I went through it all.

'I did all right in my GCSEs and felt quite pleased with myself, that I wasn't a complete failure. I would have liked to have done an NEB course, and I thought that Mum, who had a two-year-old of her own, my sister, could've looked after my baby – but she wouldn't. I am sure my sister wasn't planned! I was already thirteen when she was born, but that wasn't something Mum and I could talk about.'

The present law on abortion was passed in 1967 and there have been various modifications since. An abortion has to have the agreement of two doctors and has to be carried out in an approved place. The commonest grounds for an abortion are 'when continuing a pregnancy is more risky to the physical and mental health of the pregnant woman than if the pregnancy is terminated.' Because an abortion is slightly safer than continuing a pregnancy in statistical terms, even though both are very safe, this does allow for legal abortion almost on demand in the early stages of pregnancy.

If a teenager gets pregnant, and is not sure what to do and might want an abortion, she needs to see a GP or someone at one of the charitable abortion clinics as soon as possible. The earlier a termination is carried out, the safer are the outcomes, both physically and emotionally. If the GP is unsympathetic, she can arrange to be referred to another doctor quickly. Availability of abortion on the NHS unfortunately does depend on where you live; and if you need to consider a private abortion you must expect to pay £300 for an abortion at less than twelve weeks of pregnancy. Legally abortions can be carried out on children under the age of sixteen without their parents' consent, should the child wish it and if the doctors feel that they understand the issues. However, as with contraceptive advice, the medical professionals will make every effort to encourage the child to discuss the problem with their parents.

Early abortion is commonly performed in one of two ways, and both are very safe with few complications despite scare stories; and problems over having a baby in the future are actually very rare. The suction or aspiration method can be used up to twelve weeks after the last period. It usually involves a general anaesthetic. A thin tube is inserted through the vagina into the opening in the cervix and the contents of the uterus are sucked out. The other method involves taking a hormone pill called mifepristone. This blocks the action of the hormone which makes the lining of the uterus hold on to the fertilised egg, and so induces a miscarriage. If a teenager gets pregnant, whatever decision is made, abortion or not, the best people to give support and help will be the parents, however shocked and annoyed they initially feel. Sometimes it also helps to talk things through with a counsellor.

Sian hopes that her children are getting better sex education than she did. Sex education in schools around the country is extremely variable, and parents are advised to check what their children are being taught. You cannot assume that it is adequate. Recent research revealed depressingly that at the age of fifteen, one in three girls and one in four boys did not know where to get free condoms. Girls are generally better informed than boys and, as expected, knowledge improves in both sexes with age.

'I don't know what information is given them at school nowadays, but it is more than I had at my school which pleases me. Though I was not particularly pleased when my younger son brought it up when I was sitting with him at the hairdressers the other day. He suddenly announced to the world in general and me in particular, "Mum, we did masturbation at school today." "Oh good," I said, "shall we talk about it later?" My hairdresser didn't know where to look. Sam tried to continue with the conversation, and I kept saying, "Look, I'd rather talk about this when we get home." We did discuss it later and that was fine, though it was a bit of a shock. I had no idea that they were talking about masturbation to eleven-year-olds in PSE. Perhaps they should send a warning letter, or something.'

Statistics show that the children of a single parent are more likely to have a child outside marriage. Sian has picked up on this and is very keen that Josh should not perpetuate the cycle. She also feels that she herself missed out on her own adolescence.

'The baby son I had when I was sixteen is seventeen himself now, and my advice to him about contraception has been frank and more along the lines of a brother–sister relationship than a mother–son. It is especially difficult for me being the mother of an adolescent because I have never experienced what he's going through. I never had the freedom of being a teenager and learning things step by step. Going to nightclubs and experimenting with alcohol and drugs – I didn't have any of that because I had a baby. I missed out so much. During my adolescence I couldn't move without taking Josh with me. My mum would even ask me how long she'd have to look after Josh when I was having a bath. It's nice to be able to give Josh the support that I missed out on, but I do

*wish I could understand him more. I think that I could
talk to his girlfriend more easily than to him, but he
doesn't leave her alone with me much.'*

Sian blames herself, her youth and her inexperience, for
much of the trouble.

*'The rows we have are mainly about Josh's attitude, and I
put that down to me having him so young. He behaves as
if he is in charge of the whole household. Sometimes I feel
he doesn't even like me very much, which is very hurtful
and makes me feel guilty. I know there is a lot more I
could have done to make the relationship better. It is sad,
but I can't remember giving him a hug for I don't know
how many years. There just seems to be this barrier there.
I do love him and I don't want any harm to come to him,
but I do find it difficult to tell him so. I wish I could, but I
can't.'*

Sian also realises that for Josh, being part of a stepfamily is an
added stress. Things have changed for your average fourteen
to fifteen-year-old. Today, roughly seven out of ten teenagers
are living with both their mother and their father; one in ten
are living with only their mother; one in ten with their
mother and a step-parent; one in fifty with only their father;
and one in fifty with their father and a step-parent. She can
see Josh's point of view but does not always manage to make
things happen as he wants.

In general terms it is better if teenagers do not get pregnant at an early age. Some inevitably will, and when they do
they will need maximum support from their parents, if the
experience is to be as positive as possible for both the
teenager and their child. There is now much less stigma
attached to teenage pregnancy, and there are advantages in
making sure that teenage mothers finish their education and
obtain qualifications.

Things that may help parents if they are worried about their teenager getting pregnant:

- let children know that you will help them and won't 'kill them' if they get pregnant or get someone pregnant

- remember education and ambition are the best contraception

- for help about abortion contact the British Pregnancy Advisory Service: Tel. 01564 793225

- further details about adoption can be obtained from the Agency for Adoption and Fostering, Skyline House, 200 Union Street, London SE1 0LX. Tel. 0171 593 2000

Things that may help teenagers if they are worried that they are pregnant:

- if you think that you are pregnant, however worried you are, and however angry you think your parents might be, experience shows that your parents will be your best support

- remember education and ambition are the best contraception

- for further help about abortion contact the British Pregnancy Advisory Service. Tel. 01564 793225

- the Brook Advisory Centres give advice about contraception and abortion for young people up to the age of twenty-five. The telephone number of the central office is 0171 713 9000. They will tell you what is available locally

17

The Single Parent: Doing It Alone

As suggested earlier, even two-parent families may feel that, when it comes to bringing up a teenager, they could do with a whole team of helpers: a psychiatrist, a full-time cook, and half a dozen bouncers. Yet one in five families is now headed by a lone parent. Among the under-twenties, over eight in ten births are outside marriage; and in the twenty to twenty-four age range, five in ten births are outside marriage. So more and more teenagers will be brought up by a lone parent or in a stepfamily. Although bringing up a child alone does avoid any clash of opinions on upbringing, many single parents do find it challenging.

Pat Miller is a childminder. She had her daughter Avril when she was twenty-two, and tells of the increased feelings of vulnerability brought about by being the single mother of a sixteen-year-old.

'I grew up in a divorced family. When I was first thinking of getting married to Avril's dad it was very hard. We'd been together for some time, and Avril was three, when

*my then boyfriend slept with someone else. He wanted it
to be like it was before, but I wouldn't have that. I wasn't
going to have someone do that to me. I don't talk to my
daughter about this though. She does know I really loved
him and it took me years to get over him. It's very hard
bringing someone up by yourself because you've got no
support. You've got to keep on, and on, and on.*

*'I don't want Avril getting mixed up with the wrong
people and that does cause problems between us
sometimes. Part of that is because I am terrified of her
being exposed to drugs in a pub or a night club. I don't
think she's ever touched anything – no, no, no. She knows
what they are, but my main scare in life is for her to be
given ecstasy and for her to end up in the gutter.*

*'I'm very strict because it is a bad world for her as I've
never been married and I am still on my own. I want her
to have everything I didn't have, like her own car, a
husband who loves her, children, a career.'*

Pat has every reason to feel concerned that her daughter
might have a baby young, as women from divorced parents
are twice as likely to become teenage mothers, and are more
likely to be single or cohabiting mothers than their contemporaries. They are also more likely to form live-in
relationships at an early age. Men from divorced parents are
more likely to become fathers before they are twenty-two,
and are more likely to be unmarried fathers than their contemporaries. Pat realises that some of her conflicts with Avril
are to do with anxieties that she might get into 'trouble'.

*'The main area of conflict is that I won't let her out late
and I won't let her have too much freedom until she's
eighteen. Sometimes Avril makes me feel like an old witch
and really cruel, other times she understands that I do it
because I love her. But we do have good times when we
laugh together, have a read, go swimming together, have a*

*cuddle and lie in bed together. She tells me she loves me,
but I just wish we could have some peace in the house
sometimes. It's not that she's a monster or anything, but if
she and I start arguing, then my own mum wades in and
tells her to stop getting at me. Avril rebels against me. The
last bad argument we had was because she lied to me
about seeing her boyfriend. She told me that she was
definitely not going to see him, but she had rung his mum
up and asked if she could spend the night there. She told
her it was because she had had a really bad argument
with me. That was a lie. I found out because his mother
rang me to ask about it.'*

Many parents find the fact that their teenagers are apparently
physically and sexually mature and yet at the same time emotionally very immature difficult to cope with. Teenagers
themselves cannot believe that their parents were young
themselves once and were doing the same sorts of things –
even if generally at a slightly older age. It is because of what
Pat herself did as a teenager that makes her all the more worried for her daughter.

*'Now I've found out she's had sex with him. She's told me
about it, but what can I do? We'd already agreed that we
would go to the doctor for contraception when she was
sixteen. I thought we were going together, but then she
told me she'd already done it. I was really cross with them
both. I'm so scared because she can walk down the road
and she can look like an eighteen-year-old. If she dresses
too flirty or too revealing then I say no. When I've been
out with her, the men have all looked at her, and you can
see what's going on in their minds. We're talking about
men in their twenties and she obviously loves it. But me, I
think, "She's only sixteen, leave her alone," but what can I
do? I'm not going to let her go walking down the street
with a cigarette in one hand and a can of drink in the*

other, frightening old grannies and sleeping with every man there is. I don't really think there is any chance of her doing that because she is sensible, but what if she gets in the wrong crowd?

'The thing is she thinks she knows it all – been there and done it. She doesn't think I know anything. She's so mature for her age, I can't blame her in a way. She's very ambitious and I like that. I've always felt that I didn't want her to end up like me.'

Most lone-parent families are headed by a lone mother, and of lone mothers 37 per cent are single, 24 per cent are separated, 33 per cent are divorced, and about 6 per cent are widowed. Of lone fathers, 13 per cent are single, 30 per cent are separated, 43 per cent are divorced, and 14 per cent are widowed. Although lone parents head 21 per cent of all families with dependent children – nearly three times what it was twenty-five years ago – Pat still feels there is a stigma attached.

'It can be hard, like at school, you see all the mums and dads at parents' evening and you're the only mum by herself. But one just has to learn to live with it.'

Teenagers want freedom, object to being asked what they are up to, yet they also want boundaries and for their families to take an interest. It is difficult for both sides to get it right. Many of the feelings that Avril describes are similar to those you would expect if she had been brought up by two parents.

'I live with my mum and my nan and we get on fine most of the time, but we do have arguments, especially me with my mum about me going out. She always gives me a time to be back by, and wants to know where I am going and who with. What time I'm allowed out until depends on who I am going out with. If I'm at a party, I'm normally allowed out till 12 or half past. If I am going to be any

later she likes me to stay at the friend's house who's giving the party. As long as I phone her and tell her what I am going to do, she doesn't really mind too much. I think that's reasonable I suppose.

'I don't want to be roaming the streets all night or anything like that, but I would like to come and go with a bit more independence. If she doesn't like my friends, she doesn't let me go out with them, and I think that's too restrictive. I think my mother knows most of what I get up to, but there are some things I don't want her to know about. Sometimes I've been out with my friends to places that I know she wouldn't approve of – like clubs. And I've been to a few parties given by a good friend who my mother doesn't approve of. I just say I'm with another friend. But I think my mother knows when I'm lying – she seems to have an instinct for it. It makes me mad.

'I had a boyfriend who I split up with recently. She let me out with him alone as long as I wasn't too late back, but she wouldn't allow him up to my room. We had to sit downstairs and watch TV. That's what's considered "decent". I think she's worried that people will take advantage of me. When she wouldn't allow me upstairs with my boyfriend I did ask why and I told her, "You've got to trust me now." She thought about that and in the end she did allow us upstairs together, but my nan kept walking in to get things. Privacy is a problem in our house.'

The interpretations of the data collected about the effects on children of being brought up in different types of families continue to fill many pages of print. There is no doubt that the relative poverty experienced by many one-parent families explains some but not all of the problems. Recently the behaviours and adjustment at school of a group of children born illegitimately and a group born legitimately were compared, and it was found that most differences in outcomes between the two sets of children could be explained by social class or gender differences, rather than by their different birth statuses. Avril's views of school and her ambitions in life do not appear to have been dented by being brought up in a single-parent family.

'I'm good at school work and enjoy it, and my own group is all right, but the teachers shout at us, and there is so much pressure to do OK, but we can only go so far. There used to be pressures from classmates not to work when I was in the year below, and they used to call me "swat" – but not in the sixth form. It's too important there – everyone wants to do well. The good thing about school is my friends, and the bad thing is that it's a very long day, especially if you've got boring lessons.

'I want to be a solicitor, but after I finish school I want to take a year out just to get everything sorted. My friend said that you can work in a solicitor's office and work your way up like that, and then maybe go to college, which is the way I want to do it, so that I can earn money at the same time. I want to be independent with my own money.

'The best thing about Mum is that she is always there for me and if I am in any trouble she will back me up all the way. What I find difficult about her is that she doesn't really understand me, and says that I am too young to do things like stay out late. She is very over-protective. The nicest thing I remember her doing for me was looking after me when I was ill – she was brilliant at that. We go out shopping together – a sort of mother and daughter day – just the two of us, going to town, having something to eat, wandering around chatting. But I don't want to be like my mother. I want to be a big career woman, not like my mum who gave up any idea of nursing after she had me. She thinks of everybody else but herself.'

Many children living in single-parent families never know, or lose contact with, the other parent. Most will want to find out about both their birth parents as they grow up, as do adopted children.

> *'I've tried to contact my dad but though I've written to the address Mum gave me he's never written back. When I've got enough money I might try and find him. It hurts a bit that he doesn't want to see me.'*

Although Pat knows it is right for her daughter to want to see her father, she still finds the prospect difficult.

> *'I didn't feel comfortable when my daughter wanted to see him. It felt as if someone wanted to take something from me. I mean, it's right for her to see him but I was frightened she might want to stay with him. So far she has never got to see him.'*

Pat sums up in her own words what many, but by no means all, lone parents feel.

> *'I do know one thing though. It's very hard bringing kids up on your own. I know that they've got a Child Helpline and a Parent Helpline. One does need someone to talk to, because all the time you are asking yourself, "Am I doing it right?" "Am I too hard on her?" "What am I going to do now?" I'm proud of her because she is mine, but nervous of what she's going to do because she's very vulnerable. No, I shouldn't say that because she's not, she's very headstrong, I'm the vulnerable one. But I do worry for her because of what's happened to me. I don't want her to go through that. Nobody knows the pain I feel. I just put on a brave face.'*

Being a single parent is normally not as easy as being a pair. Nevertheless, if it does happen out of choice or through circumstance, money, friends and supporting relatives all help.

229

Things that might help lone parents with their teenagers, and the teenagers of lone parents:

- there are many reasons why people bring children up as lone parents – but the things that might help in this situation are those given at the end of Chapters 3, 5 and 7

18
Sexual Abuse

Within Europe, the English are considered to have a distinctly strange attitude to sexual matters. For instance, the Swedes have a saying: 'We do it, the English talk about it.' The English enjoy being horrified about lurid press stories of sexual abuse though, and sex and violence, as far as the press and parliament are concerned, are virtually a single word: 'sex'n'violence'.

The high rates of teenage pregnancy in the UK are frequently put down to too much sex education rather than too little – in spite of the fact that every single study on sex education shows either that it has no effect whatsoever, or that it delays the timing of first sexual intercourse.

There is another aspect to good sex education. Were sex treated as an entirely natural human occupation by which the human race survives, and taught appropriately from preschool onwards, this would enable sexually abused children to use sexual terms – penis, vagina, breasts – to explain to adults in a totally unembarrassed way what is being done to them and why they do not like it, instead of being faced with a wall of embarrassment and denial from the adults who are meant to protect them from such activities. Still, we are what we are, and we shall, at least for the moment – until we can manage to be more open and honest – have to bear the resulting pain and distress. It is not easy, as Caroline Hughes describes in an unfolding nightmare of discovery.

'When Sarah was eleven she started showing terrible signs of anger and moodiness. By twelve she was saying that she was so depressed she felt like killing herself. We went to parents' evening at her school one day and every one of her teachers said, "Sarah is depressed and she needs help." My initial response to Sarah then was, "What on earth are you on about? You've got everything. Your parents are together, we're a happy family, and you've got a lovely home." Then she became bulimic as well, and we found she was making herself vomit after every meal. We just didn't know how to handle it. OK, so we are a high-stress family in that we are somewhat driven, but we are a low-stress family in that everyone in the family is allowed to be themselves and talk about things – at least, that's what I thought at the time. We just couldn't imagine what could account for Sarah's behaviour. We'd bicker in the family once in a while but nothing to explain all of this!'

Child sexual abuse frequently presents with a sudden change in behaviour, moodiness and depression. The discovery by parents, that their child is being sexually abused, is particularly horrible because suspicion instantly falls on the nearest available male, who is considered guilty until proved otherwise, causing terrible rifts within a family.

'I took Sarah to see the family doctor, who referred us to a psychiatric hospital, and we were all interviewed as a family there. During this interview Sarah vented her anger on her father, Tom, and what started as anger

became hideous, vicious fury. Poor Tom. At that first session he thought, "she hates me" and he had absolutely no idea why. It was horrible. At the second session I said to the psychiatrist that I was completely confused and that I had no understanding of what it was that Sarah was so furious about. They took her out of the room and talked to her by herself and after an hour they came back and said, "She's been sexually abused." I instantly screamed, "But that's impossible." I was terrified they'd say that it was my husband Tom, and our family would be destroyed.'

Difficulties in diagnosing sexual abuse include the fact that the abusers are often in a powerful position over the child, that abused children do not have an appropriate knowledge of the language relating to sexual matters to explain what is happening, and that a large proportion of children who have been sexually abused show no abnormal physical signs of any kind.

Although Caroline's suspicions immediately descended on her husband, it turned out, as it does in many cases, that the sexual abuser was in fact a close friend of the family and well respected within the society in which they lived.

'They told us that it was a close friend of the family and at that instant I knew exactly who it was. It was like having a sudden revelation. He was a lawyer, a Lewis Carroll-like figure who preferred the company of children to adults. He had been a friend of our family since we came to Leeds and he had had the children over to his house many times. Sarah was six at the time we first met him, very boisterous and she loved jumping on people.'

Sexual abuse of teenage daughters occurs more commonly with stepfathers and family friends than with natural fathers. Caroline was aware that young children, in their innocence, can be sexually alluring.

> 'What was ironic was that the first time we met this guy
> Andrew, we sat down at his kitchen table and said, "Look,
> if Sarah jumps on you, you must stop her and tell her not
> to do it." We said this because we knew that Andrew
> thought children should be allowed to do exactly what
> they want and that it was wrong to restrain them. He said
> he didn't agree with stopping her doing anything she
> wanted to, but he realised this would be against the law.
> As a lawyer he wasn't about to break the law, so we didn't
> have anything to worry about.'

People who sexually abuse children are extremely skilled at
putting themselves into a position where they have access to
children on their own, and in getting both parents and children to trust them.

> 'The children went to see Andrew together. I remember
> now that he wanted Sarah and her older brother Ben to
> come separately. He suggested that they had different
> needs and he could give them individual attention if they
> came over one by one. We said, "No, whoever doesn't get
> invited will feel resentful, so you'll have to have both of
> them." It's difficult to know with hindsight whether we
> were slightly worried or what we were saying was what
> we really believed.'

Parents need to be aware that anyone who has access to their
children may use and abuse that trust. Adults who sexually
abuse children are mainly men and come from a whole range
of professional and other backgrounds. In retrospect Caroline
can see exactly how it happened.

> 'So the kids went round there about once a month, from
> when Sarah was eight until she was eleven. Ben is two
> years older. Andrew had a wonderful collection of
> children's books and a ping-pong table in his basement,

where he would take Sarah when Ben was upstairs playing on the computer. He would read to them and get them to write stories and draw pictures. They totally adored him, and I am sure that if we had forbidden Sarah to go there she would have hated us. She did actually say to us once, "I love Andrew more than Dad. I want him to be my dad. He's wiser and much nicer." He did things like the moment she got into the car he would give her a big sweet and say, "If I was your dad I would give you sweets all the time." It's so classic it hurts.'

One study found that, on average, a sexual offender had abused seven children before being caught. Sometimes, as in the present case, the sexual abuser gets away with it again and again. Sarah suddenly couldn't take it any more.

'Suddenly, when Sarah was eleven, she said that Andrew was a creep and she didn't want to see him any more. She just instantly reversed things and if she heard he was about to come round to our house, she disappeared up to her room. It was about this time that Sarah and I were driving in the car together and we heard a programme about sexual abuse. Looking back, Andrew was a classic paedophile.

'The programme said to watch out for men who prefer the company of children to the company of adults, men who want to be alone with children, and men who want to play children's games. Andrew is all those things, as well as an antisocial, unmarried weirdo. To a certain extent that was why we had all liked him. How he managed to be a lawyer with those characteristics though, God only knows.'

It is not surprising, given male sexual behaviours, that female children are targeted more often than males.

'Apparently when Sarah was with the psychiatrist, and he asked her whether a man had ever done anything to her,

she immediately told the whole story. She also told him that she thought we would prefer Andrew to her and would blame her for what had happened. It was awful. All the classic stuff came out. We wouldn't love her any more, and we would take Andrew's side. When I was told, my first feeling was of absolute disbelief, then unreality, and then violent anger. I wanted to kill Andrew, I've wanted to kill him for about a year. Interestingly I haven't seen him on the street since this has happened. I just never want to see him again. Even now, if I met him, I am sure that I would strike him.'

Studies have shown that sex offenders tend to 'target' the children who are most friendly, most receptive, most trusting, and most vulnerable, and then engage them in a relationship before beginning sexual contact. They commonly work out a way of gaining children's confidence and desensitising them to frank sexual passes by progressing from non-sexual touching to sexual touching, and through gradual development of a relationship with the child. By the time sexual abuse takes place, the child may feel that she (or he) has given consent. They use a range of very coercive behaviours over a period of time before sexually abusing. These include efforts to separate children from other adults who might protect them, using the promises of rewards and the threat of punishments, and letting children see increasingly pornographic material.

Caroline is left wondering whether Ben was also abused. Though Ben himself has always refused to admit anything took place, it was subsequently revealed that Andrew also sexually abused boys as well as girls.

'After Sarah had stopped going Ben still went for a time; but of course as soon as he heard about Sarah, he stopped going. This was hard for him because Andrew was his hero too and he adored him. Andrew was one of those people who let kids ring him at any time – day or

night. We thought, "How wonderful that our children have such a friend." If Sarah was unhappy at school, or if she was angry with me, she'd ring Andrew and tell him her troubles. They would spend hours on the phone together – no question of him being too busy for the children.

'There was the question of whether Ben had been abused. He absolutely refused to talk about it and never came to any of the therapy the rest of us have had. Tom feels that Andrew has taken his daughter away from him. Before Andrew came on the scene, Sarah had been Tom's little girl. They were extremely close. But now Sarah has gone totally anti-Tom, angry at him for everything, hurting him on every occasion she can, never touching him and never confiding in him. He is devastated.

'The whole thing has been a colossal trauma to the whole family. We've had our lives put under the microscope which was incredibly unpleasant. We've been treated as a dysfunctional family, and behind that is the assumption that there is something wrong with us, and that we were each somehow to blame. Tom came up with a whole series of ways of getting back at Andrew. He wanted to burn Andrew's house down, smash all his windows, paint 'sexual abuser' all over the front of his house. I happily shared all these revenge fantasies and more.'

In our present society, most girls in their early teens, and a smaller number of teenage boys, will almost inevitably be subjected to some form of adult sexual exposure, whether it is a flasher in a park or being rubbed up against in an underground train. These kinds of exposures, if unpleasant, are unfortunately the norm, and need to be discussed within a family and accepted as part of life. It is much more difficult to give advice to parents about how to avoid the possibility of their children being sexually abused along the lines described here. This luckily is very much rarer but, as already suggested, abusers are extremely clever and a large proportion of sex offenders are known to their victims and their victims' families.

The guilt, anger and disruption caused by finding out that one's child has been sexually abused are devastating and take a great deal of time and counselling. Discovery is only the beginning. The parents and the child need to be aware that they may have to relive the facts again and again, and still sometimes nothing gets resolved as far as punishing or stopping the offender is concerned.

> '*The police went round to see him. I know that I would have been violent if I had gone too. The psychiatrist insisted that the social services had to be involved, and they insisted – against our wishes – that the police be involved too. It was appalling. Sarah was put through the degradation of having to repeat her story to the police. Then she had to be videoed talking about it all over again. Finally there was the devastation, almost as bad as the abuse itself, when the police decided to drop the case because they didn't find that any other children were involved. They didn't even examine his books carefully, even though Ben had seen pictures of nude children in some of them. The police summed it up as "one child's word against his, and he being a lawyer – we're just not going to make the case stick with that." '*

Then there may be longer-term consequences:

> '*Sarah dropped out of school for a year. She started cutting herself and the bulimia got infinitely worse. We tried another school but it was so awful that I had to take her out again. She lost all confidence in herself and school. Even when we went on holiday recently, Sarah*

*locked herself in her room and cut herself with Ben's
penknife. She got blood all over the sheets and towels,
everywhere – it was a nightmare. Tom, Ben and I were so
upset we thought we ought to have her admitted to a
psychiatric unit. We just felt we couldn't take it, but we
did finally manage to cope.'*

One of the most devastating things for some parents is the
wall of denial put up by other people about the possibility
that someone they know well may sexually abuse young children. It goes beyond the imagination of some, and is too
repugnant for others even to allow themselves to think about
it.

*'When people knew, many behaved in a very strange way
– because he was doing it to other children as well, boys
as well as girls. Some of the parents just wouldn't allow
the police to talk to their children. One father, who had
been our friend, said, "I have known Andrew for ten
years, and I just know that he wouldn't do a thing like
that." So now we don't have him as a friend either, and
God knows what Andrew is doing to his children. The
problem was that Andrew was working with children in
other ways, and when we rang the organisations he was
involved in and told them what had happened, they just
said that they didn't want to know. He was so much loved,
we had loved him too – the guy was such a nutcase it was
difficult not to.'*

So how do parents deal with their own feelings? The answer
is 'with great difficulty and self-blame', as Caroline explains.

*'Me? When I first heard I fell apart. I just couldn't handle
it, and got my GP to put me on a huge dose of Prozac,
which allowed me to behave in a way I thought was
rational. The disadvantage was that although I was able*

to deal with Sarah's emotions quite calmly, she actually wanted me to be upset and angry along with her, instead of totally logical and controlled. I felt completely stupid for not having recognised what had been going on. I should have instantly known what the problem was. And now I feel very concerned about Sarah's sexual future. I think that is the next big hurdle.'

It is probably not only unrealistic, but also totally impossible, to protect one's children or teenagers all the time. Caroline took every reasonable precaution but it still happened. However, if a child or teenager's behaviour does suddenly change for no obvious reason, do not instantly put it down to 'teenage moodiness' or 'just trying to be difficult'. Sexual offenders put huge blackmailing and other pressures on to the children they are abusing, not to reveal what is happening. Parents must be patient with their children as they try to find their own way of explaining something that they themselves may feel guilty about and responsible for. Caroline suggests:

'If I was to advise other parents, I think the main thing in hindsight was how uncharacteristically Sarah suddenly started behaving. I should have asked her at that stage what was wrong. For a child to be as upset and angry as she was, it just wasn't normal. We thought it might be mental illness and any idea that it could have been sexual abuse just didn't occur to us. I also think one has to be very sensitive to other siblings. Ben is still very angry. He hasn't gone through releasing it all yet, and he has terrible bouts of depression. He doesn't communicate his feelings to me much though, and I still don't know whether Andrew sexually abused him or not.

'The only other advice I can give to parents is to love your children and be there for them, and help them get through it as a family. The hardest part for me was to

see my child suffering and being wrung inside out like that.'

Some things which may help parents if they are worried about their child being sexually abused:

- adults are, in almost all cases, clearly aware what the acceptable limits are between affectionate and sexual contacts

- teenagers need love and affection from their parents, including physical contacts such as hugs and kisses. These can and should be easily offered without infringing on contacts that might be considered sexual

- try to ensure that, from an early age, your child has the 'language' to express sexual matters. Use words like 'penis' and 'vagina' without embarrassment and show that sex can be discussed openly within the family if needs be

- teenagers may begin to be more wary of physical contact with their parents and others approaching, during and after puberty, as they become aware of their own sexual feelings

- young people are vulnerable to sexual approaches because they are relatively naïve about sexual feelings and frequently lack confidence in their sexual attractiveness

- in spite of anger and other sudden mood changes, try to keep on communicating as best you can, to enable your teenager to confide in you, if you think some form of sexual abuse is occurring

- sex offenders claim to have a special ability to identify vulnerable children and to manipulate that vulnerability as a means of gaining sexual access to children

- there are inherent vulnerabilities in all children and young people when it comes to adult exploitation. They are small compared with adults, they are weaker and they don't always have the language ability to explain what is happening to them

19

Brothers and Sisters: Their Loves, Hates and Fights

Relationships between brothers and sisters have, surprisingly, though with a few notable exceptions, escaped detailed examination by sociologists, psychologists and others. It is hard to know why, as the relationship is – as most of us know – both common and complex. There is no other relationship quite like it. It can range from intense love and affection to intense dislike, even hate, against a background concept within society that in families 'blood is (or should be) thicker than water'.

The feelings between siblings that are established during childhood and adolescence can last a lifetime, and may often be inexplicable to those involved. There are, after all, many different factors involved in family relationships. What is it that makes the oldest child so different from subsequent children? Was it because parents were 'practising on the job' because they had no other experience of child rearing? What is it that makes 'only' children different? Are they just 'oldest' children who were never softened up by having younger brothers and sisters, or is it something else? What makes the relationship between a child and the same sex parent different from their relationship with the opposite sex parent? What is it that makes a sibling relationship so special, and what happens to these relationships as children grow older?

One thing for sure is that many sibling relationships can be a total puzzle to parents. As one parent puts it:

> *'My children fought one another for eighteen years – from the time they were born till they moved out of our house. Sometimes, when they were fighting, I would light a cigarette and go for a long walk to get away from it all. At other times I wondered if I needed to go and see a psychiatrist to find out what I had done wrong. I just could not understand how my son and daughter, who I loved so much myself, couldn't love one another.'*

Many parents do, in fact, feel that is better to 'get out of the way' rather than interfere when siblings are fighting one another. It does appear that, on a day-to-day basis, parents interfering with these squabbles can only make things worse. Teenagers may simply use and abuse their parents' concerns to get at their rival even more effectively. The same parent says:

> *'Personally, my advice to other parents is, when your children are fighting, don't interfere until the blood is seeping under the door.'*

The question of what is the right 'gap' between children is a perennial one, voiced here by Tara Jackson (see also Chapter 10). In her first marriage she had two sons called Shane and David, now aged seventeen and thirteen. Tara is married to Tony, her sons' stepfather.

> *'The relationship between the two boys is affected by an age gap of four years. This was deliberate because I*

*wanted to avoid the age gap of twenty months between
my sister and me. Two children of the same sex close in
age inevitably get lumped together. I think the theory was
that we would amuse one another, but we just fought. I
thought a bigger age gap would sort that out. What has
actually happened is that they have very little contact at
all as they have never had the same interests at the same
time. They've always been more individuals and very
much on their own. They don't fight physically, but they
niggle and argue about who is going to sit on this
particular sofa. It is considered sort of pole position and
they have a complicated set of rules over how long you
have to be away from pole position before you lose your
rights! As long as they regulate this themselves, that's
fine by me. They drive me mad less than they do Tony. He
was an only child so he finds it more difficult to cope
with.'*

Tony, Tara's husband, sees his stepsons as being totally different personalities, but he recognises that as the boys have got
older, the four-year gap between them makes less and less difference. He thinks they've now become genuine friends (a
viewpoint less obvious to Shane and David, as will be seen).

*'The good thing about them is watching them develop
together and yet they are so totally different. The younger
one is more explosive in character, like me (although he is
a stepson), and the older one more restrained, like his
mother. They get on very well together now, but the four-
year gap was significant until the younger one reached an
age the older one was interested in. They weren't friends
before, so it makes me incredibly happy. I always hoped it
would happen.'*

Teenage sibling relationships are fraught with danger. If
teenagers are close together in years, they may compete for

the same girlfriends, at the same sports, for better exam results; or they may do the opposite, just to make sure that they feel individualistic and totally different.

However much quarrelling there is between siblings, in the majority of cases it is nothing more than companionable and mildly competitive aggression, for the sheer pleasure of seeing if you can get a rise out of a brother or sister. In most, but certainly not all cases, it is unlikely to give rise to violence (though there has been many a broken tooth, or cut lip, from testing a sibling too far!). However, the continual 'getting at one another' can cause quite deep-seated frustration in an older sibling, like Shane.

'The bad thing about having a brother like Dave is that he's always trying to copy everything I do, which I find incredibly annoying. He's four years younger than me and he is a constant presence under my feet. Some of it is just him definitely trying to annoy me, like trying to sit in the same seat as me when watching TV, or climbing over me to get out of the car at the same time when we're dropped off at school. The last bad argument we had was when we were looking at the school photo. He said my face was covered with spots. He's pretty acutely aware of my areas of sensitivity, and so am I of his, but we don't get physical with one another as he's so puny.'

One thing that siblings learn very early on is where 'Achilles' heel' weaknesses lie within the family, and how to exploit them to the full.

'It would be easier if he was closer to my own age. Four years is too big a gap for me to have him as a close friend, but he is my brother none the less. He does get on with my friends, but he definitely changes his personality for them, like he tries to be a lot more helpful towards them, but not to me. He's more eager to please

*them and they like that, but they don't see as much of
him as I have to! I prefer him not to be there when my
friends come around and I do try and arrange that. Like
I finish school earlier than he does, and he goes to bed
earlier than me.'*

Interestingly, there is a feeling that if the gap between the
two had been closer, they would not have found one another
so annoying. This is not on the whole true. Two-year gaps can
lead to more competition and more aggression.

There is also the jealousy, that somehow one sibling gets it
easier than others. It does seem that the further down a family
you are, then the more 'broken in' and 'lenient' parents are.
Shane again.

*'I think he's more spoilt than I was by Mum, my stepfather
Tony, and even Dad. He gets more new clothes, for one
thing. He's very whiney to Dad when he wants something
– the last time was over having a computer. He's allowed
to stay up later, and he gets away with things that I never
did, and he has more freedom than I ever had. Some of
that may be because our parents being older are a bit
better off now than when I was growing up. Also, my
mum and stepdad just can't remember what they used to
insist on for me, so they just more or less fit in with Dave's
life and his demands. Maybe it's for the peace and quiet.
The fight's gone out of them a bit, or maybe they are
genuinely more relaxed.'*

In most cases, when children are arguing, who is to blame is
the least of the parents' concerns, though they will often pick
on one or the other at random. They know not only that
some of the blame lies with both parties, but that there is
enjoyment and entertainment in fighting for the warring fac-
tions as well! What parents want is peace and respite from the
endless quarrelling.

'I think that all my parents see is that me and Dave are constantly trying to get at each other. I tend to get back at him with the same things that he does to me, but it's more in response to him than anything I initiate myself. I make comments about his height, which I know he's sensitive about, and yes, I do know exactly what's going to upset him. I've got a store of catch phrases for that – it's not difficult to get him wound up.

'I can't really think of any good things about having a brother. One of my friends has one, and they're much better pals, but there is only a year and a half between them. They go skateboarding together, and to films. That's just not on with Dave and me. I really keep my contact with my younger brother as brief as possible. I don't think he can relate to me at my level of interests and way of seeing things, anyhow.'

David at thirteen is, not surprisingly, more inclined to see the benefits of his position.

'Shane is not very nice to me sometimes, even though I try and be nice to him. He's a bit mean with things, like I wanted to borrow his tennis racket cover and he vetoed it and said no, because he might want to use it on his skiing holiday. That was just stupid. What we mainly argue about is where we are going to sit on the sofa, because you can lean against it in that spot and be as lazy as possible – it's just silly things like that. I'm really glad that I've got a brother but I would like there not to be such a gap.

'The advantage of being the younger brother is that things they did with Shane, that didn't go so well, they probably do differently with me. The allowance is one thing. At the beginning Shane found he had too much money to handle, and now he finds he doesn't have enough. I think my parents may give me a bit less *allowance to start with and then a bit more. He's sort of blazed the way. I do get classed with him, and my parents don't really treat me as an individual, like they said I couldn't have an allowance yet because Shane didn't get one till he was fourteen and three quarters. Also, things like, "Well, Shane never stayed up that late" or "Shane wasn't allowed to buy those kinds of trainers." I think at the moment my parents favour me, but they used to favour Shane more. That changed because he's a bit of a dollop and doesn't do anything. He doesn't seem to be working at school, though he does seem to be getting very good marks. My parents treat me as the baby at the moment, which I can twist to my favour by acting up when I want things, like I wanted a computer off my dad recently. I put on a babyish act that no one really loved me.'*

Young people are acutely aware of whom their parents favour. Luckily in many families this favouritism circulates between the siblings. As they get older, they may well be aware of this, and amused and objective enough to discuss it among themselves. What parents do also need to be aware of is the fact that teenagers, consciously or unconsciously, are ceaseless manipulators of all around them in order to achieve their own ends. It is rarely done with any wicked intent, but is rather a perfectly normal survival mechanism.

'I do sometimes tell Shane things that I don't tell my parents, like if I've been in trouble at school; and I tell him about detentions, and he says, "Oh, I've had that before." I find it helps me feel less bad about it. He wouldn't split on me – well, he might, just to annoy and tease me, but he wouldn't do it seriously. I do worry about him sometimes. Another thing is, I get a bit silly when Mum goes out and is not back when she said she would be. I start moaning, "Oh, what's happened to Mum?" Shane's reading a book, just totally unbothered, and that annoys me.'

A mixture of what appears to be all-out violence between siblings combined with huge underlying affection is what characterises many such relationships. Ryan, aged sixteen, remembers experiences with his older sister.

'My older sister tried to kill me a couple of times when I was about seven. One time she locked me in the airing cupboard and pumped its temperature up to over 40 degrees to see if she could cook me. No laughing matter, thank you very much! I think it was just jealousy of a younger brother who was diverting her parents' attention away from her. The other time she tried to stab me with a knife.

'She was a nightmare during puberty and went completely berserk. I loved her madly all the time basically, but she never had any time for me. When she had her friends around, I wanted to play with them, and join in whatever games they were playing, but she just told me to go and get stuffed. I wanted to play with them because I fancied them all, but she thought I was plain embarrassing.

'When she was younger, she and her friends made up this "fruit" language and would run around saying to one another "kiwi" or "passion fruit" or "pear", and I wouldn't know what they were talking about. They had this whole language. I talked to her a few weeks ago about that and she said, "Oh, we just shouted those things to annoy you and make you think we had a special language – but it was just rubbish. You didn't actually believe us, did you?" They had this code sheet I had seen, but she just said, "Oh that, there was nothing on it!" They had made the whole thing up to annoy me.

'I never got my own back, because you never get your own back on older brothers or sisters, simply because they are always older. She used to push me into a wardrobe and lock the door, and when we were eating together and I was

*eating something nice, she would say, "Oh look at the cat,
Ryan" and I would look, and she would snatch the food off
my plate and eat it. If I tried to do it to her, she took
absolutely no notice at all.'*

Relief from the trauma of an overwhelming sibling can come
in many different and surprising forms, as happened to Ryan.

*'But my older sister, when she was seventeen, found "The
Lord". She came down to breakfast one morning and
announced to us all, "I turned over a new leaf, I'm now a
Christian." She became totally delightful overnight and
has stayed that way ever since. I haven't taken up The
Lord at all myself and think it totally ridiculous, but I am
now close friends with my sister. All my friends, where
there is a boy and a girl in the family, they seem to fight
enormously, but not to hurt one another, and they are
actually really close. When brothers fight, they actually
aim to hurt one another, I reckon. But then they'll stop
because they'll have got their aggression out and they'll be
friends like.'*

Being the oldest, being the youngest, being elsewhere in the
family, being all boys or all girls, having big gaps or small
gaps, all play a part. How much these various factors influence the final outcome of someone's personality and their
relationship with other members of the family, when compared with other factors – like whether your parents are living
together, are rich or poor, old or young, and whether your
brother or sister has a disability – again will vary enormously.
Julia is the oldest in a family of girls, with one badly dyslexic
sister.

*'I have four younger sisters, and I never really wanted a
brother. Occasionally I did fantasise about having an older
brother, but not really. My mother was one of five girls*

and on the whole, as a family, we are really proud that we've managed to do it again! I don't think there are any disadvantages in being only girls, except that perhaps we don't understand boy things as well. Dad is OK, though I think he has a really hard time when one of us is going through puberty.

'I'm a sort of second mother to the youngest two. My next one down is sixteen and badly dyslexic, so I am OK with her and protect her. She says her earliest memory of me is me protecting her. But the one younger than her, well, we argue all the time, and we certainly had some physical fights when we were younger. I was incredibly jealous when my parents brought her home, and I wanted them to take her back to the hospital and leave her there. We are sort of friends now, but there is still a certain amount of friction. The next one down to me, well, I love her to bits.

'I am highly competitive with the second sister down. We fight about clothes absolutely all the time. We had an argument just the other day because she had taken my make-up away for the weekend, and that broke the truce we have, where we always ask before borrowing things, and she hadn't. I took back everything I had ever lent her in revenge. But the third one down, I don't mind what she borrows or whether she asks me or not, so there is obviously something else going on as well.

'It's never big things that I argue with my sisters about, we just needle one another. My parents don't really choose to do anything about it. They think that we should sort it out ourselves. Usually I'm able to pull a fast one on my parents when we're quarrelling and lay the blame on the sister I'm having the fight with; or else I feel really victimised if I'm blamed because I'm the oldest, and I feel it isn't fair and then I sulk for days. Actually I don't think it makes much difference if parents do or do not get involved – the outcome is the same. I do think that* *patterns of relationships between brothers and sisters are laid down early and in some ways don't change much over the years. If I haven't seen my sisters for some time, I just slot back into the same role with them.'*

Things which may help parents when dealing with sibling battles:

- there is no 'best interval' between children, though everyone with children will give you an opinion, and often the interval is not possible to plan

- waiting 'until the blood is seeping under the door' may be a bit extreme, but letting brothers and sisters sort things out for themselves is frequently a better learning experience for them than always trying to interfere

- each teenager needs to feel an individual, so saying 'but that is what we did with James or Mary or whichever older sibling' does not seem like sufficient justification to a younger child ('but I am me')

- the eldest sibling does often get the blame – 'you are the oldest and you should know better' – and it is frequently unfair

- younger siblings frequently cry 'wolf' in order to get the older sibling into trouble and to exert power!

- over duties around the house, get them to sort out their own rota

- relationships between brothers and sisters do change over time, so there is no need for parents to despair if things go wrong. Most, if not all, will come right or 'rightish' in the long run, especially if the parents remain fair to both

What may help teenagers handle siblings and parents:

- so much depends on where you come in the family and there are advantages and disadvantages in each position!

- if you are the oldest, be prepared to take more blame than necessary but remember you're the only one to have had the complete attention of your parents – at least for a time

- if you are not the first, you will be allowed to do things which the eldest had to wait for earlier and with less hassle – but be prepared to have hassle from above as payment!

- whatever individuals say, there are ways of getting your own back if you are a harassed younger sibling, and no doubt you will already be using them!

- you are bound to push your brothers or sisters as far as they can go at times, but don't be surprised when they bite back and you are pushed past breaking point – two can play at the same game

20
Losing a Parent

ach year, one in every hundred children under the age of sixteen will experience a parent dying. Sometimes this will be a sudden and unexpected event and sometimes the parent will have been ill for some time. This will be one of the many factors which will influence how a teenager reacts, but even if the illness has been long and unpleasant and the death is in some ways a relief and a release, the process of bereavement and grieving can be just as painful.

Stella is now nineteen, but was sixteen and still at school when her mother died from breast cancer, four years after it was first diagnosed. She is still nervous about life and uncertain of her role in relation to her father George and her sister Pauline. Stella is now at a catering college in Wales. She finds that three years on it helps to talk about her mother's death, though at the time she found it too painful.

'The thing that I miss most about Mum is having her support, not on a day-to-day basis, but her general advice and being able to talk to her about things. She was a very

easy person to talk to. Some things did shock her, stupid things like getting drunk, which I expected her to be laid back about but she wasn't. She was very good at understanding where people were coming from, and she helped me to understand what other people were about, and when and why they weren't behaving well. Dad has changed a lot since Mum died, but there is a difference between Mum and Dad. With Dad I can talk more about academic things – work, jobs, assignments. When it came to emotions I would talk to Mum. Dad is not so good at emotions as he is not as sensitive as Mum was, or rather he is sensitive in a different way.'

All the available evidence suggests that young people cope best if they are kept well informed about what is happening when a parent dies. A serious illness in a parent will change relationships within the family. There is a sudden reversal of the parent–teenager role. The parent becomes more vulnerable and the one in need of care. This can have its positive aspects, especially during an ensuing bereavement, but can also have its down side. The teenager suddenly has to take on responsibilities for the parents and/or other children, which tie them in with the family just when they are trying to separate and establish themselves in their own right. For Stella the role of carer helped her cope with her mother's illness and death.

'My sister Pauline reacted differently when Mum died. I wanted to look after Mum and decided to defer my A levels. Pauline was at university and Dad was at work, so it was my role to be Mum's carer, which was good. I looked after her for six weeks before she died and I liked doing that. She had looked after me when I was fourteen/fifteen and in a lot of trouble. This made us closer and I felt I could now give something back. I could do physical things for her and be there when she wanted

to talk. When she said goodbye to a friend – someone who had come to see her – I could sit next to her and cry with her, because it's so hard to say goodbye. When Pauline came back from university at the weekend it was harder for her because she didn't know the routine that Mum and I had built up. I knew what Mum needed, but I think that Pauline felt a bit alienated. She definitely found it harder, and was more shocked. We've talked a lot about it since, because Mum's death has brought us closer together. I miss Mum most when I hear something that I think she would find funny, or see something she would have wanted to know about.'

After the death of someone in the family, there is usually a pattern to your emotions. Initially you may feel shocked and numb. The event can seem unreal. It can be difficult to believe the death has actually happened, even if it was expected. How long each individual takes to get over this first stage varies a great deal. The ritual of a funeral may help the next few days and is well recognised as being an important supportive activity in most cultures. Few people die at home these days, so few young people see someone in the most terminal stages of an illness, and the death when it happens can appear unexpected. There is also a tendency to keep young people away from a parent who is seriously ill and not involve them in the funeral arrangements for fear of upsetting them. But feeling part of it all can actually help and quicken the grieving process. Stella felt involved at every stage and helped choose the content of the funeral service. It was she who very much wanted her mother buried with a gravestone rather than cremated. She wanted somewhere where she could go, to think about her life with her mother.

'I sometimes go and visit Mum's grave – not very often now, but I was the one who wanted her to be buried and

*not cremated. She agreed with that and it's really nice to
have her there for anniversaries and things. It is
somewhere to go, and the sun is always shining where she
is buried, and she has a lovely gravestone.'*

Immediately after a person's death and the funeral, there has
to be a shift in how one relates to others in the family. There
is a need to support each other, but for teenagers especially
there is also the need to re-establish their own lives. There
may also be a coming to terms with new relationships that the
remaining parent may develop. After her mother's death,
Stella found that the family dynamics changed again.

*'My relationship with Pauline is definitely closer now, and
with Dad too, partly because we have changed, but death
does draw people closer together. I think Dad has become
more adolescent in a way. He needs looking after as much
as I do, so it's become more like an equal friendship kind
of thing. We did have some counselling together. I was
going to a counsellor and she said I should bring Dad
along too. Well, Dad is about the worst person to try and
get to go to a counsellor – he hates them. But he did come
along and he really liked her and respected what she said.*

*'One of the things she said was that I was trying to take
on Mum's role and was trying to be more of a wife to Dad
than a daughter. That really threw me, because I am
meant to be becoming independent, separating myself
from home and branching out and living on my own. But
when I come home to Dad, I feel I ought to look after him
and cook for him and do his washing. What's more, I
think Dad quite likes it. I just feel sorry for him because
he must feel lonely. It's all right when he has a girlfriend
because she can do those kinds of things for him. I like it
when he has girlfriends because it means he is happy, but
the ones he has chosen so far have not been up to much.*

'Pauline and I judge Dad's girlfriends by what they seem

*to be after. Mum gave us strict instructions to vet them all
and make sure there weren't any money-grubbing ones.
There are lots of those around. Others are just total flirts. I
tend to argue with them a lot – especially the ones that are
highly opinionated. Some of them just talk a load of
bollocks and I argue back at them. I don't think I necessarily
want Dad to get married again. I'd rather a nice steady
girlfriend who he is happy with. We were talking about this
with him last night, and he was saying that in lots of ways
he is still totally engaged with Mum and Mum's memory.
He's always going through Mum's photos and sorting them
out. He still misses her a lot; they were together for so long
and, as far as I know, neither of them "strayed".'*

After the initial feelings of stunned shock and disbelief, these
emotions give way to feelings of loss and searching for the
person who has died. This is when the misery of someone's
death starts to feel real. Disconcertingly, as well as feeling sad, it
is common to feel angry with the person who has died. The
anger can also be directed towards other people, such as doctors and relatives, and may often be linked to feelings that they
have not done enough to help, or to prevent the person's death.
Guilt is another common feeling. There will always be sadness,
especially at birthdays and anniversaries, although sometimes
teenagers can find it difficult to express and can feel guilty, or be
made to feel guilty, that they do not feel sad enough.

Sometimes the feelings of sadness are so profound and difficult to get over that instead of passing through the stages of
grief, you get stuck with feelings of depression and fear which
may need treatment with anti-depressants. The pain of death
can also cause stress which shows itself as bad dreams, difficulty with sleeping and physical symptoms such as dizziness,
palpitations, headaches and loss of appetite. These things
usually pass in time.

Stella went through all these phases and three years on
some of the problems are still there.

'Missing Mum makes me very low and depressed. I also get bad dreams which range from people leaving to people dying and being torn between people who don't know one another. I get them all the time and they're so real and last so long that they make me feel depressed for the rest of the day. I try not to interpret them because I have been advised not to. Some people try and persuade me that God would be the answer to my problems, but I tell them to piss off because I think that's a load of bollocks.'

Another common worry is that the other parent will die or disappear. This anxiety can last for a long time and cause panic and anxiety, but recognising the problem and talking about it can help.

'The most difficult thing about Dad is when I feel that he is not there for me. I've told him this, and he's got better. There was one time I came home and he wasn't in and there was no food, and no heating on, and I didn't know where he was. I rang up all his friends and no one knew where he was and that made me really worried. He's a bit flighty at the moment. I need to know when he's going to be in and when he isn't. It's not that I have to know what he's up to – that's his business – but I need the security of knowing where he is. I think it might be a bit my fault, because I probably appear to be more independent now than I really am. It's definitely easier to talk to him about these things when he has a girlfriend, because he's more upbeat and on the level then. He's got an excellent sense of humour and gets on well with my friends. He knows I take cannabis and stuff. It's my way of coping, and he drinks a bit. He lets me do my own thing and is not judgemental. He does talk about Mum a lot.'

George was happily married to Jill for nineteen years. He runs a small family building firm in York and still lives in the family home, with his two daughters coming and going from college. He remembers clearly what it was like when his wife was first diagnosed with her breast cancer.

'When Jill first discovered it, Stella was only twelve. Jill wasn't ill of course, it was just that she had found a lump in her breast. At that time the girls didn't talk about their mother's cancer at all. She had her treatment, we all got on with our lives, and that was that. But four years later, when we suddenly knew that Jill had only a few weeks to live, we had to contact Pauline, who had just started at university. She packed her bags and came home. As soon as she arrived, the four of us went for a walk together. We walked for hours, and we talked about Jill's impending death, and what it meant to each of us. Jill explained how she felt, what she wanted us to do, and how she wanted us all to be around.

'Stella immediately took over the prominent care role. She nursed Jill day by day until she died and took care of all her most personal needs. I think that has done a lot to expiate the wounds she caused her mother earlier on. It was a reconciliation between them, sharing thoughts and experiences one to one. There was a danger there because in the past I had felt excluded from the relationship between the girls and Jill; but when Stella was looking after Jill during her last illness I didn't feel at all pushed out or rejected. I knew absolutely that I could not bring myself to do the things that Stella was doing for Jill during that last period.'

The remaining parent not only has the difficulty of coping with their children's grief but also has to deal with their own painful loss and their own needs. In retrospect George feels that in some ways he was not really there for the two girls immediately after their mother's death and has recurring 'if only' thoughts.

'Immediately after Jill died I was distracted, distraught and totally muddled. I wasn't really thinking about the girls at all. I wasn't attending to their needs or taking in what they were trying to say. I was in tears most of the time. It was a dark period with so little light. I had a great sense of destruction, of wanting to get rid of everything immediately, change everything and do something different. I wanted to be on my own, deal with my misery and find my own way in life again. Gradually, in time I became less distracted. I began working again and realising the needs of my daughters.

'But I do also remember saying to myself in those weeks of darkness after Jill's death that it should be a time of great sadness and of great joy. I was on the threshold of a new life, with the liberty to choose whatever I wanted to do, and yet I said to myself that I would trade all that liberty to have Jill back again. I still don't want that liberty. Too much liberty can be as dangerous as too little, or that is the way it appears to me.'

Friends and family usually provide most of the support in the immediate period after a death. It is after this 'busy' period that life can be lonely and difficult for the teenagers and the remaining parent. Long-term needs can be a real challenge and many bereaved families remark that the funeral is the 'easy' part. What is more difficult is the aftermath, when people stop phoning and making contact. The remaining family still feel needy and will not yet have adjusted to what is going to be a new way of life. For some people getting outside help proves useful, as it did for Stella.

'Since Jill's death the girls have changed enormously. This was clarified for me when I joined Stella for one of her counselling sessions. It provided a very helpful moment in teasing out the strands of what was going on, a year after

*Jill's death when Stella was feeling quite deeply
depressed. That session was a revelation about how, when
someone dies, other members of the family take on
different parts of the deceased person's function. Pauline,
our oldest daughter, and the one most like Jill, has taken
on her mother's persona. It is she who is now giving
advice to us both in the same understated way that her
mother did when she was alive. It is almost imperceptible
but very amusing when I recognise it. She's a natural
matriarch.*

*'For Stella, there is another figure who has become
greatly important, a grandmother and friend of the family
who at eighty has adopted Stella and acts as her
confidante. She has been an enormous support and has
probably taken over Jill's role in Stella's life.*

*'My own role is the "place of refuge" and comfort role. I
try and do what Jill would have done for them – making
up their beds with clean sheets and putting flowers in
their room when they come and stay, and sending them an
advent calendar through the post – little gestures which I
had never made before. I think they are terribly important
and I am amazed how much the girls appreciate it! They
still need a home, and one in which the memory of their
mother is still an important feature.'*

While it is normal for teenagers to get involved in new friendships and relationships during their adolescent years, it can
be very difficult for a widow or widower, especially if they
have been with one partner for many years. It is also difficult
for the children to know how to react to any new liaison.
There is a conflict between being there for the children but
also needing to start a new life.

George is very much aware of this conflict. He has had a
series of women friends since Jill died, and has mixed feelings
about handling the three-way relationship between himself,
his new women friends and his daughters.

'As far as me having new relationships is concerned, I think my daughters say one thing and mean another. They say, "Whatever makes you happy – we want you to have girlfriends," and Jill did say, before she died, that I shouldn't be inhibited about new relationships. I am sure she meant it wholeheartedly, especially as I think she had insight into the fact that I might have difficulty developing such relationships. She seemed more worried about me than about the children and I can understand that now. So that's on one level, but on another level Pauline is slightly mocking of me because she can see that, in many ways, I'm behaving like a seventeen-year-old and that a lot of my relationships are quite transient.

'My advice to other parents trying to find a new partner is that I think one should try and be reticent about one's activities because children's vulnerability in this area is great. Whether my daughters and their boyfriends are sleeping together or apart in our house has never been discussed and is never an issue. It has always been up to them, and we didn't want to know when Jill was alive. The same pertains now, but it is me who is embarrassed. It is a very tricky business which has many components, and in particular the sensitivities of the children and their loyalty to their mother.'

For most of the time, George feels he has to try to be both mother and father.

'Most of it now is using common sense to try and remain sensitive to the needs of the children and try to remember the rituals which used to go on in the family. Of course I would have to admit that those are as important for me as they are for the children. The doing of them was, and certainly is, a comfort. Things like putting flowers in their room, a continuing recognition of the girls' femininity – which is tricky for fathers left

*looking after daughters. One lasting factor though is
that Stella still gets nightmares, which feature my death
and Pauline's death, and in her dreams she sometimes
meets Jill again. These are disturbing experiences for
her.'*

It is easy to blame all the difficulties that occur after a
bereavement on the loss, rather than accepting that they are
issues which would have occurred anyway.

*'Some of the stuff we used to argue about was just
straightforward adolescent behaviour which I don't see
that I should bloody well put up with – like them doing
absolutely bugger all in terms of helping in the house, and
leaving piles of stuff they have only half eaten. They'd
come shopping with me at the supermarket and slip in
things for their own purposes. They have the ability to
turn anywhere they live into instant squalor.'*

There are some parallels between children whose parents
divorce and those who lose a parent from death, but parental
death does not carry the same risk of problems with mental
health, poverty and educational attainment. This may in part
be because when a parent dies the child does not feel so personally rejected.

George has the last word.

*'If one has children and loses a partner – from death,
separation or divorce – then the children are the reason
for continuing. Their needs cannot be denied. At the same
time it inhibits one's own personal development, one
cannot move on – sell the house, change one's life
completely, as one feels like doing. The old ways have got
to continue while the children develop. Any change of life-
style has to be suspended for the sake of the children. The
child becomes the absolute focus.'*

Things that a bereaved parent might find useful:

● teenagers may not want to talk about things immediately after the death of a parent but may want to get on with their lives. Not showing any external signs of being upset does not mean they are not grieving inside

● words may be difficult to find but hugs and other signs of affection can be just as comforting

● allow them to be teenagers still and don't expect them to behave like an adult or take on the role of the dead parent

● the remaining partner is often needy for a new relationship but this can be like a double bereavement for the children as it can be very exclusive. Try not to marry precipitously

● do not, however, become too dependent on your children

● if you remarry, many of the tips for step-parents will apply (see Chapter 10)

● seek help from your family doctor if you think your son or daughter is getting depressed

● there is some evidence that bereavement is less damaging for children than divorce as they feel less rejected

● if the parent has committed suicide, reassure the young person that it is not their fault

Things that may help bereaved teenagers

● do not feel guilty if you still want to go out and enjoy your-self

- understand that some of your friends will find it difficult to acknowledge that your mother or father has died, and will also find it hard to talk with you about your parent's death

- do not be afraid to show that you feel sad and depressed, for fear of upsetting your family

- fathers (and less often mothers) often start new relationships or remarry quickly after the death. This does not mean that they did not love your mother, or have betrayed her or you

- if the parent of a friend has died, do say something rather than pretending it has not happened for fear of upsetting them – it is much more hurtful for them to think you do not care

21

Conclusions, With Blissful and Not So Blissful Messages for Parents from Teenagers

Much of this book is based on the 'real life' experiences of teenagers and their parents – telling it like it is – rather than as the experts, or the media, see it. As can be seen, it can be great fun, it can be hell, and usually it is a combination of the two.

It is important to remember that teenagers do mature physically, emotionally and mentally at different rates in the same person, and at different rates in different people. These individual differences, which may even occur in teenagers within one family, need to be allowed for.

There is no perfect prescription for success – just hard work, sensitivity to needs, humour, and a great deal of understanding and patience on both sides. Although, as we have tried to highlight in the book, there are some things which make the relationship easier and some which make it more difficult.

If we could pick out five bits of advice from all those given they would be:

- whatever happens, make sure they know that when the chips are down you will be there to give them tender, loving care – come what may

- keep talking and communicating, however difficult that may be at times

- avoid face-offs – make sure that neither you nor your teenagers get backed into a corner

- be able to admit when you are wrong, so that they can learn to do likewise

- set parameters – within the boundaries set by their parents, teenagers can feel safe when they want to, and they can revolt when they want to test the limits of their independence

When all is said and done, if, at the end of the day, your teenagers have done some drugs, experimented with sex, smoked some tobacco and been drunk a number of times – and you and they are still talking and like one another – consider that you as parents, and they as teenagers, have done well.

We thought that teenagers themselves should have the last word and the following are a series of quotations from letters and e-mails received from young people in response to an advertisement in *Bliss* magazine (bought by girls, and read by boys and girls) asking young people what they thought of their parents.

PARENTAL 'FLAWS'

Sian, aged thirteen
Generally I like my parents. They can be funny, interesting and really nice most of the time, but they have several flaws

which are extremely annoying. My mother has no sense of privacy when it comes to me. If I go into her room without knocking, she goes berserk, but she never knocks when going into my room, and then complains when I lock the door! If she gives me a job to do around the house, she has to supervise and usually ends up doing it herself. Any corrections she makes don't stop at one sentence; they grow into a whole lecture. She and my father constantly complain about the state of my sister's room; it causes never-ending fights, but neither of us can see why it matters to them. Both me and my older sister are good at school but when we bring home a test result of maybe 97 per cent they ask, 'Where did the other three points go?' and 'Was that the highest in the class?' They take our good results for granted. When I got all As in my exams this year they both said 'well done' and went back to whatever they were doing before I told them. If that had been my friends' results their parents probably would have thrown a party. I'm seen as the good daughter in the house. My sister stays out late, drinks, never tells them where she's going, and is always losing money – so they give her more. It seems to me that she's rewarded for being bad and I'm taken for granted. Neither my father nor my mother can accept criticism or help graciously.

Having 'Respect'

Keith Janson, aged seventeen
I don't think my parents and I understand each other about anything. They cannot understand why I can be so moody and grumpy and find everything boring. They also think I am strange for getting up so late and going to bed so late (in the holidays I usually get up at about 1.30 p.m. and go to bed at 2 a.m.). They don't like the way I spend ages talking to my friends on the phone but don't really talk very much to my parents. Most of these things are classified as typical teenage

behaviour, and sometimes I cannot explain things I do, but I also find aspects of them and their behaviour annoying.

I think the best way for parents to react to their children is by respecting them and talking about things with them. For example, my dad tells me to respect him but when I say, 'You don't respect me,' he says that he doesn't have to because I am the child. This makes me very annoyed. I also disagree with violence. Sometimes small children need a smack but even then problems can be resolved by talking.

Rene Dreyfus, aged fourteen
Adults refer to teenagers as children when we feel and act older than we are. They are always speaking of how teenagers are terrible because they drink, smoke, and so on. But when I asked adult family and friends what they were like as teenagers, most of them said that they used to go to pubs when they were under-age, and used to smoke and drink. So where's the respect that we need to do the same things as they did?

Paula, aged fifteen
I hate it when parents say you're answering back, when you're voicing your opinion. Young adults should be treated with the same respect we treat our elders with. When me and my mam argue she acts really calm. I end up getting frustrated because she's not shouting back at me and I storm off, banging doors and stamping my feet. I do love my parents, but I think I shouldn't spend too much time with them, or we just annoy each other.

OLDER PARENTS AND HAVING RESPECT

Julia, aged fourteen
My parents are actually still together, so sometimes I feel in the minority! When I was born, my mum and dad were forty

years old and they are now fifty-four. The fact that my parents are quite a bit older than most never used to create many problems. Now, however, things are different. They were brought up in the 1950s and 60s. Their views and values are very different from the ones I have and the ones I'm forming. One thing I really choke on is their view on respect. My mother, especially, believes I should treat her with the utmost respect at all times, meaning that she can say and do whatever she wants towards me, but I have to be nice and polite and take everything she throws at me, which is a lot, especially when we're arguing. I believe I should be able to talk to her as I would to my sister or brother or uncle. She says she wants me to treat her like a friend, but I can't talk to her like I would to anyone else because in her eyes it's not respectful – let alone tell her my feelings. It's maddening, believe me!

'Pretty Embarrassing'

Sandra Hay, aged fourteen
My dad is pretty embarrassing. I wouldn't be seen dead with him around where we live because he gives the impression to people of being really stuck up (even though he isn't). He walks with a really straight back and his nose in the air. He also has a southern accent which some people laugh at, especially when he says 'Yah' instead of 'Yes'! He dresses OK, but is a real bore. His idea of a great day out is a visit to a museum. He also annoys me when he squeezes my cheeks. When I have boys round, he hangs around us as if we're going to do something we shouldn't. It's so embarrassing because the boys that come round are just friends. Some boys don't like coming round any more because Dad makes them feel guilty! He does have some good points. He's caring, generous, funny (well, sometimes) and I love him.

BEING 'ADOPTED'

Florence Welsh, aged sixteen
I want to be honest and praise my parents without feeling embarrassed although I know they are nothing to be embarrassed about. My parents adopted me when I was three, which was thirteen years ago, and from the first day they have given me a stable upbringing with lots of love, help and encouragement. Since me they have also adopted another child four years ago, and continued to foster in between. Having done all this didn't mean we each received less love from them, it just gave them more love for everyone. They are wonderful people who have survived through thick and thin. I sometimes find it hard to show these feelings and wish they could see how much I love and appreciate them. Things haven't always been plain sailing with me and I've had my fair share of problems, but my family has been strong and helped me through even when I acted like I didn't deserve or appreciate them. They never once turned their backs, and always tried to understand me.

BEING 'AN ONLY CHILD'

Shirley Bean, aged fourteen
All my friends think I'm lucky because I'm an only child and I get a lot, and everyone thinks my parents are safe because I've done a lot of things my friends wouldn't dare to do. They're wrong! I know they're supposed to give you advice to bring you up right, I know they have to tell you things, but I hate my dad for the way he does it. The first thing is that in February this year I was going out with a boy called James. I had been going out with him for two and a half months, but one night we all got drunk, all my mates, and we nicked £20 of alcohol from my house. It all came back on James and I couldn't ever see him again, but I don't think it's fair that he

got all the blame. My dad hates my new boyfriend, but he doesn't know enough about him to do so. I've had physical fights with him and my mum about it. All this arguing has caused fights, arguments, bad behaviour. I slit my wrists, took a drugs overdose (very close). I know I sound pretty stupid. I know I'm only a teenager and teenagers do stupid things. My dad won't listen to reason and he thinks of himself constantly. My mum is more calm, and I know that if she goes mad it's serious. I listen to her more because she doesn't go mad over petty things.

GREAT PARENTS

Ranjit Ahmed, aged thirteen
I've always been close to my parents, especially my mum. I can tell my mum anything, she's a great listener to my problems, but I know a lot of boys have trouble telling their mums. She's not only my mum, but my best friend too. We go shopping together and ice skating together and basically have a great time. I love her so much and I'm not embarrassed to tell anyone either. I'll sometimes even hold her hand when we're out shopping together. I must admit I get a few weird looks from other boys who are out as well, but I honestly don't care.

My dad, on the other hand, is very stubborn and hates it when he's wrong, where my mum is easy going. I don't have a special relationship with him, like I do with my mum. I think it's partly because he's a man like me, because I could never tell him all my problems like I tell my mum. I think I'd be embarrassed and shy.

One thing I like about both my parents is that they never pressurise me to do well in my exams or sports or anything. They just say as long as you do your best that's all that counts. If they put pressure on me I think I would do really badly!

Rhoda Smeath, aged thirteen

I'm just your average teenager, I guess! My parents? They're Pam and Stewart, but not altogether as bad as their names sound. My dad doesn't seem to like the combination of his daughter and boys! That's probably because he was once a hormone-driven teenager! Recently, while on holiday, my dad 'caught' me and my boyfriend in a 'compromising' position (kissing while lying down). He flaked and I realised that I'd just have to turn on the 'I'm a perfect daughter, you know I'm not going to do anything stupid' act. It worked! Mum reacted better to the 'situation' and I think that is because she trusts me more. I think my parents are gullible and they WANT to believe that their child is an angel. A few well-worded 'lies' and they're putty in my hands!

PARENTS 'FROM A DIFFERENT PLANET'

Katherine Spelted, aged sixteen

Parents, they come from a different planet. I mean, they always think they're right, always think they know the answer to everything. Mr and Mrs Perfect. I mean, I'm not saying we're all perfect, us children, but at least we can admit we are wrong every now and then, and don't go around thinking we are above everyone else.

Kim Krasser, aged fiteeen

It's hard enough being a young adolescent struggling through puberty, school, friends, etc. and to the everlasting list the word PARENTS is added. It's implosive! I'm sure everyone gets through it. When parents listen to your phone calls, observe your whereabouts, and question you, basically they start to cross the boundary from trusting you to examining you! I speak for all teenagers when I say we've had enough already. I mean parents, we love you dearly and we know you'd sacrifice anything for your children, but we need space and privacy to think about how we want to live our lives, not yours. Another thing that bothers me is the subject of SEX. We learn about it from books, magazines, school, television and friends. But when your mother talks to you about it, she looks more nervous than you! It's embarrassing.

Needing 'Boundaries'

Frances Penernt, aged fifteen
I'm fifteen years old and only now has Mum started to lighten up. Before, talking about periods, sex, boys was like talking to a brick wall. In fact, even now we don't talk about sex. I mean, what is it with that subject? Everybody does it at some point, so why all the embarrassment? If our parents were to be a bit more open about it, and tell us the difference between the right and wrong of having a sexual relationship, then maybe we wouldn't have such different and confused feelings towards it. I am fifteen, and was friendly with a man who was twenty-five, and I was allowed to see him. I know it might sound a bit two-faced but I wish that I wasn't allowed. Mum should have said 'no', as I do need them to set boundaries.

Parents are Great

Sheila Hadan, aged fifteen
I live with my mum and my (annoying) sister. My mum is really generous and kind and I have realised this much more as I have grown older. She usually listens to what I have to say but is often embarrassingly forgetful, like when I tell her something that one of my friends has done and then I bring it up an hour later and end up having to tell her half of the story again.

One thing I really like my mum for is giving me privacy. I have been allowed a lock on my door to stop my sister barging in, and my mum always knocks before she tries to open the door. Also, when I write letters to friends and she asks to read them and I say 'no', she just accepts it and drops the matter.

Suni Janaka, aged thirteen
I think my parents are great, they are the best. They are always there when I need them and buy me whatever I want. I go to most places with them and have a great time, like I do when I go out with my friends. They don't embarrass me like some parents do. People normally say they butt into your business, but that's only because they care.

Ruth Sunderland, aged fifteen
Everyone loves their parents differently and everyone has different standards to expect from their parents, but in the end your parents are all that you need in the world – apart from a Hi-Fi, boyfriend/girlfriend, chocolate etc.! If you didn't have parents, who would pick you up from town at 5 a.m. when you were absolutely out of your head? Who would be there for you when your mates weren't? Who changed the bed when you were little because you'd had an accident?

HATES

Susanna Breton, aged fourteen
I hate it when my mum promises to take me somewhere, and before we go there she drags me round to every other place possible and then says, 'Oh look, we haven't got time to go there now.'

Brenda Chamberlain, aged seventeen
I am seventeen, and for as long as I can remember I have hated my parents. I tried for a long time to get on with them, but nothing worked. It is not just a bad patch, nor is it me being at a difficult age, as my younger brother feels the same way.

Zoë Fanshaw, aged fourteen

She listens to my phone conversations, she asks me every day what I'm doing the next day, who I'm going out with, what's their name; and she can even read my diary when I'm not at home. How can I love a mum like this?

She used to tell me what I should wear and should not wear, it was a nightmare. Anything that is showing is not good, no short skirt, no short top, no nothing. It is OK at home, but how can I face my friends? Thank God now she doesn't care any more. You know what? Last month she bought me this white T-shirt which was very nice, but unfortunately it was kind of tight. I love it, I mean it's meant to be like that, it's the design. I put it on straightaway thinking this time Mum will be happy. When I came home she told me never ever to wear it again, because I look like a pig in it, it is too tight. I was soooo upset, what should I do? And another thing about mums is that they never say sorry. Whatever they've done wrong, they don't say sorry. I shout at her, I scream at her, I hate her, but at the end of the day I feel guilty, after all she is my mum. I want to say, 'I love you, Mum', but I don't know how.

Sian Agent, aged fourteen

My 'olds' are divorcees. I live with my mum and sister. But my dad, God, there's a subject, I could go on forever. Why do parents inflict stepfamilies on us? Why is it that dads never see the bitchiness that comes from their partners to their children? Also, why are dads so worried about short skirts and make-up? Do they think if we wear these we are going to jump into bed with whoever comes along?

Adrian Drinkwater, aged thirteen

Everyone thinks my mum and stepdad are cool! I think it's 'cos they don't care if my friends smoke or drink around them or something – but I think my parents are bloody embarrassing. OK, let's take a prime example – my twelfth birthday party! It was a really big house party and I'd made my parents stay upstairs, but then they heard the music – and horror of all horrors they started dancing! Not everyday dancing or anything, but dancing like a couple of chickens or something!

A PARENT DYING

Ruska Grieves, aged fourteen
I find it hard to write about my dad because he died about three years ago on Fathers' Day. I was staying at my friend's house overnight and we were going to the zoo the next day. In the morning my friend's mum woke me up and said that I had to go home. This was when I found out. I didn't know how my dad died until about a week later – my mum just said, 'He had an accident and it was horrible.' I was shocked still and just accepted it. My mum got my sister and me together in the lounge and explained that my dad had taken his own life but she didn't know why. I still feel confused. No one knows why he did it. I feel anger towards my dad for leaving me, but I still really miss him. I don't like talking about him and when my mum does I usually find an excuse to leave the room.

ROWING PARENTS

David Appleyard, aged twelve
I get on quite well with my parents, especially my mum. I try to stay as far away from rows as possible 'cos I hate them, so I usually just do what I'm told. My dad is quite easygoing anyway, but my mum can fly off the hook easily.

Jan Sinclair, aged fourteen
My parents continually argue. From the minute my mum gets home at 6 p.m. she is on my back about something: housework, what I am wearing, why I'm not doing homework, or

why I haven't started tea. Things don't get better at 7 p.m. when my dad gets home. Lately I have made things a bit worse by fighting back. I was thinking how pathetic it was that I am scared of my parents. To start with I thought it was because I didn't like them fighting because I love them, but then I realised that I didn't love them at all. When my dad started yelling at me the other day about why I hadn't videoed a film, I calmly said, 'Because you didn't ask me to.' I honestly was careful not to be sarcastic or rude, because I really am scared of my dad when he gets mad, but it still wasn't good enough. He turned to my mum and started having a go at her saying something was wrong with me the way I'd been brought up, and it was obviously Mum's fault. Mum then had a go at me for putting Dad in a bad mood and how I should have just let him yell at me.

Loving Bits, Hating Bits

Jeanette Barlow, aged fourteen
My dad is sweet and caring and a nice dad, and he does care about me, but he is a bit of a mess. He never tries hard enough to make it nice for us, and although I love him, sometimes his faults put me off him. My mum is the best, she really tries to make life good. But I hate the way she always has to shout at us and she always tells me off for fighting with my sisters, but she doesn't see how irritating they are. I also hate the way she always tells me to tidy my room as it is a pigsty.

'Extremely Annoying'

Jennifer Ladlow, aged sixteen
An extremely annoying thing about my mum and dad is that they absolutely hate my friends. They always say I could do

better than them, especially my dad, but my friends are really nice, most of the time. You know, we're teenagers, we go through funny phases – being obsessed with boys, make-up, stuff like that. Sometimes I do stupid things like starve myself for a few days, or go on stupid diets, and then my parents have me labelled as a psychological wreck. If it was humanly possible, I'd say my parents were born adults, that they'd never been sixteen, never been young, because they just don't understand me – no one does, but I suppose that's just me. I know this is a really horrible thing to say, but if I could choose my parents I don't think I'd choose the ones I have now. I'd choose more like Madonna and Leonardo DiCaprio.

CONFUSED MESSAGES

William Jacobs, aged thirteen
I am confused. I live with both my real parents. I do love them, but I don't really show it. My youngest sister is spoilt more than me. My parents always give my sister money and when I ask for money I get a lecture on how I should be saving my money and not spending it as soon as I get it. I am the oldest child in the family. My sister is eleven and I am thirteen. My sister keeps backchatting my mum and keeps being cheeky but she doesn't get told off or grounded. When I do it I get grounded.

BEING LET DOWN

Ian Ranson, aged thirteen
My dad upsets me sometimes because he doesn't keep his promises. At the start of the World Cup he asked me which team I was going for because Ireland weren't playing. I told him Brazil and he said that my stepmum's sister had bought

him a Brazil shirt which was too small, and that he would give it to me, even though it would be too big. I was so excited but on my next visit to my dad, my stepmum's seven-year-old son was wearing my Brazil shirt. I felt so sad I could cry. It was just another empty promise.

Appendix 1

Contraception

WHAT GCSE OR A LEVEL GRADE WOULD YOU GET IN SEX AND CONTRACEPTION?

Please answer the following questions.

1 How many hours after having unprotected intercourse can you still use emergency contraception?
  – 2 hours
  – 12 hours
  – 24 hours
  – 48 hours
  – 72 hours
  – 5 days

2 From which of the following can you get emergency contraception?
  – local chemist
  – your own GP
  – any GP
  – a family planning clinic
  – local hospital Accident and Emergency Department

3 Under which of the following circumstances should you consider using emergency contraception?
  – the pill is taken four hours late
  – when using the withdrawal method you/he fails to come out

- the condom splits or drops off – just isn't there when it should be!
- ejaculation occurs somewhere near, but not in, the vagina
- when having unprotected sex in what is considered the 'safe' period

4 At what speed does sperm leave the end of the penis during ejaculation?
- 5 miles an hour
- 13 miles an hour
- 28 miles an hour
- 39 miles an hour
- 56 miles an hour

5 How long does the average sperm hang out in the average vagina (and/or environs)?
- 4 hours
- 12 hours
- 36 hours
- 4 days
- a week

6 Which of the following are reliable methods of contraception?
- withdrawal
- the 'safe' period
- condoms
- the cap
- spermicidal jelly
- the pill
- the Femidom (the female condom)

7 Which is the best method of contraception to use?
- non penetrative sex
- condoms

- the cap
- the pill
- 'NO'
- an IUD (or coil)
- withdrawal
- 'safe' period
- Femidom

8 Two seventeen-year-olds get carried away and have
   unprotected sex once. What are the chances of her
   getting pregnant?
   - 10%
   - 20%
   - 30%
   - 40%
   - 80%
   - 100%

9 Which of the following are true about the pill?
   - it makes you fat
   - it's 100% safe
   - it helps protect you against sexually transmitted diseases
   - it causes cancer
   - it makes you infertile if you take it for a long time
   - you shouldn't smoke and be on the pill
   - it makes you depressed
   - it makes it more likely that you will have sex

10 A man who is HIV negative has vaginal intercourse
    once with a woman who is HIV positive. What are the
    chances of him catching the AIDS virus?
    - 1 in 5
    - 1 in 20
    - 1 in 50
    - 1 in 100
    - 1 in 1000

ANSWERS

1   72 hours – so don't wake the doctor at 2 a.m. but do get
    it as soon as possible the next day. If the doctor's
    receptionist won't give you an emergency appointment,
    don't take 'no' for an answer. It may help to explain
    what it's about so don't be embarrassed.

2   You can get it from:
    – your own GP
    – any GP
    – a family planning clinic
    – local hospital Accident and Emergency Department
    Sometime in the future it may be available over the
    counter from the local chemist, but not yet alas.

3   It is needed if:
    – the withdrawal method fails. It only takes a minute
      amount of sperm to get pregnant. Each 2ml of the
      stuff contains 20,000,000 or so sperms – enough to
      populate the whole of Australia at one go.
    – the condom splits or drops off. The same applies – a
      little sperm goes a long way.
    – unprotected sex occurs in what is known as the 'safe'
      period. Unless you are willing to monitor your
      periods, temperature, and vaginal mucus changes
      throughout each month, there is no such thing as an
      absolutely 'safe' period. It's just a less 'unsafe' period.

4   28 miles an hour is the average, but don't ask how it
    was measured! Trapped by a speed camera? No fines for
    over 30 mph though.

5   Most sperm are fragile little things and die off quickly.
    However, they can last for up to four days – and watch
    out for the 'seven-day' lunatic fringe.

6 Depends on what you mean by 'reliable'. There is
'reliable' for not getting pregnant and 'reliable' for not
getting a sexually transmitted infection (STI).
Condoms: good for not getting pregnant. Ninety-eight
women out of a hundred using condoms for a year
every night will not get pregnant. Also 'the best' against
getting an STI.
The Pill: 'the best' for not getting pregnant, if taken
carefully. The combined pill is virtually 100 per cent
safe. Offers no protection against STIs.
The cap: good protection against pregnancy. Ninety-six
women in a hundred using the cap every night for a
year will not get pregnant. Helps protect against STIs.
Femidom (female condom): like the male equivalent,
good for not getting pregnant and protects against
STIs – but oh dear, it's a bit noisy!
Spermicidal jelly, withdrawal and the 'safe' period: none
of these are very safe methods if you don't want to get
pregnant, but they are better than nothing. They are no
good at protecting you against STIs.

7 There is no best overall method, only a best individual
method for you and your partner. You may not want to
go on saying 'NO' indefinitely so you had better sort
something out in advance for when you want to say
'YES'. If you're an optimist, you'll be pleased at all the
different choices. If you're a pessimist, you'll feel that
all of them have their drawbacks. You have to end up
being a pragmatist and choose one of the methods. The
best method for you will be 'best' according to the type
of relationship you are involved in, your previous
experience, and your anxieties. What is best in one
relationship may not be best in another.

8 It depends on where in the woman's cycle intercourse
occurs. The egg is normally released about fourteen

days before the next period and the chances of getting pregnant at this time are 30 per cent. For about five to ten days either side of this time, the chances are 20 per cent; and for the rest of the menstrual cycle (what little there is of it) the chances are 0 to 10 per cent – but don't rely on that '0'.

9 The truth about the pill:
   – it makes you fat – NOT TRUE. A small percentage of women put on a few pounds, but you can nearly always find a pill that doesn't cause this problem.
   – it's 100 per cent safe – TRUE. If it is taken properly it is almost 100 per cent effective at stopping you getting pregnant.
   – it helps protect you against sexually transmitted infections – NOT TRUE. It does not protect you against STIs and it might be a good idea to use the pill and condoms.
   – it causes cancer – NOT TRUE AND TRUE. The pill reduces the risk of ovarian and uterine (womb) cancer, but if you take it for five years or more there is probably a small increased risk of cervical cancer (which is very rare anyway). It's therefore a good idea to have regular cervical smears from the age of twenty. The other cancer that may be affected by taking the pill is breast cancer. We still don't know exactly how breast cancer risk is altered but while you are on the pill there is a small increased risk of breast cancer which disappears ten years after stopping it.
   – it makes you infertile if you take it for a long time – NOT REALLY TRUE. The pill does not make you infertile. However, if you have taken it for many years and you stop to try to get pregnant, it might take a bit longer than usual – up to two years.
   – you shouldn't smoke and be on the pill – TRUE. It is

best not to smoke anyway, but apart from all the nasty things fags do, if you smoke and take the pill you have an increased chance of having a heart attack or a blood clot, though it's still a very small risk.

- it makes you depressed – TRUE and NOT TRUE. Most people do NOT get depressed on the pill, but a small percentage do get mood changes. If it happens to you, the best thing is to change pills and see if you can find one that suits you better (there are over ten different combinations).
- it makes it more likely that you will have sex – NOT TRUE. Whether people have sex or not doesn't seem to depend on whether they are on the pill or not. Most studies indicate that it depends on the immediate circumstances: the attraction of the partner, the time of night, alcohol, privacy, bed available, and so on.

10 The answer is between 1 in 100 and 1 in 1000 – though it is probably towards the 1 in 1000 end. These are better chances than in Russian roulette, but why take the risk when you can (a) do lots of sexy things without having intercourse or (b) use a condom. When an HIV negative woman has sex with an HIV positive man, the risk goes to the 1 in 100 end. Women have a higher risk of getting it from men than men from women.

Your grade:

If you scored 80% to 100% you get an A* or an A
If you scored 70% to 80% you get a B
If you scored 60% to 70% you get a C
If you scored 50% to 60% you get a D or an E
Below 50% is a failure and you'll have to retake – so no sex with anyone until you pass.

The two most commonly used methods of contraception that young people use are the condom and/or the pill. But surveys show that 30 to 50 per cent of young people having sex for the first time do not take any precautions.

The choices of contraception available are condoms, the combined pill, the progesterone only pill, the diaphragm or cap, spermicides, the female condom(Femidom), the 'safe' period with fertility awareness, withdrawal, progesterone injections, and the IUD or coil. Other methods are being developed but at the moment these are all variations on a theme rather than anything really revolutionary. It sounds as though there is a lot to choose from, but it's less than it seems and not all of them are ideal for young people.

A YOUNG PERSON'S GUIDE TO CONTRACEPTION

	Condoms	Pill	Cap	Withdrawal	Non-penetrative sex
For one-night stands	Excellent	OK	OK	Better than nothing!	Excellent
To avoid sexually transmitted diseases	Excellent	No good	OKish	Useless	OK
For long-term relationships	Excellent	Excellent	Good	Not reliable	OK (as long as non-penetration lasts!)
If you must smoke	Excellent	Some risks	Good	Not reliable	Excellent
'Just in case you get the urge'	Excellent	OK	OK	Not reliable	Excellent
Neither has had sex before	Excellent	Excellent	Not so easy	Not reliable	Excellent
He's had sex before, she hasn't	Excellent	OK	Not so easy	Not reliable	Excellent
She's had sex before, he hasn't	Excellent if she can get it on	OK	OK	Not reliable	Excellent
You want to end the relationship	JUST DON'T DO IT: THERE ARE MORE UNWANTED PREGNANCIES AT THE BEGINNING AND END OF RELATIONSHIPS				

'I Promise I Won't Come' is Not a Good Method of Contraception

Emergency Contraception

It is estimated that 100,000 abortions in the UK could be avoided each year if everyone who was at risk because of split condoms, getting carried away, and so on, had used emergency contraception. It works for up to seventy-two hours after the unprotected intercourse occurred, but it is more likely to work the sooner it is taken. It is available from any GP, family planning clinic, or Accident and Emergency Department. It is free, and in the future it may be available over the counter. It can be used more than once – even during one month – but if this happens, someone is not taking sex and contraception seriously and a trip to the family doctor, family planning clinic, or chemist is recommended.

There are two types of emergency contraception pills. They both work by stopping implantation of the fertilised egg. One method is to take two pills containing a combination of oestrogen and progesterone at higher doses than in the ordinary contraceptive pill taken twelve hours apart. They are 96 per cent effective in stopping pregnancy, but can cause nausea and sickness. The alternative is a high dose progesterone pill regime which is even more effective and less likely to cause sickness.

The other method of emergency contraception is to have an intra-uterine device (IUD) put in which works for up to five days after unprotected intercourse.

Condoms

Condoms are the best protection against pregnancy, STIs and AIDS. They come in different sizes, from a minimum British Standard width of 48mm (1.89 inches), length 160mm (6.2 inches) to a US brand of 65mm (2.2 inches) width and

220mm (8.66 inches) length. You can take your pick. Condoms protect women against cancer of the cervix. They come in different colours, different shapes (flared, contoured, ribbed), different flavours, and can be bought anywhere. Only two women in every hundred using condoms every night for a year will get pregnant. They can be obtained free from any family planning clinic and some family doctors.

The Combined Pill

The combined pill contains two hormones, progesterone and oestrogen, in different proportions in different makes of pill. These hormones stop the ovary producing an egg each month. The pill is the most reliable form of contraception. If taken according to instructions, less than one woman in a hundred will get pregnant in a year. While on it, women have regular periods each month and they tend to be lighter than usual. It may reduce pre-menstrual tension (PMT). It doesn't interfere with making love. It is not messy, and men like it because they don't have to take any responsibility. However, it is safer to use the pill and condoms together! The pill also protects against cancer of the womb and the ovaries, and some pelvic infections.

There are some disadvantages to the combined pill. It does not offer protection against STIs or AIDS. It needs to be taken every day. Some women do get minor side-effects, including mood changes, weight gain, tender breasts and headaches; but there is usually one pill available which will avoid these problems. Taking the pill does not mix well with smoking, as it increases the risk of developing a blood clot. It also causes a slightly increased risk of getting cancer of the breast and the cervix.

The Minipill

The minipill contains only the progesterone hormone. This is an option if the combined pill cannot be taken because of side-effects or other contra-indications. It works by changing the mucus around the cervix so that the sperm find it more difficult to enter the womb. If they do get through, the fertilised egg finds it more difficult to develop in the womb. Most people get no problems on this pill but some do get mood changes and irregular bleeding throughout the cycle. It is no good for those who are bad at time-keeping as it has to be taken at the same time every day. If taken correctly it is 99 per cent effective, but it does not protect against STIs.

The Depot (Progesterone) Injection

This is similar to the progesterone contraceptive pill, but is given as an injection which needs repeating every three months.

The Cap or Diaphragm

The cap is a rubber device which is used with spermicide. It is inserted into the vagina and covers the cervix. It can be put in some time before sex and must be left in for at least six hours afterwards. The cap gives some protection against STIs, and if it is used properly around ninety-six out of a hundred women using it regularly will not get pregnant. It does have to be fitted by a doctor or nurse and the spermicide is a bit messy.

Intra-uterine Device (IUD) or Coil

This consists of a bit of plastic covered in copper and/or a hormone, which is inserted through the cervix into the uterus. The coil is not routinely recommended for young women who have not had children as it can increase the risk of getting infected fallopian tubes, which might affect future chances of getting pregnant.

Spermicides

These can be bought over the counter. They are not very effective used alone, but they are better than nothing and they do help kill the AIDS virus as well as the sperm.

Natural Methods: Rhythm or Safe Period

Women ovulate (release an egg) fourteen to sixteen days prior to the first day of their next period and this is therefore the time when they are most likely to get pregnant.Their temperature goes up slightly and their vaginal mucus changes in character at ovulation.

Natural methods combine taking the temperature and testing the vaginal mucus with charting the timing of periods over several months to identify the more risky times to have intercourse. This is only a reliable method for those who have absolutely regular periods and are willing to be obsessional. It is not usually a good method for young people.

The Femidom (female condom)

The Femidom is very effective for the prevention of pregnancy and STIs. Users say it is noisy, but it does fit all sizes of erect penises and can be bought over the counter. It doesn't need fitting but is expensive for sex every night.

Withdrawal

This involves withdrawing the penis from the vagina before orgasm and ejaculation, and is much too reliant on men's self-control – not known to be reliable at the best of times! This method is widely used by everyone but, though it is better than nothing, it is not safe.

Appendix 2
Sexually Transmitted Infections (STIs)

Sex is fun but it can bring trouble. Sexually transmitted infections (STIs) have no regard for age. They can all be caught by having unprotected sex with someone carrying an infection. However, most, but not all of them, can be prevented by using a condom during sex. Other infections, such as cystitis, thrush and bacterial vaginosis, can occur without having sex but they are often associated with sexual activity. The sexually transmitted infections include herpes, trichomonas, chlamydia, gonorrhoea, genital warts, hepatitis B and HIV. Unfortunately they often come as a package deal and more than one infection can be caught at the same time.

This is a simple guide to sexually transmitted infections for parents and teenagers. Anyone who suspects they have been infected should get help immediately. An appointment can be arranged with a GP or at a young persons' clinic. The Brook Advisory Clinics and the Genito-Urinary Medicine Clinics (GUMs) are staffed by experts in sexually transmitted infections and all offer a totally confidential service. Some people find the anonymity of a GUM clinic less embarrassing than seeing a GP. These clinics are attached to hospitals, are free, and will not report the visit to the person's GP without permission.

Knowing whether one has a sexually transmitted infection can be a problem, particularly for a young person who may be shy or embarrassed to talk about it. But there are clues. For women the normal vaginal discharge may alter. It may get heavier, change in smell and/or colour and consistency. The normal vaginal discharge is white, but it changes to yellowish with a slight odour when it comes into contact with the air. For men there may be a discharge from the penis which should not occur except during ejaculation. For both sexes any localised sores or soreness around the genital area can also indicate an STI.

Women should seek help if they have:

- a vaginal discharge which is different from usual: smelly, of greater quantity, of different consistency, or a different colour
- pain on peeing
- sores or blisters around the vulva
- warty lumps around the vagina
- an itchy/sore vagina

Men should seek help if they have:

- a discharge from their penis
- pain on peeing
- warty lumps on the penis or around it
- painful sores or blisters on or around the penis
- an itchy penis

THE INFECTIONS

Trichomonas, Trich or TV

A tiny parasite called a protozoa and named *trichomonas vaginalis* causes a thin yellow or green frothy vaginal discharge in women. The discharge has an unpleasant fishy smell. It also causes soreness and itching around the vagina. Sometimes there are no signs at all and the infection is detected at a routine cervical smear; but cervical smears are not routine until the age of 20. Trichomonas is caught by unprotected sexual intercourse. The diagnosis is confirmed by a vaginal swab whereby a sample of the discharge is checked in the laboratory. Men may get no symptoms from this infection, but sometimes notice discomfort when urinating.

Treatment
A short course of antibiotics (metronidazole, also known as flagyl) should clear it. Partners must also be treated to prevent reinfection.

Herpes (herpes simplex virus one or HSV1)

There are many different kinds of the herpes virus. Herpes simplex (type I) usually causes cold sores, and herpes simplex (type II) usually causes genital herpes, but there is a bit of swapping around because of oral sex. Herpes can affect both men and women. It is caught by unprotected sex. Some people will have just one attack of genital herpes and then never get it again, while others get recurrent attacks from the same original infection. Small clear blisters form around the penis or vulva, in the vagina, or around the anus, and burst leaving a painful sore area. To confirm the diagnosis a swab should be taken from the blister or the sore area and sent to the laboratory. The first attack is always the worst and can be associated with a flu-like illness. Sex should be avoided if any blisters or sores are present as they are very infectious. Condoms are a must as the virus does tend to hang around even when you don't have sores. However, you are less likely to pass it on when you don't have the sores. A sign that the blisters are about to come out again is a tingling sensation around the penis or vulva, so you know not to have sex then.

Treatment

The good news is that there are now anti-viral agents, including Acyclovir and Vanciclor, which shorten the attacks of genital herpes and reduce the number of recurrences. So it is important to start treatment as soon as an attack begins. The anti-viral drugs are only available on prescription from a GP or a GUM clinic.

Genital Warts

These are common and are caused by human papilloma viruses. There are thirty different kinds of wart viruses. Some are responsible for verrucae and finger warts, while others cause genital warts around the penis, vagina or anus. Genital warts are usually caught during intercourse or by close contact. There are no routine special tests for warts but you know when you have them from the way they look! They may not appear for up to a year after being in contact with the virus, though the average interval is around three months. Most types of warts don't do much harm, but they aren't very pretty. It is now thought that some strains of the human papilloma viruses which cause genital warts are linked to cervical cancer. The types of virus that are associated with cancer, however, are not usually the ones that cause the visible fleshy lumps, but those that can be found on cervical smears.

Treatment and avoidance

Treatment depends on where they are. Warts on the vulva or penis are treated with a chemical called Podophyllin which is available on prescription. Some just disappear on their own. If the wart virus is found on the cervix at a cervical smear, you may need to have smears at more frequent intervals, and if there are any early pre-cancerous changes, these can easily be treated.

Chlamydia

This is caused by a bacteria called *Chlamydia trachomatis*. The nasty thing about this infection is that women can have it without being aware of any symptoms, although the bacteria can be causing damage to the fallopian tubes. This pelvic inflammatory disease (PID) can cause infertility in the future. With a mild attack of PID the risk of a blocked tube is 3 per cent. After three bad attacks of PID the risk is more like 75 per cent. PID can produce a vaginal discharge, or just extra moisture in the vagina, because the chlamydia has inflamed the cells of the cervix. In men it can cause inflammation of the urethra, making it sting and burn during peeing. It sometimes causes a slight white cloudy bit of fluid to ooze out from the tip of the penis. This is usually called Non-Specific Urethritis (NSU). The only way to catch it is through unprotected sexual intercourse so condoms should stop the spread of this infection. It is now being suggested that all young women should be tested for chlamydia whenever they have any abnormal vaginal discharge or when they have a new partner. GUM clinics will always test for chlamydia but a family doctor may not. The GUM clinic is therefore sometimes a better bet. Always ask to have the chlamydia test.

Treatment
A two-week course of antibiotics should clear chlamydia and partners should always be treated also.

Non Specific Urethritis (NSU)

NSU is just an overall name for inflammation of the man's urethra (the tube running down the inside of a man's penis). The result is penile discharge and pain in the penis. The commonest cause of this inflammation is chlamydia (see above). However, there is no identifiable bug to be found in all those who have NSU, and the bug causing it can have been around for a while without creating problems. This means that you could be with a steady partner and suddenly get NSU, from bugs which have been in you or your partner for some time. The discharge and urine need to be tested by a family doctor or at a GUM clinic. NSU can also be caused by the bug called *trichomonas* (see earlier).

Treatment
The treatment is a course of antibiotics (usually doxycycline). Partners also need to be treated to prevent reinfection.

Gonorrhoea

This is caused by a bacteria called *Neisseria gonorrhoea* and the infection is also known as 'the clap'. It is now more common among homosexuals in the UK. It is caught by having sex (anal, oral or vaginal) because the bacteria doesn't like living outside the body and needs a nice warm spot like the vagina or urethra. A discharge occurs between two days and three weeks after catching it, but beware, as up to 90 per cent of women do not know they have got it but can still pass it on. A discharge or soreness should always be checked. The diagnosis is made by sending swabs from the vagina and/or penis to the laboratory for testing.

Treatment
The treatment for both partners is an antibiotic, which should prevent damage to the fallopian tubes and possible infertility. As with most STIs, condoms help to stop this infection being spread.

AIDS and HIV

AIDS stands for Acquired Immune Deficiency Syndrome. It is an infectious disease caused by the Human Immuno-deficiency Virus. This virus is carried in the blood stream and is transmitted via the blood during sexual intercourse (vaginal or anal), on used needles (and before blood was tested, by blood transfusions). It cannot be caught from kissing, oral sex, touching, lavatory seats, door knobs, swimming pools, or drinking glasses. On a 'one-off' basis, the chances of catching AIDS during sexual intercourse from an infected partner is between 1 in 100 and 1 in 1000, with a woman being more likely to catch it from an infected man than vice-versa. Risk is a difficult concept. A risk of 1 in 100 to some young people might seem low, but most of them would not get in a car if they knew they had a 1 in 100 chance of dying on that particular journey. Tests are available from GUM clinics or a family doctor for the HIV virus, but it takes three months or more after being infected for the test to become positive. During that three months a person might be infectious. It can take ten or more years for someone who is HIV positive to get symptoms of AIDS, but they are infectious for all of this time; and most if not all infected people will develop AIDS. Most cases of AIDS in this country at the present time are in homosexuals, intravenous drug users and haemophiliacs, but the pattern is starting to change. More heterosexuals are now among the new cases and people found to be HIV positive.

Treatment
There are various combinations of drugs available now to treat AIDS but, though the outlook is better then previously, there is still no cure.

SEXUALLY RELATED PROBLEMS

Thrush

This is also known as a yeast infection, candida or monilia. Thrush in women is the most common cause of an itchy vaginal discharge, but it can also cause soreness and redness around the vagina, vulva or anus. Sometimes the discharge looks like cottage cheese. It may also become painful to pee or have sex because everything around the vagina is inflamed. The man's penis can get itchy, red and sore around the glans, sometimes with associated white spots.

The yeast normally lives on the skin in warm, moist places (such as armpits, under the breasts, or in the groin), in the intestines, and in the vagina of 20 per cent of women without them even knowing. It can be caught from a sexual partner who has thrush though he/she may not have any symptoms. Thrush is not strictly considered a sexually transmitted infection, as men and women can get it after taking antibiotics or steroids, or when diabetic or pregnant. All of these probably cause a change in acidity in the body encouraging the yeast to multiply. A swab from the vagina, vulva or penis is taken to check for the yeasts. Most women will experience a thrush infection some time in their lives.

Treatment

Once the thrush has been diagnosed there are a variety of creams and pessaries which can be inserted into the vagina or applied to the vulva and/or penis. One of these, clotrimazole (Canesten), can be bought without prescription. A pill called fluconazole is available with or without prescription. Self-help remedies include vinegar in the bath, eating live yoghurt and, for women, putting live yoghurt on a tampon and inserting it into the vagina.

Pubic Lice or Crabs

These are usually caught during sex. They are little parasitic insects and cause intense itching in the pubic area because of their bites. Theoretically they can be caught from towels, sheets or a toilet seat, though this is very rare.

Treatment
Disinfectant shampoos, creams and lotions are available without prescription.

Bacterial Vaginosis

This is caused by the normal bacteria which live in the vagina multiplying and making trouble. The most common of these is a bacteria called *gardnerella*. The vaginal discharge may become grey and watery with a fishy odour. The infection can be passed sexually between partners, but in men this bacteria usually does not cause problems. It is diagnosed by taking swabs from the vagina which are tested in the laboratory.

Treatment
The usual treatment is an antibiotic – usually metronidazole, or some cream called Clindamycin which can be inserted into the vagina. If the problem recurs, both partners should be treated.

Cystitis

Cystitis means inflammation of the bladder or urethra so that it hurts to pee, most often because of a bacteria, *Escherica coli*, which normally lives in the rectum but creeps up the urethra. It is commonly but not always associated with sexual intercourse. It occurs more often in women because a woman's urethra is much shorter than a man's and it is easier for the bacteria to get in. Men do get cystitis but less often, and it is more likely to be linked to an STI. Cystitis can also be caused by viruses, and allergies to soaps and vaginal deodorants. A urine test will help sort out the diagnosis, and there is now a special stick impregnated with chemicals which changes colour when dipped into urine infected by bacteria. This test does not tell you what is causing the infection, but it does help to indicate if an infection is present. A urine sample has to be cultured in a laboratory to identify the actual bug. Some women get symptoms of cystitis even though no bacteria can be cultured. Any teenager getting cystitis for the first time should get it checked out.

Treatment
Drinking lots of fluid helps flush out the bacteria. Just about anything will do, but a teaspoon of baking soda in a cup of water works especially well, as does cranberry juice. Coffee and alcohol sometimes aggravate cystitis, while aspirin or paracetamol help the pain. A short course of antibiotics may be needed.

Appendix 3
Drugs

The names of illegal drugs and the language associated with their use change rapidly but include:

Angel dust	Phencyclidine (PCP)
bingeing	prolonged bouts of using cocaine or crack
blims	small fragments of cannabis resin
brown	heroin
buzzing	being high on drugs
busted	caught with drugs by the police
caned	being high on drugs
charlie	cocaine
clucking	withdrawing from any drug
cut	mixing drugs with other substances
dope	generally cannabis but may refer to other drugs
downers	sedative-type drugs
draw	cannabis
E	ecstasy
flashback	a reappearance of sensations associated with acid taking, when not on acid, occasionally experienced by LSD takers
huffing	inhaling solvents
ice	amphetamines
'J'	joint

kak	impure
karped	being high on drugs
lick the rock	taking crack
mong	'out of it'
ninebar	nine ounces of cannabis
oil	class 'A' extract of cannabis, highly potent
pebbles	crack
poppers	amyl nitrate
puffing	smoking cannabis
reefer	joint
roach	rolled card inserted into the end of a spliff to make the draw easier
rock	crack
rush	an exhilarating physical high usually in the context of ecstasy use
skin up	make up a spliff
skunk	powerful hybrid cannabis plant
snidey up	to mix the active ingredient of 'E's with other substances
snort	sniffing drugs
speed	amphetamines
spliff	joint
stacking	taking drugs in the right mixtures and at the right timing to get maximum effect
tolerance	used in the normal sense of 'building up' tolerance so that you have to take more and more to have the same effect, whether drugs, drink or anything else!
toot	heroin
tranqs	tranquillisers
trip	prolonged high from acid or mushrooms
valis	valiums
weed	cannabis
whizz	amphetamines

Cannabis

Cannabis goes under a number of different names in the UK, including blow, grass, weed, hash, pot, dope, shit, draw, wacky-backy, gear, puff and spiff. In the East it has a number of other names: bhang, charas, ganja, kif, dagga, kabak and hashish. The names for the form in which it is usually smoked (mixed with tobacco surrounded by a cigarette paper) are a joint (now out of fashion), spliff, bifter, cone or two-skin. When rolling a spliff (skinning up), the gear is first 'roasted' and then put in rolling papers with the tobacco and a roach.

The Law

Penalties are up to a maximum of five years in prison for possession. Dealing can bring an unlimited fine and up to fourteen years in prison.

Forms and Content

More than 400 chemicals have been found in the resin, including sixty compounds (canniboids) which have an effect on our perceptions.

The most active ingredient is called delta-9-tetrahydro-cannabinol (THC). Dope comes in many different forms with different THC levels (between 1 and 30 per cent THC per weight). These include herbal material (marijuana or grass), resin compressed into blocks and thick oil (hash).

New forms of the plant called hybrids are being developed all the time around the world. The strongest is currently called Northern lights, but other varieties are Purple haze, Sumatran red, Durban poison and Skunk.

Effects

Cannabis tends to heighten whatever mood was prevalent

prior to taking the drug. If you are in a positive mood this is potentiated but if you are depressed or anxious you may feel worse. The effects of smoking come on within a few minutes, peak after about thirty minutes, and last for three to four hours. If you eat hash, onset is within one to two hours and the effects last longer. Cannabis affects your mood, concentration and memory, perception and patterns of thinking. Its physical affects are that your heart rate increases, you may become more clumsy, your speech may slur and your eyes may become reddened. Overdose from dope alone has never been reliably reported. There is no evidence that one can become physically addicted to cannabis.

Side effects are, on the whole, rare considering how commonly the drug is used. One worrying effect of cannabis use is a condition called 'amotivational syndrome', which is a state of apathy, passivity, not wanting to do anything. But dope use may be as much a consequence of this condition as a cause. Other side effects are panic attacks and anxiety, 'flashbacks', loss of mental control and paranoia. A serious source of concern is the associated loss of memory, in particular the ability to learn new information. Recent research suggests that memory loss continues for several weeks after stopping using dope. 'Caned' or 'karped' (stoned) people are more likely to be accident prone; reaction time, depth estimation, tracking moving objects and recovery from glare are all impaired.

INHALANTS/SOLVENTS

The Law

It is not illegal to inhale solvents but the Intoxicating Substances Supply Act introduced in 1985 makes it an offence to supply someone under the age of eighteen with a substance known to 'achieve intoxication'.

Forms and Content

There are many examples of products containing solvents which can be inhaled, including glues and adhesives (toluene, benzene, xylene, acetone); cleaning fluids; aerosols; petrol; rubber solution; correcting fluid; paint; varnish; nail polish; dyes; fire extinguishers; and room fresheners.

Effects

The commonest age to sniff for the first time is between twelve and fourteen.The solvent tends to be rapidly absorbed from the lungs into the blood stream after inhalation. The chemicals reach the brain via the blood and produce a variety of sensations. The active chemical substances disappear from the blood stream two to three hours after the last inhalation as the chemicals are broken down in the liver.

The effects include feelings of power, exhilaration and excitement. Use is often accompanied by blurred vision and slurred speech, a buzzing in the ears and marked clumsiness. During sex, orgasm feels prolonged and intensified. These peak effects usually only last for a few minutes or so, and are followed by a relaxed sense of well-being for half an hour or more. The worst side effect is sudden death, and solvents contribute to more deaths in people under twenty than any other drug. Other side effects include palpitations, unpleasant headaches, buzzing in the ears, nausea and abdominal pains. The fumes of the solvent may cause coughing bouts, sneezing and streaming eyes. After the high comes the hangover characterised by lethargy, depression, irritability, restlessness, poor appetite and altered sleeping patterns.

ECSTASY

Less than half the substances sold as ecstasy actually contain any substance even vaguely related to the basic drug. The drug is commonly known as 'E' and when it does contain a relative substance it may come in many different forms:

'Power packs'	=	MDEA
'Triple Xs'	=	MDEA
'Adam and Eves'	=	MDEA
'White burgers'	=	MDEA
'Snowballs'	=	MDA
'White caps'	=	MDA
'Love hearts'	=	decongestant
'Splits'	=	decongestants
'White callys'	=	antihistamine
'California sunrise'	=	amphetamine/caffeine
'Green burgers'	=	amphetamine/caffeine

The Law

Ecstasy is a class 'A' drug which means, for both possession and supplying, anything from six months plus £5000 fine up to life and an unlimited fine.

Forms and Content

There are more than a thousand variants of the basic amphetamine chemical, but the most common of these in current circulation are: methylenedioxyamphetamine (MDA), methylenedioxymethamphetamine (MDMA, Ecstasy), and methylenedioxyethamphetamine (MDEA, 'Eve'). MDMA is available as a powder, tablets and capsules of various shapes, colours and sizes, with names like Doves, Dennis the Menace, Disco biscuits, Burgers, M25s and Pink skuds.

Effects

The drugs (MDA and MDMA) work through their effects on the chemical messengers (neurotransmitters). They both cause a massive release of 5-hydroxytryptamine (5HT, serotonin), and then seem to inhibit its synthesis so that the brain becomes temporarily depleted. 5HT is thought to play an important role in regulating mood, sleep, aggression, hunger and sexual activity. The results of an oral dose become apparent within thirty minutes, peak at between sixty and ninety minutes, and disappear in about four hours. The effects have been described as 'an easily controlled altered state of consciousness with emotional and sensual overtones'. There is an increased sense of alertness, dryness in the mouth, a tingling of the skin or 'rushes' and an increased heart rate. The drug certainly increases the sensual experience of sex, but can cause erectile failure in men and delay orgasm in both sexes.

Twenty to twenty-five deaths in the UK have been directly related to the effects of MDMA, in spite of millions of people having taken the drug. Facts about its long-term side effects are still emerging, but appear to be increasingly serious and include very long-term memory loss. More immediate side effects include clumsiness and lack of co-ordination, disorientation, nausea and vomiting. Interactions with other illicit drugs or prescribed drugs may prove fatal. A rare but serious effect is a rapid rise in body temperature.

Lysergic Acid (LSD)

The Law

Lysergic Acid is a class 'A' drug which means, for both possession and supplying, anything from six months plus £5000 fine up to life and an unlimited fine.

Forms and Content

LSD is a white, tasteless powder which dissolves easily in water to produce a colourless solution. It is highly potent. Tablets or capsules presented as LSD are more likely to contain a variety of substances other than LSD itself. This drug belongs to the group of substances called indolealkylamines, which are similar in structure to the brain's chemical messengers.

Effects

Effects begin within twenty minutes and last for up to eight hours, peaking at about three hours. People have an 'out of body' mystical sensation in which colours intensify, moving objects leave tracks, patterns appear and disappear. Vision, hearing and touch are distorted but the user remains aware that these are the effects of the drug itself. No one has died from the direct effects of LSD, and prolonged depression and paranoia are only known to have occurred in previous sufferers who then try the drug. Sensitivity to the drug rapidly decreases but returns after a brief abstinence. A bad trip can induce acute anxiety, paranoia, fear and, at high doses, hallucinations. There is no physical or psychological dependence associated with the drug.

MAGIC MUSHROOMS

These are a specific type of mushroom which grow wild in damp fields and heaths around the UK between September and November.

The Law

It is not illegal to possess magic mushrooms but it is illegal to 'make them into a preparation'.

Forms and Content

The most common type is popularly known as 'liberty cap'. It is white and rocket shaped, but it is very hard to tell one type of mushroom from another. The technical names for the two most common are 'Psylocybe' and 'Fly Agaric'.

Effects

The strength of the hallucinations depends on how many mushrooms you eat. The effects of a mushroom trip are similar to 'acid', but less mentally intense and shorter lasting. The use of mushrooms extends back thousands of years to when ancient people used them on quests for spiritual enlightenment. They were adopted in the West in the 1960s as a natural alternative to LSD. If you pick the wrong ones, you can poison yourself. Even the right ones can give you stomach ache as well as hallucinations.

AMPHETAMINES

Amphetamine sulphate is also known as speed, uppers, sulphate, sulph, whizz and billy. In the UK, the use of speed is second only to the use of cannabis. The average purity of what is sold as amphetamines is around 10 per cent. The other 90 per cent is 'cut', and contains glucose, caffeine, milk powder, or talc.

The Law

The law can give you penalties of up to a maximum of five years in prison for possession, and for supplying an unlimited fine and up to fourteen years in prison. Although speed is normally a class 'B' drug, if it is prepared for injection it is a class 'A'.

Forms and Content

Speed is made artificially and frequently cut with other substances. The powder can be eaten, snorted, stirred into a drink, rubbed into your gums, or dissolved in water and injected.

Effects

The effects come on within an hour and last for about four hours. The drug makes you feel self-confident, alert, powerful and energetic. It keeps you going without food or sleep but then you finally collapse and have to catch up with both. The pharmacological effects of speed are very similar to cocaine but last longer. Amphetamines raise the blood pressure, cause rashes and may cause teeth to rot and fall out because of loss of dentine. They also severely reduce calcium levels. They are more toxic than cocaine in a physical sense especially in the damage they can cause to the liver. The persistent use of amphetamines and alcohol together can lead to a dual dependency on both drugs; and increasing tolerance to amphetamines leads addicts to take several grams a day. Seesawing moods, poor concentration, insomnia and a sense of being persecuted are common. A physical withdrawal may manifest itself in depression, fatigue, an extreme craving for drugs and sleep disturbance that may last for weeks or even months.

COCAINE

Other names for cocaine include coke, snow, charlie and Bolivian marching powder.

The Law

Cocaine is a class 'A' drug, incurring up to seven years in

prison for possession and life for supplying.

Forms and Content

It normally comes as a white powder. When the powder is sniffed (snorted) absorption may be delayed because the drug narrows the blood vessels in the nose. The powder may also be injected after being dissolved in water. If injected, it hits the brain within sixteen seconds but this practice is extremely dangerous because you never know what it has been 'cut' with.

Effects

Cocaine gives a terrific sense of well-being within minutes, which gradually increases. Confidence is raised, as are feelings of optimism, enthusiasm and energy. Self-esteem and sex-drive are also enhanced. There is an overall feeling of exhilaration and happiness. Most normal pleasures are augmented but there is a reduced need for food, rest and sleep. The duration of its effect can be measured in minutes rather than hours, however, because cocaine is broken down by the body very quickly. With increased use comes decreased sensitivity to the drug. Excessive doses are likely to produce sweating, dizziness, irritability, a high body temperature, a dry mouth, trembling hands, ringing ears, involuntary teeth grinding and skin picking. Blood pressure may go up to the point of producing a stroke. Fits can occur, and injectors expose themselves to other life-threatening diseases including HIV infections and hepatitis in addition to the dangers that inevitably accompany such a life-style, such as violent crime.

CRACK

Street names for crack include pebbles, scud, wash and rock.

It got its original name of 'crack' because of the popping and clicking given off by exploding impurities during smoking.

The Law

Like cocaine, crack is a class 'A' drug, incurring up to seven years in prison for possession and life for supplying.

Form and Content

Crack is a specific form of cocaine which when smoked delivers the drug to the brain at least as rapidly as would be achieved by injection. This is because, in this specific form, it goes straight from the lungs to the brain within seconds, without having to pass the liver.

Effects

The 'rushes' it produces are like a very intense form of the effects of cocaine which are so extreme that people using the drug often fail to find suitable words to describe it. It is said to be like 'a thousand simultaneous orgasms'. The high lasts just ten minutes or so, and may be followed by a rapid downswing in mood. Regular smokers feel irritable or 'wired' and take heroin to ease this. Crack smoking is extremely damaging to the lungs and is associated with severe chest pains, bronchitis and asthma. In pregnant mothers we also see the phenomenon of 'crack babies'. Crack is exceedingly addictive, especially for people who don't feel too good about themselves in the first place.

HEROIN AND THE OPIATES

Heroin is also known as smack, junk, gear, brown or skag. It has gradually become clear that the body produces its own natural opiates called endorphins. These substances are produced by the body in response to pain and moderate its perception.

The Law

Heroin is a class 'A' drug, incurring up to seven years in prison for possession and life for supplying.

Forms and Content

Raw opium is obtained from the seed capsule of the poppy, *Papaver somniferum*. When the capsule is slit after the petals have fallen, a white juice oozes out which soon thickens and darkens to a tar-like substance with a bitter taste and a pungent smell. Prepared opium for selling is usually presented as this material resembling treacle, or compressed into pills or sticks. Street heroin usually consists of an off-white or brown powder, although occasionally it is granular in consistency and has a bitter taste. The powder can be snorted up the nose, smoked in a cigarette, heated in foil ('chasing the dragon'), or dissolved and injected. In one analytic study, the average purity of street heroin was found to be about 40 per cent, with the drug becoming more adulterated at every stage of its journey.

Effects

Opiates exert an inhibitory effect upon the brain and nervous system, with a wide range of results. Perception of and concern about pain is reduced; the pupils of the eyes are constricted; drowsiness or sleep is induced with larger doses; anxiety, panic and fear are inhibited, as is the 'fight or flight' mechanism; the cough reflex is suppressed; breathing is depressed; body temperature is reduced; sex hormones are reined in. The blood vessels in the skin tend to relax and blood pressure falls, the guts slow down, muscles loosen and sphincters tighten. The organism slows up to a state akin to hibernation.

The feeling associated with taking opiates has been described as 'a sensation of fullness in the head, soon followed by a universal feeling of delicious ease and comfort, with an elevation and expansion of the whole moral and intellectual nature which is, I think, the most characteristic of its effects . . . along with this emotional and intellectual elevation, there is also increased muscular energy; and the capacity to act, and to bear fatigue, is greatly augmented.'

Anxieties and stresses disappear, the user may droop and his eyes close as he 'goes on the nod' or 'gouches out'. The body feels heavy, and if problems come into the mind at all, they are suffused with optimism and confidence that all will turn out well. Unless overdosed into unconsciousness, the mind remains functioning although it may not seem to do so to an outside observer. It is virtually impossible to use heroin or any opiate without becoming physically and mentally dependent. There are risks of overdose, infection and serious accidents.

FURTHER READING ON DRUGS

Balding, John, 'Young people and drug-taking: facts and trends', in *Education and Health*, 12(4), 1994. The best summary of the rate of drug taking in young people in the UK.

Cocaine and Crack and other leaflets from the Institute for the Study of Drug Dependency, 1 Hatton Place, London EC1N 8ND.

Cohen, Julian and Kay, James, *Taking Drugs Seriously: a Parent's Guide to Young People's Drug Use*, Thorsons, 1994.

Drugs and Solvents: Things You Should Know: the Facts for Young People and *Drugs: A Parent's Guide: The Dangers:*

What to Do. Both from BAPS, Health Publications Unit, DSS Distribution Centre, Heywood Stores, Manchester Road, Heywood, Lancs OL10 2PZ. Free. Tel: 0800 555 777.

'Drugs: Who Takes Them, Why We Use Them, What the Future Holds?' in *Life*, The *Observer* Magazine 9, 16 and 23 October 1994.

Many frequently asked questions and answers can be found via anonymous FTP from http://www.hypereal.org/drugs

'Peanut Pete' productions: *The Big Blue Book of Booze, In the Zone, The Lads Go Mad in Amsterdam, Everything You Wanted to Know about Cannabis, Amphetamine, MDA Snowballs*, and many other brilliant books. Lifeline Manchester, 101–103 Oldham Street, Manchester M4 1LW. These are rated very high by young people themselves.

Robson, Philip, *Forbidden Drugs: Understanding Drugs and Why People Take Them*, Oxford Medical Publications, 1994. An outstandlingly informative book on the subject of drugs.

'Roots of Addiction', in *New Scientist*, 1 October 1994.

Tackling Drugs Together. HMSO, A Strategy for England 1995/1998.

WHAT HAPPENS WHEN YOU GIVE UP CIGARETTES

Within 20 minutes   your blood pressure drops
your pulse rate drops to normal
the temperature of your hands and
feet increases to normal

After 8 hours   the carbon monoxide level in your
blood drops to normal
the oxygen level in your blood
increases to normal

After 24 hours   the chances of having a heart attack
decrease

After 48 hours   your nerve ends start regrowing
your ability to smell and to taste
things improves

After 72 hours   your bronchial tubes begin to relax
your breathing becomes easier
your lung capacity increases

After 2 weeks to   your circulation improves
3 months   your lung functions are improved by
30 per cent

After 1 to 9 months   coughing, sinus congestion,
tiredness, shortness of breath, all
improve
the linings of your lungs regrow
normally
your overall energy is improved

After 5 years	lung cancer death risk for the average smoker decreases from 137 per 100,000 people to 72, and then (after 10 years) to 12, which is almost the rate of non-smokers
After 10 years	most pre-cancerous cells have been replaced other cancer risks, such as those of the mouth, throat, bladder, kidney and cervix, are decreased as well

THE EFFECTS OF AN EVENING'S DRINKING A ROUGH GUIDE

Thus:

– at midnight after an evening's drinking you will still have 200 mg per ml of alcohol in the blood

– at 7.30 a.m. as you lie there with your hangover, your alcohol level is still at 130 mg per ml, still well over the driving limit

– at midday after the night before, your level will be down to 80 mg per ml, only just the legal limit to drive

– at 8 p.m. not all the alcohol has gone, but it is OK to drive again

REMEMBER this is a rough guide and is proportional to factors such as your **age**, **sex** and **weight**

Appendix 4
Health and Fitness

CHECK YOUR STAMINA

Find a reasonably flat route about a mile long (a bit of road, park or running track). Walking, running or with a mixture of both, cover the mile as quickly as you can without becoming uncomfortably breathless.

If you take:

20 minutes or over	desperately unfit
15–20 minutes	just unfit
12–15 minutes	fairly fit
10–12 minutes	fit
10 minutes or under	very fit
under 4 minutes	join your school team now

TIPS ABOUT EXERCISING

– try to choose active ways of doing daily tasks – running upstairs, jogging instead of walking, bicycling rather than going by car or bus

– choose a form of exercise that you enjoy enough to do it regularly

– you need 20 to 30 minutes of exercise three times a week

– start gently and build up gradually

– you don't have to choose just one form of exercise, try lots of different ones

HEIGHT AND WEIGHT CHARTS

Adolescents grow at very different rates, and how tall or short they are usually also reflects parental height. The height and weight centile charts for boys and girls included in this book give an idea of the variations that can occur.

If your son or daughter is on the middle line of the chart called the fiftieth centile this means that of every hundred teenagers of that age 49 will be taller or heavier, and 49 will be shorter or lighter. If a teenager is on the 98th line only two other teenagers will be taller or heavier, and 97 will be shorter or lighter. Similarly, if a teenager is on the 2nd line (centile) 97 will be taller or heavier and two will be shorter or lighter. If the young person is above the 98th line or below the second line on either chart there could be something wrong, but not necessarily so. However, it would be a good idea in these circumstances to contact your doctor.

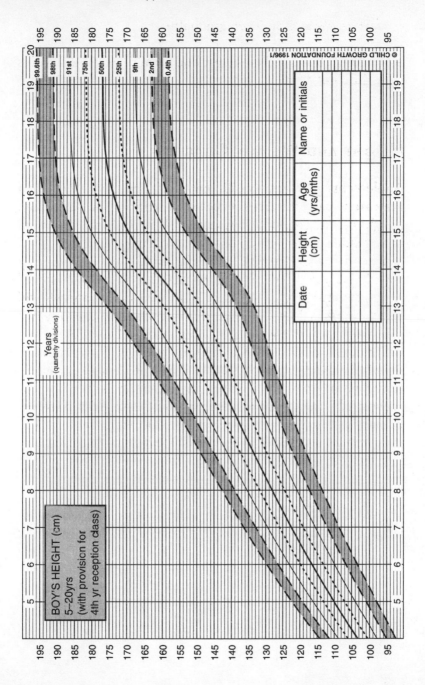

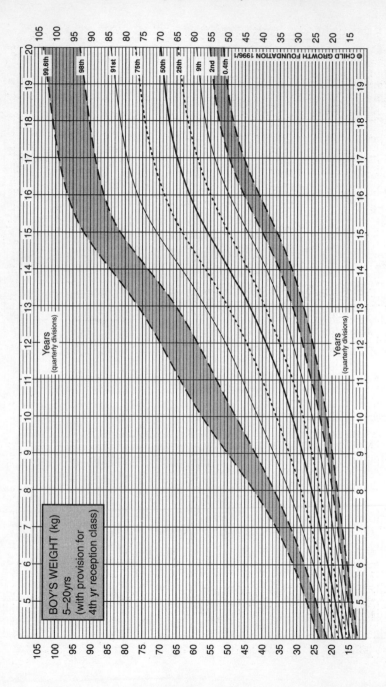

BOY'S WEIGHT (kg)
5–20yrs
(with provision for
4th yr reception class)

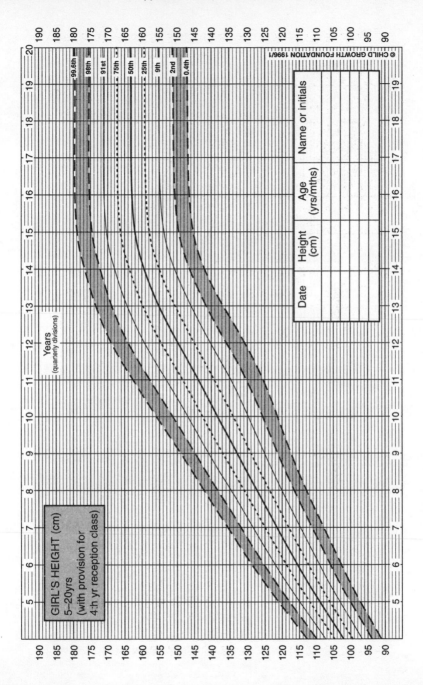

GIRL'S HEIGHT (cm)
5–20yrs
(with provision for
4th yr reception class)

Years
(quarterly divisions)

99.6th
98th
91st
75th
50th
25th
9th
2nd
0.4th

© CHILD GROWTH FOUNDATION 1996/1

Date	Height (cm)	Age (yrs/mths)	Name or initials

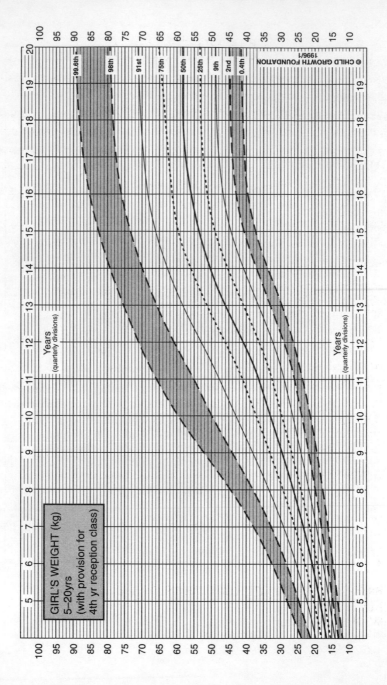

GIRL'S WEIGHT (kg)
5–20yrs
(with provision for
4th yr reception class)

© CHILD GROWTH FOUNDATION
1996/1

99.6th
98th
91st
75th
50th
25th
9th
2nd
0.4th

Years
(quarterly divisions)

Years
(quarterly divisions)

Appendix 5
Useful Organisations

ADFAM NATIONAL
Waterbridge House
32–36 Loman Street
London SE1 0EE
Helpline: 0171 928 8900
Offers information and confidential support to families of drug users

AL ANON/ALATEEN FAMILY GROUPS
61 Great Dover Street
London SE1 4YF
Tel: 0171 403 0888
Provides understanding and support for friends and relatives of problem drinkers

ALCOHOLICS ANONYMOUS
Tel: 0171 833 0022
Helps alcoholics to stay sober

ANTI-BULLYING CAMPAIGN
185 Tower Bridge Road
London SE1 2UF
Tel: 0171 378 1446
Helps parents with step-by-step guidelines on how to work with schools to combat the problem of bullying

THE BRITISH DIABETIC ASSOCIATION
10 Queen Anne Street
London W1M 0BD
Tel: 0171 323 1531

BRITISH PREGNANCY ADVISORY SERVICE
Austy Manor
Wooten on Wawen
Solihull, W. Midlands B95 6BX
Tel: 01564 793 225

BROOK ADVISORY SERVICE HELPLINE
Tel: 0171 617 8000
Offers a counselling and advice service covering all aspects of sexuality for all age groups

CHILDLINE
Freepost 1111
London N1 0BR
Tel: 0800 1111
A national telephone helpline for children and young people in danger or distress

COMPASSIONATE FRIENDS
53 North Street
Bristol BS3 1EN
Helpline: 0117 953 9639
Self-help organisation of parents whose child has died

CONTACT A FAMILY
170 Tottenham Court Road
London W1P 0HA
Tel: 0171 383 3555
Brings families whose children have disabilities together

THE COUNCIL FOR DISABLED CHILDREN
8 Wakley Street
London EC1V 7QE
Tel: 0171 843 6000

CRIMESTOPPERS SNAP (Say No And Phone) CAMPAIGN
Tel: 0800 555111
Nationwide crimestoppers campaign aimed at tackling the drug problem

CRUSE (Bereavement Care)
Cruse House
126 Sheen Road
Richmond
Surrey TW9 1UR
Tel: 0181 940 4818
Bereavement Line: 0345 585565
Provides free help and support to all bereaved people

THE CYSTIC FIBROSIS TRUST
11 London Road
Bromley
Kent BR1 1BY
Tel: 0181 464 7211

DIAL UK
Tel: 01302 310123
Telephone advice lines and a drop-in information service for people with disabilities, their families or carers, and professionals

DIVERT
33 King Street
London WC2E 8JD
Tel: 0171 379 6071
Charity aimed at helping those aged under twenty-five

DRINKLINE
National Alcohol Helpline
London only: 0171 332 0202
All UK: 0345 320202
Freecall Dial and Listen Line: 0500 801 802
Provides confidential help to callers worried about their own drinking, and supports the family and friends of people who are drinking

EATING DISORDERS ASSOCIATION
First Floor
Wensum House
103 Prince of Wales Road
Norwich NR1 1DW
General Helpline: 01603 621414
Youth Helpline: 01603 765050
Helps and supports all those affected by anorexia and bulimia

FAMILY PLANNING ASSOCIATION
2–12 Pentonville Road
London N1 9FP
Tel: 0171 837 5432
Helpline: 0171 837 4044
Offers information on all aspects of family planning and sexual health

FFLAG (Friends and Families of Lesbians and Gays)
PO Box 153
Manchester M60 1LP
Helplines: 0181 467 0309/01223 315 745
Offers confidential support for parents and their gay, lesbian and bi-sexual sons or daughters

GENITO-URINARY MEDICINE CLINIC (GUM)
Your local clinic can be found in the phone book under 'G' for Genito-Urinary Medicine Clinics, 'S' for Sexually Transmitted Diseases Clinic and 'V' for Venereal Diseases Clinic.
GUMs not only provide counselling about sexual problems, but also give information about contraception, pregnancy, infection and other sexual matters

GINGERBREAD
16–17 Clerkenwell Close
London EC1R 0AA
Tel: 0171 336 8183
Day-to-day support and practical help for lone parents and their children

JEWISH LESBIAN AND GAY HELPLINE
Tel: 0171 706 3123
Offers counselling and information to lesbians and gay men and their families and friends

LESBIAN AND GAY SWITCHBOARD
Tel: 0171 837 7324
Offers information and advice to lesbians and gay men and their families and friends

NATIONAL AIDS HELPLINE
Tel: 0800 567123
Worries about AIDS can be discussed with trained advisers

NATIONAL DRUGS HELPLINE
Tel: 0800 776600
A free, confidential service available in English and other languages

NATIONAL SOCIETY FOR EPILEPSY
Chalfont Centre
Chalfont St. Peter
Gerrards Cross
Bucks SL9 0RJ
Tel: 01494 873 899

PAPYRUS (Prevention of Suicides)
Rossendale G H
Union Road
Rawtenstall
Rossendale BB4 6NE
Tel/Fax: 01706 214449
Parents for the prevention of young suicide

PARENTLINE
National Office
Endway House
The Endway
Hadleigh
Essex SS7 2AN
Helpline: 01702 559900
Provides support for parents under stress

PARENT NETWORK
Room 2
Winchester House
11 Cranmer Road
London SW9 6EJ
Tel: 0171 735 1214
Provides support and education groups for parents in their local communities

PARENTS ANONYMOUS
The Hanlycrouch Community Centre
Sparsholt Road
Islington
London N19 4EL
Tel: 0171 263 8918
Offers a telephone counselling service for parents

RAPE CRISIS HELPLINES
Look in the phone book or ring Directory Enquiries on 192 for the helpline number in your area.
Provides free confidential support and advice to victims of rape

RELEASE
388 Old Street
London EC1V 9LT
Advice Line: 0171 729 9904
24-hour Emergency Line: 0171 603 8654
Drugs in Schools: 0345 366666
Confidential service for drug-related legal problems

THE SAMARITANS
Helpline: 0345 909090
A 24-hour confidential telephone helpline for people who are in despair

STEPFAMILY (National Stepfamily Association)
Chapel House
18 Hatton Place
London EC1N 8RU
Tel: 0171 209 2460
Helpline: 0990 168 388
Support, advice and information for all members of stepfamilies

TRUST FOR THE STUDY OF ADOLESCENCE
23 New Road
Brighton BN1 1WZ
Tel: 01273 693311
Promotes the study of adolescence by undertaking research on adolescent development

YOUNG MINDS
The National Association for Child and Family Mental Health
102–108 Clerkenwell Road
London EC1M 5SA
Tel: 0171 336 8445
Helpline: 0800 018 2138
Aims to raise awareness about the emotional and behavioural problems of children and young people

YOUTH ACCESS
1a Taylor's Yard
67 Alderbrook Road
London SW12 8AD
Tel: 0181 772 9900
An independent association of agencies and individuals providing information, advice and counselling

Index